SOCIAL PROGRAMS THAT WORK

SOCIAL PROGRAMS THAT WORK

Jonathan Crane, editor

Russell Sage Foundation ▽ New York

The Russell Sage Foundation

Library of Congress Cataloging-in-Publication Data

Social programs that work / edited by Jonathan Crane
   p. cm.
   Includes bibliographical references and indexes.
   ISBN 0-87154-173-4 (cloth)   ISBN 0-87154-174-2 (paper)
   1.Socially handicapped—Services for—United States—Case Studies. 2. Social work with the socially handicapped—United States—Evaluation. 3.Social work with the socially handicapped—United States—Case Studies. 4. Social work with the socially handicapped—United States—Evaluation. 5.Evaluation research (social action programs)—United States. I. Crane, Jonathan, 1959– .
HV91.S615   1998   97-44908
362.5'8'0973—dc21   CIP

Text Design by Suzanne Nichols.

RUSSELL SAGE FOUNDATION
112 East 64th Street, New York, New York 10021
10   9   8   7   6   5   4   3   2   1

To Hana and Alyssa, for all their love and support.

Contents

Contributors

JONATHAN CRANE is domestic policy advisor in the office of the Vice President of the United States.

CLANCY BLAIR is postdoctoral fellow in the Department of Psychology at the University of Miami.

GILBERT J. BOTVIN is professor of public health at Cornell University Medical College. He is also director of the Institute for Prevention Research at Cornell University.

FRANCES A. CAMPBELL is senior investigator at the Frank Porter Child Development Center of the University of North Carolina at Chapel Hill.

PATRICIA CHAMBERLAIN is director of clinical programs at the Oregon Social Learning Center (OSLC).

BARBARA DEVANEY is senior fellow at Mathematica Policy Research in Princeton, New Jersey.

MARCELLA DIANDA is senior program associate at the National Education Association.

LAWRENCE J. DOLAN currently works for the College Board.

PHYLLIS L. ELLICKSON is director of the Center for Research on Maternal, Child, and Adolescent Health and senior behavioral scientist at RAND.

GEORGE FARKAS is professor of sociology and political economy and director of the Center for Education and Social Policy at the University of Texas at Dallas in Richardson, Texas.

NANCY A. MADDEN is principal research scientist at the Center for Research on the Education of Students Placed at Risk at Johns Hopkins University. She is also codirector of the Success for All/Roots and Wings project.

LAWRENCE M. MEAD is professor of politics at New York University.

KEVIN MOORE is project director for the Allies Program at the Oregon Social Learning Center (OSLC).

CRAIG T. RAMEY is University Professor of Psychology, Pediatrics, Public Health, and Neurobiology and director of the Civitan International Research Center of the University of Alabama at Birmingham.

ARTHUR J. REYNOLDS is associate professor in the School of Social Work and in the Department of Child and Family Studies at the University of Wisconsin–Madison.

STEVEN M. ROSS is professor of educational psychology and research at the University of Memphis.

LAWRENCE J. SCHWEINHART is chair of the research division at the High/Scope Educational Research Foundation and codirector of the High/Scope Perry Preschool Study.

ROBERT E. SLAVIN is codirector of the Center for Research on the Education of Students Placed at Risk at Johns Hopkins University. He is also codirector of the Success for All/Roots and Wings programs.

LANA J. SMITH is professor of reading and language arts, Department of Instruction and Curriculum Leadership, The University of Memphis.

BARBARA A. WASIK is principal research scientist and codirector of the Early Learning Program at the Center for Research on the Education of Students Placed at Risk at the Johns Hopkins University.

DAVID P. WEIKART is president of the High/Scope Educational Research Foundation and codirector of the High/Scope Perry Preschool Study.

Acknowledgments

This book is based on a conference entitled "Social Programs That Really Work," which was held at the University of Illinois at Chicago in October of 1995. The conference was sponsored by the Institute of Government and Public Affairs at the University of Illinois, the Russell Sage Foundation, The Chicago Urban League, and the Chicago Council on Urban Affairs. Anna Merrit, Robert Rich, and Cedric Herring of the Institute of Government and Public Affairs and Nancy Casey of the Russell Sage Foundation were instrumental in putting that conference together. David Haproff and Suzanne Nichols of the Russell Sage Foundation and an anonymous reviewer offered invaluable comments and suggestions on the manuscript. Finally, I would like to thank Keith Higdon for his tireless efforts, above and beyond the call of duty, on both the conference and the book.

JONATHAN CRANE

CHAPTER 1

Building on Success

Jonathan Crane

In recent years, social programs for the poor clearly have lost the support of the American public. At the same time, public opinion polls show that the vast majority of Americans remain sympathetic to the plight of the poor or, at least, to the plight of poor people who adhere to mainstream values and social norms. How are we to reconcile these two facts? The answer is simple. Most Americans are convinced that social programs simply do not work and that many existing programs encourage antisocial behavior and attitudes.

Certainly many programs have failed. Even worse, some of the failures have become apparent only after extravagant claims of success have been made. This has made the public exceedingly skeptical of all social programs and given rise to an increasingly popular myth that nothing works. This is simply not true.

A number of programs have had a substantial, positive impact on the lives of the people they have served and have benefited society as a whole. These programs are not miraculous. They do not completely solve any social problem. They do not help all of the people they serve or anything close to 100 percent. But they do substantially reduce the rates and severity of particular social problems among participants.

This volume describes some of the very best programs and documents their benefits. Chapters 2 through 10 each presents a description and formal evaluation of a single program. These particular programs were chosen after reviewing several hundred formal evaluations, because, according to a subjective interpretation of objective evidence, they stand out in one or more of five ways.[1]

Each program offers at least one of the following: (a) extraordinarily large benefits per dollar of cost (chapters 3, 5, 8, and 9); (b) unusually convincing evidence that the program delivers substantial benefits, regardless of cost (chapter 2); (c) convincing evidence of

1

long-term effects (chapters 4, 5, 6, and 9); (d) evidence of cost-effectiveness on a national scale (chapter 7); and (e) new hope of making progress to solve a seemingly intractable social problem (chapter 10).

Chapter 11 is different from the rest. It does not evaluate a single program. No work and training program "really works," because even the best ones produce only small benefits. Yet this volume discusses them because they play a key role in the Personal Responsibility and Work Opportunity Reconciliation Act of 1996. Completely changing the national welfare system, this is one of the most important pieces of social legislation ever passed in this country. In chapter 11, Lawrence Mead challenges the consensus by reinterpreting old data and presenting new data from numerous work and training programs. His arguments have important implications for the welfare revolution that is just beginning.

Thirteen criteria are used to determine whether a particular social program meets one or more of the five standards. They are also used to interpret the policy relevance of evaluation results. These criteria are detailed in the following section of this chapter. Although used to judge the objective findings of the evaluations, most of these criteria cannot be applied without some degree of subjective interpretation.

CRITERIA

The first criterion is whether a program has statistically significant effects on the treatment group. This is a necessary, but clearly not a sufficient, condition for a program to be judged successful. It is necessary because we cannot be confident that a finding is valid unless it is statistically significant. But it is insufficient because a significant effect can be so small that it has no practical importance or policy relevance whatsoever. All findings presented in this chapter are statistically significant, unless otherwise noted. Therefore, few references are made to this criterion.

The second criterion is effect size. A program that works must have "substantial" effects on participants' lives. Unfortunately, the definition of what constitutes a substantial effect size is completely subjective. Therefore, each reader must ultimately decide whether the effect of a particular program is substantial. As a broad rule of thumb, the following changes can be considered substantial: a reduction in the incidence of a serious social problem by more than 20 percent, a change in a behavior or an outcome of more than 0.25 standard deviation, and an income gain of more than two thousand dollars a year. In cases where more than one of these standards is relevant, the effect should meet the most stringent one. The first standard is a 20 *percent* change, not a 20 *percentage point* change. Thus, for example, reducing the proportion of individuals in a group who have committed a felony from 30 to 20 percent is only a 10 percentage point reduction, but it is a 50 percent reduction, which is substantial. Small percentage point reductions sometimes seem trivial, but they can be important when dealing with a national problem, because the total number of people involved is large. For instance, reducing the use of hard drugs from 2 to 1 percent is only a 1 percentage point decrease. But in a population of 250 million, this 50 percent reduction would imply that 2.5 million fewer people were using hard drugs.

The third criterion is a program's cost-benefit relationship. If the monetary value of all costs and benefits could be determined for all programs being compared, it would be possible to ascertain which ones produce the most dollars of benefit for each dollar invested. In theory, this is the best way to judge programs and the best criterion for determining which programs should be funded. Unfortunately, determining the cost-benefit relationship is easier said than done. Although the costs are usually easy enough to measure, determining the monetary value of benefits is often difficult. Formal cost-benefit analyses have not been done for most of the programs presented here, but they are discussed where they are available. For the other programs, cost estimates and qualitative judgments are presented about the size of the benefits and their overall relationship to cost. In some cases, these judgments are necessarily quite rough, but in others the costs are either so large or so small that we can be fairly confident about whether the benefits exceed them or not. Some might question the value of imprecise estimates. However, in cases where the costs are extreme, in one direction or the other, subjective judgments about whether benefits exceed costs have a high probability of being correct. The opportunity costs of ignoring such information simply because we cannot generate a precise numerical estimate are potentially very large. Thus, despite the lack of precise estimates, the relationship between costs and benefits is the single most important criterion used here to judge how well each program works.

The fourth criterion is the length of time that effects last. This is directly related to the third criterion. The longer an effect lasts, the more benefits it is likely to generate. It is common for short-term effects to fade out over time. Some effects, such as temporary increases in academic achievement, may have no benefit at all. However, this does not imply that all short-term effects are worthless. Temporary academic gains that reduce grade retentions and special education placements clearly do save money. In chapter 5, Lawrence Schweinhart and David Weikart argue that although academic gains disappear, they contribute indirectly to other long-term benefits. Short-term health improvements reduce suffering and save money. Temporary reductions in drug use probably reduce crime and improve health outcomes. Nevertheless, all other things being equal, the longer effects last, the better.

The fifth criterion is the quality of the evaluation. No matter how large or long term a particular program effect is, it is meaningless if its estimate was not generated in a methodologically sound way. A pure experimental design in which evaluation participants are randomly assigned to treatment and control groups is the universally accepted gold standard in evaluation research. Results generated from studies using this design have a lot of credibility, although even they may suffer from problems such as attrition bias or issues of external validity.[2] When random assignment is not feasible, evaluators typically select a comparison group, using any one of a number of techniques designed to make it as similar as possible to the treatment population.

Unfortunately, it is impossible to be sure that the distinctions between the treatment and comparison groups are produced by the program and not by initial differences in the makeup of the groups. Even if the two groups appear to be similar or if statistical controls are used, unobservable differences could be generating variable outcomes. Thus nonexperimental evaluations always carry less weight. However, if there is evidence of equivalence between the comparison and treatment groups, and if other factors lend credence to the results, nonexperimental results should be taken seriously.

The sixth criterion is the relationship between the evaluator and the program. Evaluations done by program developers tend to yield larger effects than ones done by independent evaluators. Therefore, results are always more credible when produced by independent researchers. This is not to say that we should discount evaluations done by program developers. But large investments in such programs should be made only after the results have been verified by someone else.

The seventh criterion is replication. No matter how impressive the results, no matter how good the study design, and no matter how objective the researchers, a single evaluation of a single program is never enough to prove that it really works. The value of replication is a matter of simple multiplication. If the odds of generating a particular result are 1 in 20, the odds are 1 in 400 of generating it twice, 1 in 8,000 of generating it three times, and 1 in 160,000 of generating it four times. If a program is replicated many times, and the results are consistently the same, we can be very confident that the findings are real, unless they can be traced to a common design flaw in every evaluation.

The eighth criterion is a variation of the seventh. Some studies have not been replicated per se, but they can be compared to programs that are similar enough to be considered "near replications." If such near replications produce similar effects, the original findings become more credible. Naturally, real replications are preferable, because what appear to be small differences among similar programs may turn out to be critical ones.

The ninth criterion is uniqueness. It is in a sense the opposite of the eighth. Several of the programs presented here have been included precisely because there are no similar programs with comparable results. They are uniquely successful. In statistical terms, they are outliers. This begs the question of whether their success may simply be a product of good luck. Even if all programs were completely ineffectual, it is likely that some of them would appear to be successful by random chance alone. To confirm that an unusually good result is valid, we should be able to distinguish features of the program that could explain its unique success—something that shows the program to be an orange in a distribution of apples, rather than just an apple that by chance is unusually juicy. Unfortunately, this is a highly subjective exercise. It is always possible to point to certain unique components or combinations of features that could account for a uniquely successful result. So the seventh criterion supersedes the ninth one. All results, no matter how impressive, need to be replicated.

The tenth, eleventh, and twelfth criteria are all related to internal consistency. Certain patterns of findings can strengthen our confidence in the overall results.

The tenth criterion involves the relationship between effect size and program intensity or time of participation. A positive relationship between the size of effect and the intensity of the program or the amount of time participants spend in it lends credence to an overall finding of beneficial effects. In other words, if more of the program works better than less of it, it tends to confirm that the program really does work. Of course, a program's benefits may reach a saturation point. Thus the absence of a relationship is not necessarily a problem, but it clearly is a problem if more participation or greater intensity reduces the effects. If more of a program is worse than less of it, any positive effects are called into question.

The eleventh criterion has to do with implementation fidelity. No replication of a program is ever a perfect copy of the original model. Whenever there are many replications, there is always some variation in the degree to which the copies remain faithful to the original design, when they are implemented. If a program really works, there should be a positive relationship between implementation fidelity and the similarity of the replication's results to the original's.

The twelfth criterion involves the relationship between the effect size and "site experience," that is, the time a program has been in existence at a particular site. If a program really works, more experience with applying it could improve its effectiveness. So a positive relationship between a site's experience with a program and the effect size is a good indicator of the program's overall effectiveness. This criterion may, in part, be a variation on the eleventh. In many replications, it takes time to implement a program fully or to learn how to use it correctly. So site experience may sometimes be a proxy for implementation fidelity.

The thirteenth and final criterion has to do with scale. Even if a program really works at one or two sites, it will not necessarily be successful if replicated on a substantially larger scale. Although success on a small scale does have some value, particularly if it proves a concept or suggests a promising strategy, the ultimate goal of social program research is to develop good programs that can benefit lots of people. Programs that have already been "upscaled" successfully have a leg up on pilots, because they have shown that they can work outside a "hothouse" environment. This final criterion is not the same as the seventh. Although upscaling almost always involves replication, it presents the program with new obstacles and problems that only emerge once a certain size has been reached.[3]

Having detailed the criteria for judging success, we can now apply them, in the following section, to determine whether the social programs presented in this volume really work. We can also use the criteria to decide whether each program merits the investment that would be required to scale it up substantially.

THE PROGRAMS

Success for All, presented in chapter 2, is aimed at improving the reading skills of children in the early grades of elementary school. Although the program is multifaceted, its main component is individualized tutoring, with one tutor teaching one child. This is crucial, because individualized tutoring is the key ingredient that makes the program successful.

A huge number of programs have been developed to raise the academic achievement of disadvantaged children. It is probably the single most common goal of social programs. For the most part, these program have proven disappointing. There are isolated cases of gains, but very little in the way of consistent patterns of success that would demonstrate convincingly that a particular strategy works. *There is one clear exception:* individualized tutoring has consistently raised children's reading levels. Three different tutoring programs have improved the reading test scores of thousands of children at scores of sites.

Reading Recovery was the first of these programs, and it served as the model for the other two. It remains perhaps the best known and most widely acclaimed of all reading programs. It probably deserves that acclaim, although Success for All is even more effective.

In Success for All, tutors work with individual students in twenty-minute sessions. The tutors are certified teachers who have experience working with disadvantaged children. They cover the same material and teach the same concepts addressed in the regular curriculum, although they often use different approaches.

The program has components besides tutoring, but individualized tutoring appears to be a necessary element for a successful reading program. Many programs include one or more of the other components of Success for All, but only those programs with tutoring consistently increase reading test scores by substantial amounts. What we do not know is whether tutoring is sufficient. Each of the three successful tutoring programs provides additional services. Until we vary the ancillary services in some kind of systematic experiment, there is no way to know for sure whether any of these services or any of the mixes of services unique to each program add to the overall impact.

What is the overall impact of Success for All? This has been assessed many times in many places with various kinds of children. These evaluations demonstrate a consistent pattern of positive and statistically significant effects on reading test scores. In chapter 2, Robert Slavin and his coauthors report the results of a meta-analysis of Success for All. A meta-analysis is a study that attempts to determine the average effect size of a large number of individual evaluations. The meta-analysis presented here includes evaluations of Success for All in nineteen schools, involving roughly four thousand children (and a comparable number in comparison schools that did not use the program).

The average effect of Success for All was to increase children's reading test scores by about half a standard deviation. This effect is not huge, but it is enough to bring a child reading in the middle of the bottom half of the distribution up close to average. For example, an increase of half a standard deviation would bring a child from the twenty-fifth percentile up to the forty-third. It would not bring a child at the very bottom to anywhere near the average.

However, the impact of Success for All on the very poorest readers was much larger. The average effect size for children reading below the twenty-fifth percentile ranged from 1 standard deviation for first graders to 1.7 standard deviation for fourth graders. A full standard deviation is a big effect by any measure, and a 1.7 standard deviation effect is huge. Consider, for example, a child reading at the tenth percentile, close to the very bottom. An increase of 1 standard deviation would boost him to the thirty-eighth percentile, while an increase of 1.7 standard deviation would catapult him to the sixty-fifth percentile, almost into the upper third of the population. Follow-up studies suggest that the effects are maintained through grade seven, at least two years after the final treatment. No data are available yet for older children.

Impacts of this size are impressive. But large effects do not in and of themselves guarantee that a program really works. The evaluations did not assign children randomly to treatment and control groups. Instead, they selected comparison groups composed of children from schools that were chosen because they were similar to the Success for All schools in terms of demographics and test scores. This kind of comparison is a lot better than none at all, but it is not as good as one predicated on random assignment. It increases the chances that systematic differences between the Success for All and comparison children could bias the results. In addition, because children were the unit of analysis, while schools were the unit of assignment, significance tests should have been adjusted for within-school correlations, but they were not. Also, Success for All is only adopted in a school if 80 percent of teachers vote to have it. Thus there is a chance that the treatment schools have teachers who are more motivated on average than the comparison schools. This, too, could bias the evaluation results, making the program look more effective than it really is.

However, a number of factors lend credence to the positive results. First, the program has been successfully replicated and upscaled. It has consistently generated statistically significant effects of substantial size across numerous evaluations, sites, cohorts, and grade levels. Second, the results have been strongly significant in most cases, so it is unlikely that the bias in the significance tests have affected their outcomes. Third, the two similar tutoring programs that have been tested on a large scale have also consistently generated positive results. And fourth, there is evidence of a learning curve in the implementation process. The effects are larger in schools that have used the program longer. An increase occurs each year from the first through the fourth year of implementation. In this case, site experience may be a proxy for implementation fidelity, although there is no direct analysis of the relationship between implementation fidelity and the effect size.

In short, the lion's share of the evidence suggests that Success for All is a program that really works. However, at least two issues remain. One is that most of the evaluations were done by the program's founders or their protégés, at schools in which they were closely involved. We would have even greater confidence in the program's effectiveness if more studies had been done by independent evaluators. The second, and more important, issue is that we do not know if the benefits of Success for All exceed its costs.

It is hard to value the benefits of educational programs that have not followed participants into adulthood, because the main outcome variables are test scores. Surprisingly, very little research has been done on the effects of test scores on long-term adult outcomes, such as earnings. Jencks and Phillips (1996) find that the effects of increases in high school mathematics scores on earnings can be fairly large, particularly at the bottom of the distribution. However, they only find significant effects of reading gains for girls. This work, although important, is too preliminary and too removed from the kinds of effects discussed here to use in estimating benefits.

The only direct monetary value that raising childhood test scores has is that it typically reduces grade retentions and special education placements, both of which are quite expensive. Success for All does reduce special education placements, but that alone is by no means enough to pay for the program in and of itself. The program may have long-term benefits. The cognitive gains may endure into adulthood and contribute to increases in income, reductions in welfare dependency, and other positive outcomes. Even if the reading gains fade away, valuable behavioral changes may emerge later. If so, the total benefits may ultimately exceed the costs, even when the long-term gains are discounted at a reasonable interest rate. Unfortunately, we simply do not know right now.

We have a little more information on the program's costs. Slavin and his coauthors do not provide data on the total cost of Success for All. But based on experience from his own program, George Farkas (chapter 3) conservatively estimates that it costs at least three thousand dollars a year to deliver a full complement of tutoring sessions to the average child. The other services provided by the program add to this cost. If this were a one-time expenditure that yielded permanent effects, it would almost certainly be worth the investment. However, if that amount had to be spent several times in a child's school years and if the gains completely faded out before adulthood, the program almost certainly would not be cost-effective. At this point, we do not know if effects tend to cumulate for children who receive multiple years of treatment, how much would have to be spent per child to generate permanent effects, or indeed if the program can generate enduring changes at all.

Until these questions have been answered, it will be impossible to determine whether the benefits of Success for All outweigh the costs. However, Slavin and his coauthors note in chapter 2 that because virtually all schools who adopt Success for All reallocate Title I resources to it, the incremental cost of the program is quite small. Evaluations suggest that Title I programs have, on average, small effects at best and perhaps none at all (Arroyo and Zigler 1993; Slavin, Karweit, and Madden 1989). This is not to say that no Title I programs work, but on the whole, Title I is not an effective social program. It is likely that replacing Title I with a national Success for All program would improve educational outcomes for poor children.

It is also possible that Success for All might be too expensive to provide to all disadvantaged children but might still be cost-effective for the bottom quartile of readers. If the large gains for the poorest readers hold up over time and contribute to improvements in earnings and other adult outcomes, they might very well justify a large investment.

At the very least, Success for All offers great hope. It demonstrates convincingly that an educational program can raise the academic achievement levels of disadvantaged children by substantial amounts. Moreover, a new program suggests that its principles can be applied in a more general way to completely restructure schools. Roots and Wings, discussed briefly in chapter 2, is a complete elementary school model that evolved out of Success for All. It is too early to pass judgment, but the preliminary results are extremely promising. They suggest that elementary schools with large proportions of disadvantaged children can raise achievement levels at least close to average in every subject.

Despite Success for All's promise, the issues of cost and permanency are problematic. They are also intimately related. Most social programs attempt to deliver a one-shot intervention that will have permanent effects. There is evidence, described here, that such a strategy can reduce criminal behavior and other social problems. But this approach has never succeeded in generating long-term gains in academic achievement or cognitive skills. A different approach may be needed. Rather than attempting to "inoculate" students against academic failure, perhaps we should try to raise educational productivity on an ongoing basis. In other words, we may need to increase the amount that disadvantaged children learn every year that they are in school or at least increase it several times during their educational careers.

To be cost-effective, such an approach would have to be relatively inexpensive in terms of expenditures per child per year. As George Farkas shows in chapter 3, Reading One-to-One successfully delivers individualized tutoring at a fraction of the cost of Success for All. It does so by using part-time workers (often college students) as tutors, rather than experienced teachers.

Given its reliance on less-experienced tutors, one would expect the effects of Reading One-to-One to fall short of those of Success for All. But the evidence suggests otherwise. On average, each Reading One-to-One tutoring session increased students' reading achievement 0.073 grade levels.[4] Thus sixty sessions, which was about the average amount received by full-time program participants, generated gains of 0.44 grade equivalents (0.51 standard deviation). This is roughly equivalent to the average effect of Success for All. If the marginal effectiveness of the tutoring sessions held up as the number of sessions increased, then 100 sessions generated increases of

0.73 grade equivalents (0.85 standard deviation). These are large gains, although not as large as the ones that Success for All generated for the poorest readers.

What is most impressive about Reading One-to-One is that it delivers a large "bang for the buck." The total cost, including administrative overhead, is about $8.38 per session. Thus sixty sessions of tutoring cost just $503, and 100 sessions cost $838. As noted, it is hard to do a true cost-benefit analysis of educational programs, because it is difficult to determine the monetary benefit of improved test scores. But if these numbers are accurate, Reading One-to-One delivers far greater gains in academic achievement per dollar spent than have ever been documented before.

These results suggest a number of exciting possibilities. At this rate, for example, one could deliver a sixty-session tutoring module to a child every year from grade one to grade twelve at a total cost of six thousand dollars, roughly the cost of one year of public school. If the marginal effectiveness of the program held up every year, the total increase in reading achievement would be five to six years by the time the child graduated. This would constitute a huge improvement in the productivity of the overall educational system for the child, clearly worth the 8.3 percent increase in overall cost.[5]

Unfortunately, we do not know whether the effectiveness of tutoring sessions would remain at such a high level as the total number of sessions increased and as the child moved past the third grade. The marginal effectiveness of tutoring is calculated from a sample of students who received an average of sixty sessions. So we cannot even be completely confident of the estimates for one hundred sessions in one year, much less for the seven hundred and twenty sessions over twelve years. However, even if we remain cautious in extrapolating from Reading One-to-One's basic results, they suggest that the reading skills of disadvantaged children can probably be improved at a reasonable cost.

The fundamental question is whether these basic results are credible. Farkas was not able to assign students randomly to treatment and control groups. He did not attempt to establish a nonrandom comparison group. Instead, he measured effectiveness by analyzing the relationship between variation in the number of tutoring sessions and changes in the level of reading achievement. This is a systematic way of using the relationship between time of participation in the program and the effect size (the tenth criterion) as an evaluation tool. The validity of this approach depends on the assumption that the number of tutoring sessions is not correlated with the students' abilities or motivation.

Farkas argues that this assumption is warranted, because the number of tutoring sessions that students received was determined by "accidents of scheduling" and thus was determined in an essentially random way. His case is strong, because he finds no relationship between the number of tutoring sessions and initial reading ability. Of course, there could still be unobserved differences in potential among students of comparable initial ability. Farkas eliminated one possible difference by having tutors rate students' levels of concentration in sessions and then controlling for this variable in his estimates. But it is impossible to eliminate all conceivable differences.

For example, one possibility is that frequent absence was associated with both fewer sessions and lower potential, even among those with comparable initial ability. But offsetting this concern is a selection process for participation in the program that may have biased estimates of the program effects in the opposite direction. When regular tutees were unavailable because of accidents of scheduling, alternates were chosen. Farkas notes that these alternates were typically the students who received the fewest number of sessions in the sample. Teachers selected both the regular tutees and the alternates. If teachers used subtle unobserved differences to select those most in need of tutoring as the primary tutees and those somewhat less in need as alternates, the estimated effect size would have been biased downward.

All in all, Farkas's evaluation design is probably as good as one using a matched comparison group, but clearly not as good as one using a randomly assigned control group. The results presented here are reinforced, however, by related ones. Similar tutoring programs, such as Reading Recovery and Success for All, have also been successful. But, of course, because the unique use of low-cost tutors makes Reading One-to-One potentially more cost-effective than its peers, the relevance of results from the other programs is limited. Reading One-to-One itself has been replicated and upscaled. Farkas has analyzed different sites, cohorts, and time periods, with consistently positive results. Although the relationship between implementation fidelity and effectiveness has not been analyzed directly, the effects have grown over time as sites have gained more experience with the program. This is a good sign. Nevertheless, a good deal more work needs to be done to prove the concept, all the more so because the program is so extraordinarily promising.

Three separate lines of research, with different time frames, should be established as quickly as possible. The first line of research should be aimed at determining whether Reading One-to-One, in its present form, merits being turned into a national-scale program over the next several years. As Farkas notes in chapter 3, we spend more than five billion dollars a year on educational programs for poor children through Title I, even though Title I is not an effective program. Farkas calculates that if we used all of the Title I money, we could provide sixty Reading One-to-One sessions to ten million children a year (or one hundred sessions to six million students a year). Therefore it would be quite feasible simply to replace Title I with a national Reading One-to-One program. This would be a bold step, but since the current program is ineffective, the risk is relatively small.

Nevertheless, we would naturally want to be as confident about the program's effectiveness as we reasonably could be before making such a major investment. Therefore, numerous evaluations of different sites and cohorts should be undertaken. As many evaluations as possible should be done by independent evaluators using a pure experimental design. If these evaluations yielded consistently positive results, we would probably have enough evidence in two or three years to justify making a major investment to expand the program.

Even with the best of results, the program should be ratcheted up in steps. Even if the program works extremely well at its present size, it might lose its effectiveness if its scale were increased substantially. It has already grown successfully from a single site to thirty-two schools and twenty-four hundred children at its height. However, that is a long way from being a national-scale program serving millions of children. To reduce the risk of wasting large amounts of money, the program should grow in stages. Evaluations should be done at each stage, and ensuing steps should be taken only if those evaluations indicate that the program still works.

The second and third lines of research should have longer time frames. The second should be made up of long-term studies that follow various cohorts from numerous sites into adulthood. This would enable us to determine whether Reading One-to-One's effects endure or fade out.

The third line of research should be structured to push the limits of Reading One-to-One's potential to raise the productivity of the

American educational system. This would involve developing equally inexpensive versions of Reading One-to-One for children in grades four through twelve. Planned variation studies should then be structured to determine how the program's impact varies with the duration and timing of interventions over the course of twelve years. At the earliest sign of success, we would probably also want to develop a "Math One-to-One" program and do similar planned variation studies on it, if the initial results prove promising.

One could certainly argue that no major investments should be made in Reading One-to-One before results from the long-term studies in the second and third lines of research have generated positive results. After all, numerous other programs have raised academic achievement in the short run only to see those gains fade out. There is a good chance that the second line of research will show that the gains of Reading One-to-One fade out sooner or later. It would be prudent to wait to make major investments in the program, were it not for two facts. First, the low cost of Reading One-to-One offers hope that we can intervene whenever gains begin to fade out. And second, in the plan described here, money would be reallocated from an ineffective program (Title I), so there is little risk of making the current situation worse. This seems like a good risk to take when measured against the opportunity cost of delaying implementation for the ten to fifteen years that it would take for the long-term follow-up studies to yield results.

One reason we can be hopeful that multiple years of intervention can produce long-term gains is that this has been the case with the Chicago public schools' Child-Parent Center (CPC) and Expansion Program. The CPCs offer a combination of educational enrichment and family support services to children between the ages of three and nine (preschool through third grade). The key components of the program are small class sizes, parental involvement, an emphasis on basic skills, and most notably, the opportunity to receive up to six years of services.

The effects of the CPCs are evaluated by Arthur Reynolds using the Chicago Longitudinal Study in chapter 4. This study included all 1,152 children enrolled in twenty CPC preschools and kindergartens between 1983 and 1986 as well as a comparison group. The children in the comparison group attended different full-day kindergartens at six randomly selected schools in high-poverty areas of Chicago. The study continues to follow both groups as they move through the school system.

Reynolds finds that the CPCs generate long-term gains in academic achievement, but only for children who participated for at least three years. The effects for those children who participated for six years are quite substantial. By eighth grade, the effect for six-year participants was 0.56 standard deviation in reading and 0.50 standard deviation in math. These long-term participants gained about one full grade level in achievement, making up roughly half the gap to the national average. Only 11 percent were held back a grade in school versus 34 percent in the comparison group. They also averaged half a year less in special education and developed more practical life skills.

Gains tended to fade out over time, but only partially. Effect sizes fell between third and fifth grade but stabilized thereafter. There is no way to know yet whether the gains achieved through eighth grade are permanent, but by that point the gains had survived for five years after the final intervention.

The most striking feature of these results is the consistent relationship between the size of gains and the duration of participation. Each extra year of participation after the first tends to raise performance on each one of five measures of achievement. The correlation is not perfect, but we would not expect it to be, given random error. The positive trend is quite strong, particularly when all five measures are considered. This pattern is important for two reasons. It suggests that long-lasting improvements in academic performance can be achieved through sustained intervention, and it lends a great deal of credibility to the results. Thus the program confers tangible benefits that accrue slowly, but consistently, over time.

This pattern is all the more important, because the evaluation did not have a pure experimental design. Reynolds and Temple (1995), who are both independent evaluators, go to great lengths to identify and adjust for any biasing effects that nonrandom selection might have on these findings. The results appear to be robust, but without random assignment it is hard to be completely confident. Also, the significance tests are biased, because they do not adjust for within-school correlations.

Reynolds analyzes the CPC data as if it were all from one medium-size program, in part because it provides him with enough cases and variation with which to assess the relationship between duration of participation and effect size. But the CPCs have essentially been replicated and scaled up. There are twenty sites in Chicago, which have served thousands of children. An analysis that defines each cohort at each site as a single case (as is done by Slavin and his coauthors in chapter 2) should be carried out to replicate the basic results. It would be preferable for such a study to use different cohorts, so that those findings are completely independent of the ones presented here. That study could also examine the relationship between effect size and implementation fidelity or site experience.

Most programs similar to the CPCs have not yielded long-term gains in academic achievement. This fact begs the question of whether CPC results are those of a random outlier. In chapter 4, Reynolds attempts to identify a number of components of CPCs that could explain their relatively unique success, but each of the elements he cites, such as parental involvement, has been used by other programs that did not generate enduring gains. Therefore, if future studies replicate Reynolds's results, we would have to ascribe the program's success to either the unique mix of components or the duration of intervention itself or both.

The CPCs are expensive. They cost $3,600 more than the regular educational program for the primary grades and $4,180 more for kindergarten. Because five or six years of intervention are needed to generate substantial long-term gains, the overall cost is in the range of $18,000 to $22,000. This is mitigated somewhat by reductions in grade retentions and special education. We will not be able to determine whether the benefits outweigh the costs until the current cohorts reach adulthood, although it is quite possible that they will, given the gains in both academic achievement and practical life skills. Offhand, it might seem that the total cost would be politically and financially infeasible. Yet the Chicago public school system has provided this program to thousands of children over many years, so we should not be quick to write off the program as being too costly. Long-term interventions may be necessary to generate enduring academic gains, so it is vital that we follow up with these cohorts to determine whether the investment pays off in the end. However, until we can replicate these results and measure the long-term benefits, it is not advisable to spend large amounts on upscaling this program.

Although sustained intervention may be necessary to raise academic achievement, results from evaluations of the High/Scope Perry Preschool Program suggest that the "inoculation" approach may be extremely effective in dealing with other important social problems. The Perry Preschool is described by Lawrence Schweinhart and David Weikart in chapter 5. It is, in many senses of the word, the mother of all social programs. Initiated in 1962, it was one of the first rigorously planned social experiments. Its evaluation was one of the first to use a pure experimental design. It was a model for Head Start and, in a looser sense, for much social policy and experimentation that evolved over the ensuing decades. The consistency and duration of follow-up studies of the long-term effects of the program are unparalleled. In fact, the participants and controls are still being followed today, more than thirty years after the experimental treatment ended. Thus it offers as much or more evidence on the question of the permanence of effects than any program ever has. The evaluation's only real weakness is that it was not carried out by independent analysts.

The program itself was the archetypal early intervention program for preschoolers. Three- and four-year-old children participated for one or two school years. The program applied classic principles of child development to create a nurturing environment fostering social, emotional, and cognitive growth. Student-teacher ratios were very low, with four teachers in each class of twenty to twenty-five children. Teachers made weekly ninety-minute home visits to every family. All teachers were certified in both early childhood and special education.

In the early years after the treatment was completed, the program was deemed a failure, because most of the early academic gains faded out in the later grades. But long-term follow-ups revealed successes in other areas.

The most recent data were generated when the participants were twenty-seven years old. By that age, there were a number of large effects, several of which were truly dramatic. The program quadrupled the proportion of individuals who were earning more than two thousand dollars a month, from 7 to 29 percent. It almost tripled home ownership, raising it from 13 to 36 percent. It reduced the proportion who had ever received welfare by a quarter, from 80 to 59 percent. And in what is probably the single most extraordinary gain ever achieved by a social program, it reduced the rate of hard-core criminality (defined as having five or more arrests) by four-fifths, from 35 to 7 percent. For males, the reduction was from 49 to 12 percent. There were no significant differences between children who spent one year in the program and those who spent two years, so time of participation had neither a positive nor a negative influence.

The program was expensive, but cost-effective. The total cost was $12,356 per participant in constant 1992 dollars, but the savings to the public, in terms of lower taxes and reduced crime, was $88,433 (assuming an annual discount rate of 3 percent). In other words, the program saved the general public $7.16 for each dollar invested. And this does not even take into account any psychological benefits that accrued to the participants and their families, which common sense tells us were huge.

If these results are replicable, the policy prescription is clear. We should turn Head Start into a copy of the Perry Preschool Program and make it available to every poor child. This would involve a substantial up-front investment that would pay for itself many times over by significantly reducing the incidence of some of America's worst social problems down the road.

The problem is that we cannot yet be sure that the results are replicable, and we need to have a high degree of confidence to justify a multibillion dollar investment. Despite the high quality of the evaluation design, a single study is never enough to be sure of a program's efficacy. And because the program was done at a single site, we do not know whether it would work as well for poor children in other places and situations or whether quality would suffer in the process of upscaling it. The lack of replication also means that there is no information on the relationship between effect size and either implementation fidelity or site experience.

Recently, however, Schweinhart and Weikart (1997) have published results from one near replication, as part of the High/Scope Preschool Curriculum Comparison. In that study, children were randomly assigned to three preschools, each with a different curriculum design. One was based on the High/Scope (Perry Preschool) model, a second was a more intensive academic program called Direct Instruction, and a third was a traditional nursery school. In short, the study was structured specifically to determine whether the unique design of the Perry Preschool was responsible for its outcomes. Unfortunately, although the original program was replicated, the original evaluation cannot be. There was no pure control group of individuals who did not receive any treatment at all.

The basic result was that by age twenty-three, the High/Scope group had better outcomes on a number of social (but not academic) measures than the Direct Instruction group. As with the original Perry Preschool children, the largest and most consistent effects were in the area of crime and delinquency. For example, the High/Scope individuals had less than half the total number of arrests. And just 10 percent of the High/Scope group had been arrested for a felony compared with 39 percent for the Direct Instruction group. But there was no clear pattern of statistically significant differences between the High/Scope group and the traditional nursery school group, with respect to crime or any other outcomes. Therefore, given the absence of a pure control group, it is hard to know whether the High/Scope and traditional nursery schools reduced crime, whether the Direct Instruction Program increased it, or both. As it happens, the arrest rates at age twenty-three were roughly the same for the original Perry Preschool group as for the new High/Scope group. They were also roughly the same for the no-treatment control group in the original Perry study and the new Direct Instruction group. These facts hint that the later results may reflect improvement in the High/Scope and traditional nursery groups rather than deterioration in the Direct Instruction group. However, there is no sound methodological basis for making such comparisons.

The similarity in outcomes between the High/Scope and the traditional nursery school groups is also an important result. On the one hand, it is bad news in the sense that it calls into question whether the unique features of the Perry Preschool model add any value at all above and beyond what traditional nursery schools provide. On the other hand, it is good news in the sense that it suggests that any preschool offering a high-quality program emphasizing social and emotional development may reduce crime and delinquency among individuals who grow up poor.

A major research effort is needed to determine the effects of various types of preschools on crime and delinquency over the life cycle. Part of this research should be devoted to developing new studies similar to the High/Scope Preschool Curriculum Comparison (but with a no-treatment control group in which parents chose between the options available in the general community). But we cannot rely on this approach exclusively. It takes too long for the major potential benefits of such programs to manifest themselves. Fortunately, both the first and the second studies find that reductions in early adolescent misconduct presaged later reductions in crime and delinquency. Even so, if we started now, it would take a minimum of ten years to get any clear indication of effectiveness.

Thus another part of this research effort should be aimed at following up on adolescents and adults who were in other preschool studies. Numerous evaluations of various kinds of preschool programs were conducted over the past thirty years. Unfortunately, most of them focused on academic outcomes. Follow-up studies that focus on criminality and other behavioral outcomes in adolescence and adulthood are needed on as many of these programs as possible. Even data from projects with poor evaluation designs would be of some value in meta-analyses. If such a research effort reveals a strong relationship between certain types of preschool and crime, a large-scale investment in early intervention programs might be justified. Depending on the nature of the results, this might take the form of expanding, standardizing, or intensifying Head Start.

The Perry Preschool was originally considered a disappointment because most of the early cognitive benefits it generated faded out over time. This is a consistent pattern in early intervention programs. They typically raise IQ (intelligence quotient) and achievement test scores by large amounts, but these gains disappear by the third or fourth grade.

The Abecedarian (ABC) Project, described by Craig Ramey, Frances Campbell, and Clancy Blair in chapter 6, is an exception. It increased cognitive test scores, and these increases held up through the latest evaluation, at age fifteen. ABC is somewhat unusual in that it intervened extremely early, at six weeks of age. Children who were randomly assigned to the control group received nutritional supplements and screening for developmental problems. Children who were randomly assigned to the treatment group received these services and were enrolled in an intensive educational day care program. On reaching kindergarten age, half of the treatment and control groups were randomly assigned to a follow-up home enrichment program that lasted for an additional three years. The other half received no further treatment and began attending public school kindergarten. Because time spent in the program and the age of intervention are confounded, there is no way to determine the relationship between effect size and duration of participation.

Seven to ten years after the final treatment, at age fifteen, those children who attended the preschool program had IQs that were 0.35 standard deviation (4.6 points) higher than those who did not. This difference is not large, but it is not trivial either. The program's overall effect on achievement test scores was comparable. The effect on the IQs of the children of mothers with very low IQs was quite large (11.7 points), but there were just six such cases each in the treatment and control groups. The program reduced grade retentions by about 40 percent and special education placements by half. The follow-up program had no effect on IQ or mathematics scores, but it did raise reading achievement by a small amount.

These findings are promising, but there are reasons to be cautious. The evaluation was not done by independent researchers, although the design was excellent. The program has not been formally upscaled or replicated.[6] Because of the lack of replication, there is no information on the relationship between effect size and implementation fidelity or site experience. The most important reason for pause is that similar early intervention programs have not had consistent long-term effects on cognitive test scores (although they have reduced grade retentions and special education placements; Consortium for Longitudinal Studies 1983). It is possible that the Abecedarian Project is simply one of two random outliers (along with the *Milwaukee Project*, Garber 1988). One factor that may distinguish ABC as an "orange" in this distribution of apples is its initiation of intervention in early infancy. Most of the IQ difference between treatment and controls was already present by six months of age.

Even if ABC's results are replicable, the program may not be cost-effective on the basis of cognitive gains alone. The annual cost of the program is six thousand dollars per child. Because the elementary school intervention had virtually no impact, the effective part of the program involved five years of intervention, for a total cost of thirty thousand dollars. Even if the cognitive gains hold up through adulthood, they would not justify that kind of investment, unless they spin off other positive outcomes. We should not rush out and spent lots of money replicating ABC on a larger scale, although it may hold some promise as a medium-scale program targeted specifically to mothers with very low IQs.

The next follow-up is scheduled to be done when the individuals are twenty-one years old. At that point, it will be important to determine whether economic and behavioral outcomes similar to those generated by the Perry Preschool have manifested themselves. If so, ABC might turn out to be highly cost-effective. Unfortunately, results from the early follow-ups on childhood misconduct show that the treatment group exhibited more problem behavior than the controls. So it may be that ABC had too strong an academic orientation, like the Direct Instruction model.

Regardless of whether we would ever want to replicate ABC on a large scale, the program is important because it suggests that we should not completely abandon the hope of inoculating children against cognitive deficits through early intervention. The results are favorable enough to justify further research. In particular, we should continue examining the cognitive effects of very early intervention in infancy and the effects of intervention on the children of mothers with very low IQs. If we can identify the particular elements of the Abecedarian Project that generate the effects, we may be able to develop a program that can deliver the same impact for a fraction of the cost or a larger impact for the same price.

The programs discussed so far have all been small to medium scale. But at least one national-scale federal program can offer evidence of both substantial benefits and cost-effectiveness: the Special Supplemental Nutrition Program for Women, Infants, and Children, better known as WIC, which is analyzed by Barbara Devaney in chapter 7.[7] The WIC program serves low-income pregnant women and mothers as well as children under the age of five. It provides its clients with vouchers for food supplements, nutrition education, and referrals to health care and social service providers. WIC is one of the largest social programs in existence. In fiscal 1993, it served almost six million people and cost 2.8 billion dollars.

WIC appears to have substantial impacts on gestational age and birthweight, outcomes that are associated with various health risks. Devaney, an independent evaluator, finds that the incidence of preterm births was 18 to 31 percent lower for the WIC participants. The incidence of low birthweight was 22 to 31 percent lower. And the average birthweight was 51 to 117 grams higher for WIC children.

WIC also seems to save more money than it costs. And unlike some other programs in which the benefits do not start to accrue until years after the investments are made, WIC appears to be cost-effective almost from the beginning. Devaney finds that in the first sixty days after birth, the Medicaid costs of WIC newborns and mothers were $277 to $598 lower than those of newborns and mothers who did not participate in WIC. Thus the program saved between $1.77 and $3.13 in Medicaid for every dollar spent on the program. Savings were even larger for a subset of infants whose mothers were not eligible for Medicaid during pregnancy, but who became eligible after birth because the newborns suffered health problems requiring expensive medical care.

We need to be cautious about these results. They were not generated from a controlled experiment, but rather from a comparison between WIC participants and nonparticipants on Medicaid.[8] Because nonparticipants were eligible for WIC, selection was based largely on choice and access. Such nonrandom selection may bias the results, although it is not clear in which direction. To the extent that WIC mothers were volunteers who were motivated to maintain the health of themselves and their children, the effects of WIC are probably overstated. To the extent that WIC tends to target the highest-risk mothers, the effects are probably understated. WIC participants do tend to be more disadvantaged than eligible nonparticipants in comparison groups.

Since WIC is a national program, there are no replications of it or anything remotely comparable to it in terms of scale. It is so unique that it does not fit into any distribution of programs. It has essentially been almost fully scaled up already. Although the program has not been replicated, Buescher and others (1993) applied similar methods to North Carolina data and generated results comparable to Devaney's. There is no information on the relationship between effect size and implementation fidelity or duration. There is some information in other studies on time of participation, but it is confounded by the child's age at intervention, so its relationship to effect size cannot be distinguished (Rush and others 1988).

A multisite analysis could shed light on these issues. Devaney does this to a limited extent by conducting separate analyses for each of five states. She finds a positive effect on each of five outcomes in five states, with twenty-three of the twenty-five results statistically significant and one other nearly so. This consistency lends credence to the overall findings. However, if selection biases the effects upward, it could very well affect every outcome in every state.

Because WIC is an ongoing national program, it will be hard to design an evaluation that is free of selection bias. Nevertheless, further research using quasi-experimental methodologies is warranted, because the program is so large. If Devaney's results are valid, there is a least one large-scale federal social program that really works. And this would be true, even though the cost-benefit analysis completely omitted any possible medium- and long-term medical and social gains. Taking these into account, it is quite possible that the benefit-cost ratio of WIC could be much higher than Devaney's upper bound of 3:1.

Even many people who believe that social programs can work if they reach children early, like WIC does, are all too ready to write off older children and adolescents. This is particularly true with respect to delinquency and drug abuse. Yet there is hope that these terrible problems are not necessarily intractable, even if we get a late start.

Two drug prevention programs offer sound evidence that they reduce rates of substance use and abuse among adolescents. Phyllis Ellickson describes one of these programs, Project ALERT, in chapter 8. Project ALERT is a module of eleven classes offered to seventh graders and a booster set of three sessions to eighth graders. The curriculum is designed to increase students' motivation to abstain from drug use and to give them the social skills needed to resist peer pressure.

Relative to students in randomly assigned control schools, Project ALERT lowered the proportion of students who started using marijuana in junior high school by about 30 percent. It also substantially reduced the frequency of both marijuana and cigarette smoking among individuals who had already been using the drugs. Effect sizes were roughly the same at schools with high percentages of minorities as they were at largely white schools. The evaluation design was based on random assignment of schools, but not of individuals. Significance tests were adjusted for within-school correlations.

There are a number of reasons to be cautious about the results. There was one anomalous finding. The most committed smokers in the treatment schools actually smoked more than their counterparts in control schools. This weakens our confidence in the positive results obtained. The evaluator was also the developer of the program. The results have not yet been replicated, and the program has not been upscaled. Thus there is no information on the relationship between effect size and implementation fidelity or site experience. There are also no data on the association between effects and time of participation. And perhaps most important, all of the effects faded away during high school.

There are also reasons to be hopeful. Project ALERT is by no means unique. A number of similar programs have also reduced various kinds of drug use in the short run (Botvin, chapter 9 in this volume; Murray and others 1984; Perry and others 1980). And the fade-out of effects does not make the program a failure, by any means, because the costs of treatment are trivial. In chapter 8, Ellickson estimates that the entire cost of the program is $1.50 per student, assuming that teaching time is drawn from other drug prevention uses. Even if we impute the value of the teaching time, the total cost of the program is probably no more than thirty-five dollars per student.[9] The fact that such a low-intensity, inexpensive program may have reduced several types of drug use by fairly large amounts for two years is quite extraordinary. It is very likely that even the short-run medical and social benefits of the reduced drug use amount to more than thirty-five dollars per person. More important, the amazing "bang for the buck" that the program yields suggests the possibility that permanent results might be achieved either by increasing its intensity or by offering additional boosters in later years. The Life Skills Training (LST) Program, presented by Gilbert Botvin in chapter 9, offers a chance to test that hypothesis.

LST is similar to Project ALERT, but it provides twice as many sessions and an additional year of boosters. It consists of fifteen classes of forty-five minutes each in the seventh grade and boosters of ten classes in the eighth grade and five in the ninth grade. Its curriculum covers drug information, self-management skills, general social skills, and social resistance skills.

LST has been replicated many times over and implemented on a medium scale. There have been numerous evaluations of it, involving several thousand students. These evaluations consistently demonstrate large, and in some cases huge, short-term reductions in both overall use and heavy use of cigarettes, alcohol, marijuana, and hard drugs. Scaling the program up reduced the effect size a bit, but the impacts were still large. There was some tendency for effects to fade out over the long term, but at least some effects remained three years after the last boosters. At the end of high school, the program reduced cigarette smoking by more than 20 percent. It lowered the incidence of drunkenness by about 15 percent. It reduced weekly marijuana use by 33 percent, but the effect was not significant. There were small reductions in casual use of alcohol and marijuana, but they were inconsistent and not significant. Every combination of multiple use of these three drugs was lower in each of two treatment groups, but only about half of these effects were significant. Implementation fidelity was systematically measured in a random sample of classes. Effects were consistently larger for students who received treatments that were more faithful to the program design. Of the thirty-four long-term effects measured for the high-fidelity sample, twenty-nine were significant, and the other five were all positive (Botvin et al. 1995).

There are some problems with the LST evaluations. All of them were done by Botvin, the program's developer. They were based on random assignment, but with schools as the unit of assignment and students as the unit of analysis. Because no adjustments were made for within-school correlations, the tests of significance are biased. Also, long-term results are not yet available for samples with high percentages of minorities.

However, there are factors that lend credence to the results. Project ALERT and similar programs have generated similar results, so LST is not an outlier. LST is distinct from Project ALERT in offering more sessions over more years. The fact that it produces larger effects suggests that there may be a relationship between program intensity and effect size. There is no analysis of the relationship between site experience and effect size.

By far the most impressive aspect of the program is the extraordinary relationship between cost and long-term effects. Including the value of teachers' time, the entire program probably costs less than seventy-five dollars per student.[10] Yet it generates substantial long-term reductions in various kinds of drug use. Although no formal analysis of the value of such reductions has been performed, the benefit-cost ratio is probably very large.

Some work remains to be done. First, the tests of significance in the studies need to be adjusted for within-school correlations. Second, it would be nice to have at least one evaluation in which students were the unit of assignment as well as the unit of analysis. Third, we need long-term results from at least one study in a population with a substantial proportion of minorities. And fourth, a formal cost-benefit analysis should be done.

If all of those analyses corroborate the findings presented here, ratcheting up the scale of LST would be justified, with the goal of turning it into a national program over the course of several years. Given the low cost of the program, the risks are small relative to the huge potential benefits.

While conducting further analysis of the basic LST program, we should also be developing and piloting new, more intensive versions. Versions that offer three or five or even ten times as many sessions over several years would still be relatively cheap. Given the record of the current version, these "super-LSTs" could potentially yield huge long-term reductions in drug use. Of course, there are no guarantees that increasing the intensity would enlarge the impact. But the findings to date offer ample justification for investing in a planned variation study that would compare several versions of different intensity levels to each other and to a "no-treatment" control group.

The success of the drug programs with heavy users offers hope that social programs can do some good even if intervention begins after people have developed serious social problems. The Treatment Foster Care (TFC) Program, described by Patricia Chamberlain and

Kevin Moore in chapter 10, suggests that even chronic juvenile delinquents can be helped. TFC placed eighty delinquent boys between the ages of twelve and seventeen into foster families recruited from the community. The boys had been ordered into residential treatment by a juvenile court and randomly assigned to either a group home or TFC. The average age of the boys was 14.3 years, and their mean number of arrests prior to beginning treatment was thirteen. The program trained the foster parents in the use of behavior management skills and monitored them closely throughout the program. It emphasized the importance of preventing contact between the boy and any delinquent peers. Only one boy was placed with each particular TFC family. The average treatment period was seven months in both TFC and group care.

TFC had very large effects both during the treatment period and one year after it ended. Six months into treatment, arrest rates were more than two-thirds lower for the TFC group. There was some fade-out of the effect during the post-treatment year. But at the one-year follow-up, TFC arrest rates were still 52 percent lower. Most of this gain was attributable to the relatively large proportion of TFC boys who stayed completely "clean": 41 percent of the TFC boys had no arrests by the follow-up compared with only 7 percent of the group-care teens, an extraordinary ratio of almost 6:1. TFC tripled the proportion of boys who returned to their original families and decreased the number of days of incarceration by 59 percent (from 129 to 53) during the follow-up period.

The average cost of TFC was $18,620 for a full course of treatment. This was 29 to 47 percent lower than the cost of group care. So, with substantially lower costs and much larger benefits, the program is clearly superior to group care. Because TFC was not compared to a control group that received no treatment at all, we do not know if TFC is cost-effective relative to doing nothing for the boys.[11] But given its large advantages over group care and the high costs of arrest, trial, and incarceration, TFC is an extremely promising program.

The version of TFC evaluated here was itself a replication. The first two pilots were also successful, which lends credence to the results. But all three trials were small, so we do not know if quality would suffer if the program were enlarged. The approach of the program is fairly unique, so it is clearly not a random outlier in a large distribution. Of course, this means that there are no corroborating results from similar programs. We do not have any information on the relationship between site experience or fidelity of implementation and effect size. We also do not know if longer or more intense treatment would improve the results. Overall, the design of the evaluation was quite good, although the evaluators were also the program developers.

A good deal of additional research on the program needs to be done. A formal cost-benefit analysis should be carried out. The boys from the original program should be followed to determine how long the effects last. A long-term study could also determine whether any other benefits, such as gains in education or employment, emerge. And, of course, the program should be replicated at other sites with larger samples and different populations. Some of these evaluations should use a "no-treatment" control group (which would probably necessitate applying a selection process other than court mandate). Clearly, it is too early to recommend that this program be implemented on a large scale. Nevertheless, TFC is a tremendously exciting program that offers hope for teenagers who currently seem out of reach.

If early intervention programs occupy one end of the spectrum of social programs, work and training programs occupy the other. They attempt to intervene late in the game, in adulthood or late adolescence. There is a long history of experiments with and evaluations of work and training programs. These programs have generated a set of results that are consistent enough to have created a fairly widespread consensus among scholars with regard to their potential.

On the one hand, the best programs can be cost-effective. On the other hand, their effects are small. By investing a small amount of money per participant, it is possible to increase the amount that the individuals work, to reduce their welfare dependence, and to raise their earnings by enough to justify the cost of the program. However, the earnings gains typically amount to just several hundred dollars a year. Increasing the intensity (and cost) of the program beyond a certain point does not increase the size of those gains (Friedlander and Gueron 1992). No matter how much is invested, these programs cannot come close to making a typical welfare recipient financially self-sufficient. The consensus is that work and training programs cannot possibly move large numbers of people off welfare and into jobs in the private labor market.

Lawrence Mead challenges this consensus in chapter 11. Chapter 11 is unique in this volume in that it does not present an evaluation or a meta-analysis of a single program. Instead it reinterprets the body of evidence generated from all research on one type of program. Mead contends that a combination of good training programs and stringent work requirements in welfare programs can reduce welfare dependence. He supports this contention in three ways. First, he argues that the results from work and training evaluations understate the potential of the approach, for technical reasons. Second, he cites results from recent programs suggesting that we are learning how to generate larger gains. And third, he presents data suggesting that the combination of strict work requirements and good programs has reduced welfare caseloads by substantial amounts in various localities.

Some of Mead's technical arguments have merit, but even if he is right on every count, the overall picture remains the same. It is unlikely that all of these factors together could have led to underestimates of potential income gains from work and training programs by more than five hundred dollars per year and certainly not by more than a thousand dollars. Even at the upper end of that range, the programs would not make most welfare recipients financially self-sufficient.

The recent successes that Mead cites clearly offer hope. He argues that there was a clear pattern of learning and improvement over time in California. The Saturation Work Initiative Model in San Diego improved on an earlier generation of programs by enforcing participation more aggressively. Then the Greater Avenues for Independence (GAIN) in Riverside got even better results by emphasizing job search. Indeed, Riverside GAIN is probably the most successful work and training program ever done. It increased earnings by 40 percent. Two other sites using the same basic "labor force attachment" strategy also achieved unusually good results. So there is reason to hope that the unique features of that strategy make it genuinely superior. If so, work and training programs should start producing better results by using this approach. Nevertheless, even Riverside GAIN, which is the most successful program on record, increased earnings by just $1,010 a year. So if the goal is to make families self-sufficient, we clearly have a long way to go up the learning curve.

Mead also presents evidence that a combination of well-run programs and strict work requirements can reduce welfare caseloads by substantial amounts. In particular, he cites data from Wisconsin, which established programs with strict work requirements and saw its caseload fall by half between 1987 and 1996. Given the effect sizes of work and training programs, the larger declines could only have been the result of a diversion effect, that is, people getting thrown off welfare, leaving it voluntarily, or choosing not to go on it in the first place because of the work requirements.

Unfortunately, there is no way to be sure whether the caseload declines were actually the result of the programs and the requirements, for a number of reasons. No experimental evaluation has been done. Much of the decrease in some of the counties occurred before the particular programs or requirements were instituted. And Wisconsin's economy was growing strongly during most of the period, while welfare benefits were being cut. But Mead's statistical analyses suggest that these factors cannot account for the large declines in caseloads (Mead 1997).

We need to do more rigorous evaluations of the diversion effect of work requirements. Mead's evidence suggests that the effect may well be substantial. But this evidence is by no means strong enough, in and of itself, to justify major policy decisions.

Even if all of the reduction in Wisconsin's caseloads could be attributed to the programs and work requirements, we still could not use them as stand-alone alternatives to a guaranteed benefit program, without decreasing incomes of the poor by a large amount. Unfortunately, this is essentially what our new welfare system, enacted by the Personal Responsibility and Work Opportunity Reconciliation Act of 1996 (PRWORA), does. Thus it seems very likely that this legislation will lead to large losses of income among the poorest Americans and perhaps a catastrophic rise in abject poverty.

The reason for this is that the numbers just do not add up. The 1996 legislation has "ended welfare as we know it" in the simplest possible way—by ending it, without offering any viable alternative. Although this legislation has a number of components, some good and some bad, ultimately they all pale in comparison to the provision that places a five-year lifetime limit on welfare benefits. This provision is implicitly predicated on the assumption that given strong incentives and enough time, we can prepare 100 percent of welfare recipients to become self-sufficient in the private labor market. But every bit of research ever done on welfare and training programs clearly suggests that nothing could be further from the truth. A large proportion of welfare recipients, probably somewhere in the range of 25 to 50 percent, are not capable of sustaining regular employment in a competitive labor market. There is absolutely no evidence that any amount of training can change that fact. And although the most optimistic interpretation of Mead's evidence suggests that work requirements may divert large numbers of recipients away from welfare, it does nothing to offer hope for the substantial portions that would be left without any alternative sources of income.

Mead suggests that friends and relatives and other programs can pick up the slack. With respect to friends and relatives, only time will tell. With respect to programs, current alternatives are clearly inadequate. State-funded general assistance programs are the main alternative to federal welfare programs. None of them offers benefits even remotely close to what is necessary to support a family. Traditionally, individuals who have depended on these programs for support have been single men who are either homeless or living in single-room-occupancy hotels. Recent cuts in these programs have created substantial hardship among that population (Danziger and Kossoudji 1994/95).

PRWORA does allow states to exempt 20 percent of its welfare population from the five-year time limit. This will no doubt help to prevent some suffering. But not all states will use this exemption, and even the ones that do will not be able to ensure that every one of those spots will go to people who really need them.

Mead's analysis in chapter 11 offers some hope of a viable compromise between the new system and the old. This compromise involves the resurrection of an old reform proposal—workfare. In workfare, welfare recipients have to work to receive their benefits. This is radically different from the five-year time limit, because it guarantees all recipients a job.

PRWORA will almost inevitably appear to be a great success on the surface. There is no doubt that caseloads and welfare costs will fall dramatically. It is easy to cut caseloads and costs simply by kicking people out of the program. Another result will be that work will increase among the poor, which will probably be the greatest legitimate benefit of the new system. At the same time, however, PRWORA will almost certainly reduce the income of the poor substantially. And it may consign large numbers of American families to abject poverty without any choice at all or, in some cases, perhaps with a choice to remain in abusive domestic situations. In evaluating the success of the new system, it will be vital to weigh the lost income and other hardships suffered by the poor against the governmental savings and the increases in work.

Workfare would offer most of the upside of PRWORA, without most of the downside. It would provide a reasonable alternative to every adult welfare recipient, while dealing with the one complaint that the overwhelming majority of Americans have with the old system—that people can receive money without working. Critics have argued that workfare is too expensive. Administering work programs certainly costs more per participant than simply writing benefit checks. It may well be that most Americans are willing to pay that price in order to balance their concern for the poor with their resentment of idleness. The most important contribution of chapter 11 is its suggestion that we might not have to pay that price. If work requirements have a strong diversionary effect, then workfare might not be more expensive overall than welfare, because it would cut caseloads substantially. It would steer the more capable people into the private labor market, while guaranteeing a public job and a living wage to those who need that guarantee.

SUMMARY AND POLICY IMPLICATIONS

Table 1.1 encapsulates the analysis presented here. It summarizes how each of the programs evaluated in this volume stack up when judged according to the thirteen criteria.

Only a small percentage of social programs offer convincing evidence that they generate both substantial effects and benefits that exceed costs (Crane, in preparation). This conclusion has important implications for social policy. It suggests that a decentralized approach to program development, which is increasingly our de facto national policy as the federal government continues to hand off responsibilities to the states, is sensible in the early stages of program development. If only a small fraction of the approaches that are tried work, many different approaches need to be tried to yield even a single success. However, it also suggests that once a successful model has been developed, it is probably necessary to recentralize control over the implementation process. *If the overall success rate is low, using social programs as an instrument of social policy will never be cost-effective unless the very best programs are replicated on a large scale.*

Title I illustrates this principle. Although federally funded, it is a highly decentralized program. Every school chooses what programs to use to help disadvantaged students. Because only a small percentage of the programs used actually work, the overall impact of Title I is virtually zero. As long as we had no alternatives, this approach served a valuable purpose. It enabled us to try lots of different methods and, ultimately, provided funds that contributed to the develop-

Table 1.1 Performance of Programs Judged According to Thirteen Criteria

Criteria	Success for All	Reading One-to-One	Chicago Child-Parent Centers	High/Scope Perry Preschool	Abecedarian Project	WIC[a]	Project Alert	Life Skills Training	Treatment Foster Care
Key outcomes are significant[b]	Yes	Yes	Yes	Yes	Yes	Yes	Yes	Yes	Yes
Effect sizes for key outcomes[c]	Substantial-huge	Substantial-large	Substantial	Substantial-huge	Substantial	Substantial	Substantial	Substantial-large	Large-huge
Cost-benefit relationship[d]	Uncertain	Promising	Uncertain	Excellent	Unpromising	Good	Promising	Promising	Promising
Long-term effects[e]	2 years +	—	5 years +	22 years +	7 years +	—	No	3 years +	—
Evaluation design[f]	Good	Good	Good	Excellent	Excellent	Good	Good	Good	Excellent
Independent evaluators[g]	No	No	Yes	No	No	Yes	No	No	No
Successful replications[h]	Yes	Yes	No	No	No	No	In progress	Yes	Yes
Success of similar programs[i]	Yes	Yes	No	No	No	No	Yes	Yes	No
Unique qualities explain success[j]	—	Probably	Probably not	Probably not	Maybe	—	—	Probably	Probably

More of program is better[k]	—	—	Yes	No	—	—	—	Maybe	—
Implementation fidelity helps[l]	—	—	—	—	—	—	—	Yes	—
Site experience help[m]	Yes	Yes	—	—	Yes	—	—	—	No
Program has been upscaled[n]	Yes	Yes	Yes	No	Yes	Yes	No	Yes	No

— Not available in all cases.

a Special Supplemental Nutrition Program for Women and Infant Children.

b Yes was the minimum standard for inclusion in this volume.

c Effect sizes were given as a rating or a range, and the minimum standard for inclusion in the volume was substantial (other categories were large and huge).

d If a formal cost-benefit analysis was done, the categories were good or excellent (none was worse than good); if no formal analysis was done, the categories were promising, uncertain, or unpromising.

e The number of years indicates the period after the last treatment for which effects remain significant, and a plus sign indicates that the effects were significant at the time of follow-up.

f The categories were excellent or good (none was worse than good); this does not reflect the quality of the work of the evaluators so much as the practical opportunities for developing a control or comparison group.

g Yes means that the evaluators were not involved in program development or implementation; no means that they were.

h Yes means that at least one replication was implemented and an evaluation of it, as an independent experiment, successfully generated results similar to those of the original program; in progress means that such a replication is in progress; no means that no successful replications have been documented.

i Yes means that most similar programs have yielded similar results; no means that they have not.

j Applicable if the program yields at least one result that is different from those of similar programs; the categories are probably (if the unique results seem clearly linked to a unique feature of the program), probably not (if there does not appear to be a link between the unique results and a feature of the program), and maybe (if there is a possible link).

k Yes means that the time of participation or program intensity was significantly correlated with effect size; no means that the time of participation and program intensity were not significantly correlated with effect size; maybe, in the case of Life Skills Training, means that although no formal analysis was done, the fact that the program provided more sessions than Project ALERT may explain why its effects lasted longer.

l Yes means that implementation fidelity was significantly correlated with effect size; no means that it was not.

m Yes means that size experience was significantly correlated with effect size; no means that it was not.

n Yes means that the program increased in size from one to at least ten sites; no means that it did not.

ment of good programs like Success for All and Reading One-to-One. As we become more and more convinced that at least one of these programs can work on a large scale, continuing local control over program selection in Title I will make less and less sense.

Of the nine programs evaluated here, WIC is the only national program, and it does appear to work. None of the others offers "plug and play" solutions that can be applied immediately on a national scale, although two seem to have that potential. Three others are also promising, but they need substantially more confirmation of their effectiveness. Three programs have less potential to be scaled up dramatically, mainly because of their high costs. They are important nonetheless, because they demonstrate that certain outcomes appear to be attainable. In each of these cases, further evidence of long-term benefits could change the prognosis.

The two programs that are closest to being ready for large-scale application are Reading One-to-One and the Life Skills Training drug prevention program. Both of them have had large effects in evaluations with quasi-experimental designs. Both of them are extremely cheap in terms of cost per participant per year. Both have been implemented on a medium scale, having served thousands of students. And in both cases, similar programs, like Success for All and Project ALERT, have proven successful using similar strategies.

However, neither one of them has been evaluated in a study using an experimental design in which individuals are the unit of assignment. If either one of these proves successful in such a study, and if some of the smaller issues are adequately addressed, it should be turned into a national program, serving millions of people. That growth process should be carried out in steps, and it should only be continued as long as evaluations show that the program remains successful at each step.

The three programs that are also promising but further away are Project ALERT, Treatment Foster Care, and the Perry Preschool. Project ALERT is similar to LST, but at an earlier stage of development. We would not need national versions of both. The new version of Project Alert, with a booster session in high school, bears watching and could prove even more effective than LST.

Treatment Foster Care appears to have the potential to reduce crime and delinquency by large amounts, but it is too early in the testing process to be fully confident of its impressive results. We need to determine how long its effects last and to conduct a cost-benefit analysis. If the analysis yields positive results, a multisite replication should be done. Only if that proves successful could we begin to think about developing it into a large-scale program.

The Perry Preschool is a conundrum. It has as much or more potential than any social program anywhere. If its long-term effects on crime, employment, earnings, and welfare receipt could be replicated on a national scale, some of the nation's worst social problems would be dramatically reduced. However, we simply do not know if such replication is possible. Thus, it is absolutely vital that we do as many long-term follow-up studies of other preschool programs as possible. This opportunity is far too important to waste.

Success for All, the Chicago Child-Parent Centers, and the Abecedarian Project may be too expensive to be turned into national programs, at least given our current state of knowledge about the benefits. Nonetheless, each makes an important contribution to the state of knowledge in the field, which could lead to the development of programs that have national potential. Success for All has demonstrated that at least one technique (one-on-one tutoring) increases the amount that children learn. If Reading One-to-One is successful on a national scale, it will be because it found a cheaper way to do what Success for All did first. This does not mean that we should abandon Success for All. Long-term follow-up studies may reveal that it yields greater benefits than its cheaper cousin, particularly for the poorest readers. These benefits may ultimately justify the high cost. Success for All has also given birth to Roots and Wings, a tremendously promising model of school reform.

The Chicago Child-Parent Centers and the Abecedarian Project have demonstrated the possibility of generating substantial long-term academic gains if the intervention lasts long enough, starts early enough, or is intensive enough. Unfortunately, the costs of these programs are too high to justify expanding them, given our current knowledge about their benefits. However, this could change, if the benefits increase substantially over the long term.

With respect to the work and training programs discussed in chapter 11, current research clearly indicates that we should not invest the money needed to run them on a national scale. Unfortunately, the new welfare legislation specifically mandates that we do just that. Mead's analysis suggests that work requirements may divert large numbers of people away from the welfare system. If that is true, the cost of guaranteeing people public jobs, rather than just kicking them off the rolls, might not be prohibitive.

In sum, we, as a nation, can benefit from social programs if we use rigorous evaluation methods to identify the very best programs and then replicate them (and only them) on a large scale. Critics of social programs often argue that such large-scale replication is impossible, typically predicating this argument on one or both of two premises. One premise is that social experiments are usually done in university settings by extraordinarily skilled people using unusually skilled labor. The other is that a large, centralized federal bureaucracy inevitably screws up anything that it attempts to do.

There is no systematic evidence to suggest that either of these premises is true. Critics often cite the failure of specific federal social programs as evidence, but this argument is not germane. There are no instances in which a specific federal program has been developed by faithfully replicating a small successful program on a large scale. Some might contend that Head Start essentially replicates the Perry Preschool model, but that is simply not the case. No attempt was made in Head Start to copy the Perry Preschool or any other model in a uniform way. Moreover, Head Start's funding levels are substantially lower than Perry Preschool's on a per child basis, so it could not offer all of the same services regardless of its design.

The dearth of evidence to support these claims does not mean that they are wrong. There is enough anecdotal evidence of bureaucratic inefficiency to justify skepticism, but not enough to warrant giving up without conducting a reasonable trial on programs that may have the potential to ameliorate serious social problems.

The little evidence that does exist on the question of scale is in fact promising. WIC is a national program that appears to work quite well. And a number of good smaller programs, including Reading One-to-One, Success for All, Reading Recovery, the Child-Parent Centers, and Life Skills Training, have been successfully scaled up from a single site to numerous sites serving thousands of individuals. Clearly there are differences between the scale of thousands and the scale of millions. But successful replications on a medium scale tend to disprove the premise that a hothouse environment is necessary to produce good results.

The pattern of success and failure of replications also bears on the second premise. One factor that tends to be positively correlated with the outcome of a replication is implementation fidelity. When a successful program is duplicated, the closer the copies are to the original, the more successful they tend to be.

This suggests that, contrary to the conventional wisdom, tight centralized control may actually be a necessary condition for success rather than a barrier to it. When control is decentralized, there is a tendency for changes to occur in implementation. People who implement programs like to throw in their pet ideas or adapt the program to the unique circumstances of a particular site. Schorr (1988) even cites such flexibility as an important ingredient of success. Also, funders and legislators may try to expand participation without increasing the budget or try to cut the budget without decreasing participation. Either modification yields a less intense version of the successful model.

Every change increases the probability of failure. The best way to turn a successful small program into a successful large one is to ensure that each replication is as faithful as possible to the original design. Accomplishing this may require the establishment of some centralized authority that oversees the expansion process, acting as the guardian of the model. Ultimately, we will never know whether an effective program can be implemented on a large scale until we identify a genuinely successful program and attempt to scale it up with an absolute commitment to be faithful to the original design.

Because we have not tried it, there is clearly an element of risk in the process. Therefore, any attempt to scale up a successful model should be done in steps, evaluating outcomes at each level. This would enable us to identify and fix any problems that crop up along the way or to scrap the project if it seems destined to failure. There is no formula for the optimal size of each step, but an order of magnitude seems reasonable. A program that has worked with hundreds of participants should be tried with thousands, then tens of thousands, then hundreds of thousands, then millions, and if necessary, then tens of millions.

All evaluations should be done using pure experimental designs. All funding of programs, whether private or public, should be made conditional on this. At first glance that requirement might seem unrealistic. What legislator would pay attention to esoteric issues of social science methodology? Yet this was precisely what was done in the 1988 round of welfare reform legislation, the Family Support Act of 1988. In ordering evaluations of the Job Opportunities and Basic Skills Training Program, Congress mandated that "a demonstration project conducted under this subparagraph shall use experimental and control groups that are composed of a random sample of participants in the program" (Public Law 100-485 [October 13, 1988], sec. 203, 102 statute 2380).

We have invested at least thirty-five years and billions of dollars in developing good social programs. Most of them have failed, but some of them have worked. If there is a chance that the few successes can be applied on a large scale, it makes no sense to continue developing hundreds of new programs, knowing that the vast majority will fail.

We stand poised at a watershed in the history of social policy. The most important lesson of this volume is that the time has come to focus substantial energy and resources on attempting to turn small successes into large ones. Although there have been many disappointments in the past thirty-five years, we have learned a tremendous amount. If we let this knowledge go to waste, then the money spent on programs over the years will have gone for naught. If, instead, we capitalize on the handful of successes that we have worked so hard to develop, then all the money, the failures, and the disappointments will have been worthwhile after all.

NOTES

1. These programs were originally selected for a conference. The evaluators of eleven programs were invited to present papers at the conference, and those papers indicated that ten of the programs met at least one of the standards described here. The evaluators for each of those ten were invited to contribute chapters to this volume. One group, the evaluators of the Elmira home-visiting program (Olds and others 1988), declined, leaving the nine programs presented here.

2. Even if experimental results are valid for the participants in the study, they may not be applicable to the population at-large.

3. It is possible to enlarge a program at the original site without replicating it, but this is not how programs typically grow.

4. This estimate and those for Reading One-to-One are averages for grades one through three.

5. The average cost for a year of school is assumed to be $6,000, so twelve years of tutoring would increase the overall cost of a child's primary and secondary education from $72,000 (that is, 12 × $6,000) to $78,000, or 8.3 percent.

6. Many features of the Abecedarian Project were applied in the multisite Infant Health and Development Project. Early results from that program are consistent with those of the Abecedarian Project, but the long-term effects will not be known for several years.

7. This is not to say that WIC is the only federal poverty program that works. There is some evidence that Head Start raises test scores (Cur-

rie and Thomas 1993), and both Aid to Families with Dependent Children and Food Stamps clearly reduce material deprivation. But there is more controversy about the overall cost-effectiveness of those programs, as well as the size and value of the benefits they confer.

8. This was not the result of a design error on the part of the evaluator but rather was necessary because WIC eligibility is legally mandated.
9. If a teacher earns forty thousand dollars a year in salary and benefits, averages five classes of twenty-five students a day for one hundred and eighty days a year, then the personnel cost is $24.89 per student for the fourteen-session program. Training, materials, and administrative costs add a little more.
10. This figure is generated using the same assumptions used for Project ALERT.
11. Because boys were placed in TFC by court order, it would be difficult to create an experimental control group that received no treatment at all.

REFERENCES

Arroyo, C. B., and Edward Zigler. 1993. "America's Title I/Chapter I Programs: Why the Promise Has Not Been Met." In *Head Start and Beyond: A National Plan for Extended Childhood Intervention*, edited by Edward Zigler and Sally Styfco. New Haven, Conn.: Yale University Press.

Botvin, Gilbert J., E. Baker, L. Dusenbury, F. M. Botvin, and T. Diaz. 1995. "Long-term Follow-up Results of a Randomized Drug Abuse Prevention Trial in a White Middle-Class Population." *Journal of the American Medical Association* 273(14):1106–12.

Buescher, Paul A., Linnea C. Larson, M. D. Nelson, and Alice J. Lenihan. 1993. "Prenatal WIC Participation Can Reduce Low Birth Weight and Newborn Medical Costs: A Cost-Benefit Analysis of WIC Participation in North Carolina." *Journal of the American Dietetic Association* 93(2): 163–6.

Consortium for Longitudinal Studies. 1983. *As the Twig Is Bent: Lasting Effects of Preschool Programs*. Hillsdale, N.J.: Lawrence Erlbaum Associates, Inc.

Crane, Jonathan. In preparation. *Social Programs: What Works and What Doesn't*. Unpublished manuscript.

Currie, Janet, and Duncan Thomas. 1993. "Does Head Start Make a Difference?" Working Paper 4406. Cambridge, Mass.: National Bureau of Economic Research.

Danziger, Sandra K., and Sherrie A. Kossoudji. 1994/95. "What Happened to General Assistance Recipients in Michigan?" *Focus* 16(2, winter): 31–34.

Friedlander, Daniel, and J. M. Gueron. 1992. "Are High-Cost Services More Effective than Low-Cost Services?" In *Evaluating Work and Training Programs*, edited by Charles F. Manski and Irwin Garfinkel. Cambridge, Mass.: Harvard University Press.

Garber, H. L. 1988. *The Milwaukee Project*. Washington, D.C.: American Association on Mental Retardation.

Jencks, Christopher, and Meredith Phillips. 1996. "Does Learning Pay off in the Job Market?" Northwestern University. Unpublished paper.

Mead, Lawrence M. 1997. "The Decline of Welfare in Wisconsin." Paper presented to the Midwest Political Science Association, annual conference. Chicago, Ill.(April 11, 1997).

Murray, D. M., C. A. Johnson, R. V. Luepker, and M. B. Mittelmark. 1984. "The Prevention of Cigarette Smoking in Children: A Comparison of Four Strategies." *Journal of Applied Social Psychology* 14(3): 274–89.

Olds, D. L., C. R. Henderson, Jr., Robert Tatelbaum, Robert Chamberlin. 1988. "Improving the Life-Course Development of Socially Disadvantaged Mothers: A Randomized Trial of Nurse Home Visitation." *American Journal of Public Health* 78(11): 1436–45.

Perry, C. L., and others. 1980. "Modifying Smoking Behavior of Teenagers: A School-Based Intervention." *American Journal of Public Health* 70: 722–25.

Reynolds, Arthur J., and J. A. Temple. 1995. "Quasi-Experimental Estimates of the Effects of a Preschool Intervention: Psychometric and Econometric Comparisons." *Evaluation Review* 19(4): 347–73.

Rush, D., D. G. Horvitz, W. B. Seaver, J. M. Avir, G. C. Grabowski, J. Leighton, N. L. Sloan, S. S. Johnson, R. A. Kulka, and D. S. Shanklin. 1988. "The National WIC Evaluation: Evaluation of the Special Supplemental Food Program for Women, Infants, and Children. Study of Infants and Children." *American Journal of Clinical Nutrition (supplement)* 48(2, August): 484–511.

Schorr, Lisbeth B., with Daniel Schorr. 1988. *Within Our Reach: Breaking the Cycle of Disadvantage*. New York: Anchor Books.

Schweinhart, Lawrence J., and David P. Weikart. 1997. *Lasting Differences: The High/Scope Preschool Curriculum Comparison through Age 23*. Ypsilanti, Mich.: High/Scope Educational Research Foundation.

Slavin, Robert E., Nancy L. Karweit, and Nancy A. Madden. 1989. *Effective Programs for Students at Risk*. Needham Heights, Mass.: Allyn and Bacon.

CHAPTER 2

Success for All: Achievement Outcomes of a Schoolwide Reform Model

Robert E. Slavin, Nancy A. Madden,
Lawrence J. Dolan, Barbara A. Wasik,
Steven M. Ross, Lana J. Smith, and Marcella Dianda

Ms. Martin's kindergarten class has some of the brightest, happiest, friendliest, and most optimistic kids you will ever meet. Students in her class are glad to be in school, proud of their accomplishments, certain that they will succeed at whatever the school has to offer. Every one of them is a natural scientist, a storyteller, a creative thinker, a curious seeker of knowledge. Ms. Martin's class could be anywhere, in suburb or ghetto, small town or barrio. Kindergartners everywhere are just as bright, enthusiastic, and confident as her kids are.

Only a few years from now, many of these same children will have lost the spark with which they began school. Some will have failed a grade. Some will be in special education. Some will be in long-term remediation, such as Title I. Some will be bored or anxious or unmotivated. Many will see school as a chore rather than a pleasure and will no longer expect to excel. In a very brief span of time, Ms. Martin's children will have defined themselves as successes or failures in school. All too often, only a few will still have a sense of excitement and positive self-expectations about learning. We cannot predict very well which of Ms. Martin's students will succeed and which will fail, but we can predict, based on the past, that if nothing changes, far too many will fail. This is especially true if Ms. Martin's kindergarten happens to be located in a high-poverty neighborhood, in which there are typically fewer resources with which to provide top-quality instruction to every child, fewer forms of rescue if children run into academic difficulties, and fewer supports for learning at home. Preventable failures occur in all schools, but in high-poverty schools failure can be endemic, so widespread that it is difficult to treat each child at risk of failure as a person of value who simply needs emergency assistance to get back on track. Instead, many such schools do their best to provide the greatest benefit to the greatest number of children possible but have an unfortunately well-founded expectation that a certain percentage of students will fall by the wayside during the elementary years.

Any discussion of school reform should begin with Ms. Martin's kindergartners. The first goal of reform should be to ensure that every child, regardless of home background, home language, or learning style, achieves the success that he or she so confidently expected in kindergarten, that all children maintain their motivation, enthusiasm, and optimism because they are objectively succeeding at the school's tasks. Any reform that does less than this is hollow and self-defeating.

What does it mean to succeed in the early grades? The elementary school's definition of success, and therefore the parents' and children's definition as well, is success in reading. Very few children who are reading adequately are retained, assigned to special education, or given long-term remedial services. Other subjects are important, of course, but reading and language arts form the core of what school success means in the early grades.

When a child fails to read well in the early grades, he or she begins a downward progression. In first grade, some children begin to notice that they are not reading adequately. They may fail first grade or be assigned to long-term remediation. As they proceed through the elementary grades, many students begin to see that they are failing at their full-time jobs. When this happens, things begin to unravel. Failing students begin to have poor motivation and poor self-expectations, which lead to poor achievement and a declining spiral that ultimately leads to despair, delinquency, and dropout.

Remediating learning deficits after they have become well established is extremely difficult. Children who have already failed to learn to read, for example, are now anxious about reading and doubt their ability to learn to read. Their motivation to read may be low. They may ultimately learn to read, but reading will always be a chore, not a pleasure. Clearly, the time to provide additional help to children who are at risk is early, when children are still motivated and confident and when any learning deficits are relatively small and remediable. The most important goal in educational programming for students at risk of school failure is to try to make certain that we do not squander the greatest resource we have: the enthusiasm and positive self-expectations of young children themselves.

In practical terms, this perspective implies that schools, and especially Title I, special education, and other services for at-risk children, must be shifted from an emphasis on remediation to an emphasis on prevention and early intervention. Prevention means providing developmentally appropriate preschool and kindergarten programs so that students will enter first grade ready to succeed, and it means providing regular classroom teachers with effective instructional programs, curricula, and professional development to enable them to see that most students are successful the first time they are taught. Early intervention means that supplementary instructional services are provided early in students' schooling and that they are intensive enough to bring at-risk students quickly to a level at which they can profit from good-quality classroom instruction.

This chapter describes the current state of research on Success for All, a program built around the idea that every child can and must succeed in the early grades, no matter what this takes. Success for All seeks to use everything we know about effective instruction for students at risk in an effort to direct all aspects of school and classroom organization toward the goals of preventing academic deficits from appearing in the first place, recognizing and intensively intervening when any deficits do appear, and providing students with a rich and full curriculum to enable them to build on their firm foundation in basic skills. Success for All is committed to doing whatever it takes to see that every child becomes a skilled, strategic, and enthusiastic reader as he or she progresses through the elementary grades.

PROGRAM DESCRIPTION

Success for All is built around the assumption that every child can read. We mean this not as wishful thinking or as philosophical statement, but as a practical, attainable reality. In particular, every child without organic retardation can learn to read. Some children need more help than others and may need different approaches than those needed by others, but one way or another every child can become a successful reader.

The first requirement for the success of every child is *prevention*. This means providing excellent preschool and kindergarten programs, improving curriculum, instruction, and classroom management throughout the grades, assessing students frequently to make sure they are making adequate progress, and establishing cooperative relationships with parents so they can support students' learning at home.

Top-quality curriculum and instruction beginning at age four will ensure the success of most students, but not all of them. The next requirement for the success of *all* students is *intensive early intervention*. This means one-to-one tutoring by certified teachers for first graders having reading problems. It means working with parents and social service agencies to be sure that all students attend school, have medical services or eyeglasses if they need them, have help with behavioral problems, and so on.

The most important idea in Success for All is that the school must work relentlessly with every child until that child is succeeding. If prevention is not enough, the child may need tutoring. If this is not enough, he or she may need help with behavior or attendance or eyeglasses. If this is not enough, he or she may need a modified approach to reading. The school does not merely provide services to children; it constantly assesses the results of the services it provides and keeps varying or adding services until every child is successful.

Success for All began in one Baltimore elementary school in 1987 to 1988 and since then has expanded each year to additional schools. As of fall 1997, it is in more than seven hundred fifty schools in thirty-seven states throughout the United States. The districts range from some of the largest in the country, such as Baltimore, Chicago, Cincinnati, Houston, Memphis, Miami, New York, Philadelphia, and San Antonio, to middle-size districts, such as Galveston (Texas), Rockford (Illinois), and Modesto and Riverside (California), to tiny rural districts, including two on the Navajo reservation in Arizona. Success for All reading curricula in Spanish have been developed and researched and are used in bilingual programs in Arizona, California, Florida, Illinois, New Jersey, New York, Pennsylvania, and Texas. Almost all Success for All schools are high-poverty Title I schools, and the majority are schoolwide projects. Otherwise, the schools vary widely.

OVERVIEW OF PROGRAM COMPONENTS

Success for All has somewhat different components at different sites, depending on the school's needs and resources available to implement the program (Slavin and others 1996). However, a common set of elements is characteristic of all.

READING PROGRAM

Success for All uses a reading curriculum based on research and effective practices in beginning reading (for example, Adams 1990) and on effective use of cooperative learning (Slavin 1995; Stevens and others 1987).

Reading teachers at every grade level begin the reading time by reading children's literature to students and engaging them in a discussion to enhance their understanding of the story, their listening and speaking vocabulary, and their knowledge of story structure. In kindergarten and first grade, the program emphasizes the development of oral language and pre-reading skills through the use of thematically based units that incorporate areas such as language, art, and writing under a science or social studies topic. A component called Story Telling and Retelling (STaR) involves the students in listening to, retelling, and dramatizing children's literature. Big books as well as oral and written composition activities allow students to develop concepts of print as they also develop knowledge of story structure. Strong emphasis is also placed on phonetic awareness activities that develop auditory discrimination and support the development of reading readiness strategies.

Reading Roots is typically introduced in the second semester of kindergarten or in first grade. This kindergarten-through-first-grade beginning reading program uses a series of phonetically regular but meaningful and interesting minibooks and emphasizes repeated oral reading to partners as well as to the teacher. The minibooks begin with a set of "shared stories," in which part of a story is written in small type (read by the teacher) and part is written in large type (read by the students). The student portion uses a phonetically controlled vocabulary. Taken together, the teacher and student portions create interesting, worthwhile stories. Over time, the teacher portion diminishes and the student portion lengthens, until students are reading the entire book. This scaffolding allows students to read literature when they only have a few letter sounds.

Letters and letter sounds are introduced in an active, engaging set of activities that begin with oral language and move into written symbols. Individual sounds are integrated into a context of words, sentences, and stories. Instruction is provided in story structure, specific comprehension skills, meta-cognitive strategies for self-assessment and self-correction, and the integration of reading and writing.

Spanish bilingual programs use an adaptation of Reading Roots called *Lee Conmigo* ("Read with Me"). *Lee Conmigo* uses the same instructional strategies as Reading Roots but is built around the Macmillan *Campanitas de Oro* series.

When students reach the primer reading level, they use a program called Reading Wings, an adaptation of Cooperative Integrated Reading and Composition (CIRC; Stevens and others 1987). Reading Wings uses cooperative learning activities built around story structure, prediction, summarization, vocabulary building, decoding practice, and story-related writing. Students read with a partner, engage in structured discussion of stories or novels, and work toward mastering the vocabulary and content of the story in teams. Story-related writing is also conducted within teams. Cooperative learning both increases students' motivation and engages students in cognitive activities known to contribute to reading comprehension, such as elaboration, summarization, and rephrasing (see Slavin 1995). Research has found that CIRC significantly increases students' reading comprehension and language skills (Stevens and others 1987).

In addition to these story-related activities, teachers provide direct instruction in reading comprehension skills, and students practice these skills in teams. Classroom libraries of trade books at various reading levels are provided for each teacher, and students read books of their choice for homework for twenty minutes each night. Home readings are shared via presentations, summaries, puppet shows, and other formats twice a week during "book club" sessions.

Materials to support Reading Wings through the sixth grade (or beyond) exist in English and Spanish. The English materials are built around children's literature and around the most widely used reading texts and anthologies. Supportive materials have been developed for more than a hundred children's novels and for most current basal series. Spanish materials are similarly built around Spanish-language novels and the *Campanitas* basal program.

Beginning in the second semester of program implementation, Success for All schools usually implement a writing and language arts program based primarily on cooperative learning principles (see Slavin, Madden, and Stevens 1989/90).

Students in grades one to three (and sometimes four to five or four to six) are regrouped for reading. The students are assigned to heterogeneous, age-grouped classes most of the day, but during a regular ninety-minute reading period they are regrouped by reading performance levels into reading classes of students all at the same level. For example, a two to one reading class might contain first-, second-, and third-grade students all reading at the same level. The reading classes are smaller than homerooms because tutors and other certified staff (such as librarians or art teachers) teach reading during this common reading period. Regrouping allows teachers to teach the whole reading class without having to break it into groups. This greatly reduces the time spent in independent seatwork and increases direct instruction time, eliminating workbooks, dittos, or other follow-up activities, which are needed in classes that have multiple reading groups. The regrouping is a form of the Joplin Plan, which has been found to increase reading achievement in the elementary grades (Slavin 1987).

EIGHT-WEEK READING ASSESSMENTS

At eight-week intervals, reading teachers assess their students' progress through the program. The results of the assessments are used to determine who is to receive tutoring, to change students' reading groups, to suggest other adaptations in students' programs, and to identify students who need other types of assistance, such as family interventions or screening for vision and hearing problems. The assessments are curriculum-based measures that include teacher observations and judgments as well as more formal measures of reading comprehension.

READING TUTORS

One of the most important elements of the Success for All model is the use of tutors. One-to-one tutoring is the most effective form of instruction known (see Wasik and Slavin 1993). The tutors are certified teachers with experience teaching Title I, special education, or primary reading. Often, well-qualified paraprofessionals also tutor children with less-severe reading problems. In this case, a certified tutor monitors their work and assists with the diagnostic assessment and intervention strategies. Tutors work one-on-one with students who are having difficulties keeping up with their reading groups. The tutoring occurs in twenty-minute sessions during times other than reading or math periods.

In general, tutors support students' success in the regular reading curriculum, rather than teaching different objectives. For example, the tutor will work with a student on the same story and concepts being read and taught in the regular reading class. However, tutors seek to identify learning problems and use different strategies to teach the same skills. They also teach meta-cognitive skills beyond those taught in the classroom program (Wasik and Madden 1995). Schools may have as many as six or more teachers serving as tutors, depending on the school's size, need for tutoring, and other factors.

During daily ninety-minute reading periods, certified tutors serve as additional reading teachers to reduce class size for reading. Reading teachers and tutors use brief forms to communicate about students' specific problems and needs and meet at regular times to coordinate their approaches with individual children.

Initial decisions about reading group placement and the need for tutoring are based on informal reading inventories that the tutors give to each child. Subsequent reading group placements and tutoring assignments are made using the curriculum-based assessments. First graders receive priority for tutoring, on the assumption that the primary function of tutors is to help all students be successful in reading the first time, before they fail and become remedial readers.

PRESCHOOL AND KINDERGARTEN

Most Success for All schools provide a half-day preschool or a full-day kindergarten for eligible students. The preschool and kindergarten programs focus on providing a balanced and developmentally appropriate learning experience for young children. The curriculum emphasizes the development and use of language. It provides a balance of academic readiness and nonacademic music, art, and movement activities in a series of thematic units. Readiness activities include use of the Peabody Language Development Kits and STaR in which students retell stories read by the teachers. Pre-reading activities begin during the second semester of kindergarten.

FAMILY SUPPORT TEAM

Parents are an essential part of Success for All. A family support team works in each school, making families feel comfortable in the school, encouraging them to become active supporters of their child's education, and providing specific services. The family support team consists of the Title I parent liaison, vice principal (if any), counselor (if any), facilitator, and any other appropriate staff already present in the school or added to the school staff.

The family support team first works to establish good relations with parents and to increase involvement in the schools. Members may complete "welcome" visits for new families. They organize many programs in the school, such as parenting skills workshops. Many schools use a program called Raising Readers in which parents are given strategies to use in reading with their own children.

The family support team also intervenes to solve problems. For example, they may contact parents whose children are frequently absent to see what resources can be provided to assist the family in getting their child to school. Family support staff, teachers, and parents work together to solve behavioral problems. Also, family support staff are called on to provide assistance when students seem to be working at less than their full potential because of problems at home. Families of students who are not receiving adequate sleep or nutrition, need glasses, are not attending school regularly, or are exhibiting serious behavioral problems may receive family support assistance.

The family support team is strongly integrated into the academic program of the school. It receives referrals from teachers and tutors regarding children who are not making adequate academic progress and thereby constitutes an additional stage of intervention for students in need above and beyond that provided by the classroom teacher or tutor. The family support team also encourages and trains the parents to fulfill numerous volunteer roles within the school, such as providing a listening ear to emerging readers or helping in the school cafeteria.

PROGRAM FACILITATOR

A program facilitator works at each school to oversee (with the principal) the operation of the Success for All model. The facilitator helps plan the Success for All program, helps the principal with scheduling, and visits classes and tutoring sessions frequently to help teachers and tutors with individual problems. He or she works directly with the teachers on implementation of the curriculum, classroom management, and other issues, helps teachers and tutors deal with any behavioral or other special problems, and coordinates the activities of the family support team with those of the instructional staff.

TEACHERS AND TEACHER TRAINING

The teachers and tutors are regular certified teachers. They receive detailed teachers' manuals supplemented by three days of in-service at the beginning of the school year. For classroom teachers of grades one through three and for reading tutors, these training sessions focus on implementation of the reading program, and their detailed teachers' manuals cover general teaching strategies as well as specific lessons. Preschool and kindergarten teachers and aides are trained in use of the STaR and Peabody programs, thematic units, and other aspects of the preschool and kindergarten models. Tutors later receive two additional days of training on tutoring strategies and reading assessment.

Throughout the year, facilitators and other project staff make in-service presentations on topics such as classroom management, instructional pace, and cooperative learning. Facilitators also organize informal sessions to allow teachers to share problems and their solutions, suggest changes, and discuss individual children. The staff development model used in Success for All emphasizes relatively brief initial training with extensive classroom follow-up, coaching, and group discussion.

ADVISORY COMMITTEE

An advisory committee composed of the school principal, program facilitator, teacher representatives, parent representatives, and family support staff meets regularly to review the progress of the program and to identify and solve any problems that arise. In most schools, existing site-based management teams are adapted to fulfill this function. In addition, grade-level teams and the family support team meet regularly to discuss common problems and solutions and to make decisions in their areas of responsibility.

SPECIAL EDUCATION

Every effort is made to deal with students' learning problems within the context of the regular classroom, as supplemented by tutors. Tutors evaluate students' strengths and weaknesses and develop strategies to teach in the most effective way. In some schools, special education teachers work as tutors and reading teachers with students identified as learning disabled as well as with students experiencing learning problems who are at risk for special education placement. One major goal of Success for All is to keep students with learning problems out of special education if at all possible and to serve any students who do qualify for special education in a way that does not disrupt their regular classroom experience (see Slavin and others 1991).

RELENTLESSNESS

Although the particular elements of Success for All may vary from school to school, one feature is consistent in all: a relentless focus on the success of every child. It would be entirely possible to have tutoring, new curricula, and family support and other services and still not ensure the success of at-risk children. Success does not come from piling on additional services but rather from coordinating human resources around a well-defined goal, constantly assessing progress toward that goal, and never giving up until success is achieved.

No element is completely new or unique to Success for All. What is most distinctive is its schoolwide, coordinated, and proactive plan for translating positive expectations into concrete success for all children. Every child can complete elementary school reading confidently, strategically, and joyfully and can maintain the enthusiasm and positive self-expectations with which he or she came to first grade. The purpose of Success for All is to see that this vision can become a practical reality in every school.

RESEARCH AND EVALUATION

From the very beginning, Success for All has focused on research and evaluation. We began longitudinal evaluations of the program in its earliest sites: six schools in Baltimore and Philadelphia and one in Charleston. Later, third-party evaluators at the University of Memphis—Steve Ross, Lana Smith, and their colleagues—added evaluations in Memphis (Tennessee), Montgomery (Alabama), Ft. Wayne (Indiana), and Caldwell (Idaho). Marcella Dianda, then at the Southwest Regional Laboratory, conducted studies focusing on English language learners in Modesto and Riverside (California). Each of these evaluations compared Success for All schools to matched comparison schools on measures of reading performance, starting with cohorts in kindergarten or in first grade and following these students as long as possible. Vagaries of funding and other local problems ended some evaluations prematurely, but most followed Success for All schools for many years. As of this writing, there are nine years of continuous data from the six original schools in Baltimore and Philadelphia and varying years of data from seven other districts, a total of twenty-three schools (and their matched control schools).

Earlier evaluations of Success for All schools found almost uniformly positive outcomes for all schools on all reading measures (see Slavin and others 1990, 1992; Madden and others 1993). Smaller special-purpose studies also found positive effects of Success for All on such outcomes as attendance and reduced special education placement and referrals (Slavin and others 1992, 1994).

In order to summarize the outcomes from all schools and all years involved in experimental control comparisons, this chapter uses a method of analysis, called a multisite replicated experiment (Slavin and Madden 1993), in which each grade-level *cohort* (students in all classes in that grade in a given year) in each school is considered a replication. In other words, if the three first grades have proceeded through school X, each first-grade cohort (compared to its control group) produces an effect size representing the experimental-control difference in student achievement that year. For example, across twenty-three schools ever involved in Success for All evaluations, there are a total of sixty first-grade cohorts (about five-thousand students in experimental schools and a similar number in control schools) from which experimental and control achievement data have been collected. This procedure applies a procedure common in medical research called a multicenter clinical trial (Horwitz 1987). In such studies, small-scale experiments located in different sites over extended periods of time are combined into one large-scale experiment. For example, patients with a given disease entering any of several hospitals might be given an experimental drug or a placebo at random. If the disease is relatively rare, no one hospital's experiment will have an adequate sample size with which to assess the drug's effects, but combining results over many hospitals over time will provide an adequate sample. In schoolwide reform, the "patient" is an entire grade level in a school, perhaps one hundred children. Obtaining an adequate sample of schools at any point in time would involve thousands of children and hundreds of teachers.

The idea of combining results across experiments is not, of course, foreign to educational research. This is the essence of meta-analysis (Glass, McGaw, and Smith 1981). However, meta-analyses combine effect sizes (proportions of a standard deviation separating experimental and control groups) across studies with different designs, measures, samples, and other features, leading to charges that they mislead readers by "combining apples and oranges" or by missing unwritten or unpublished studies in which effects were zero or negative (Matt and Cook 1994; Slavin 1986).

Combining results across geographically separated experiments into one study is also not unheard-of in educational research. For example, Pinnell and others (1994) studied the Reading Recovery tutoring model in ten Ohio districts. Three variations of Reading Recovery were compared to control groups in each district, and results were then aggregated using the cohort of tutored first graders as the unit of analysis. A multisite replicated experiment adds the accumulation of experimental-control differences over time.

In addition to applying the multisite replicated experiment design to data from Success for All schools, this chapter also summarizes the results of several studies in particular subsets of schools. These include studies of outcomes of the Spanish version of Success for All, *Lee Conmigo*; studies of Success for All with students in English as a Second Language (ESL) programs; studies of special education outcomes of the model; and studies comparing Success for All and Reading Recovery. This chapter summarizes the state of research on Success for All in all study sites as of the tenth year of program implementation.

EVALUATION DESIGN AND RESULTS

A common evaluation design, with variations due to local circumstances, was used in all Success for All evaluations. Every Success for All school involved in a formal evaluation was matched with a control school that is similar in poverty level (percentage of students qualifying for free lunch), historical achievement level, ethnicity, and other factors. Children in the Success for All schools were matched on district-administered standardized test scores given in kindergarten or (starting in 1991 in six districts) on Peabody Picture Vocabulary Test scores given by the project in the fall of kindergarten or first grade. In some cases, analyses of covariance rather than individual child matches were used.

The measures used in the evaluations were as follows:

* *Woodcock Reading Mastery Test*   Three Woodcock scales—Word Identification, Word Attack, and Passage Comprehension—were administered individually to students by trained testers. Word Identification assesses recognition of common sight words, Word Attack assesses phonetic synthesis skills, and Passage Comprehension assesses comprehension in con-

text. Students in Spanish bilingual programs were given the Spanish versions of these scales.

• *Durrell Analysis of Reading Difficulty*   The Durrell Oral Reading scale was administered individually to students in grades one through three. It presents a series of graded reading passages that students read aloud, followed by comprehension questions.

• *Gray Oral Reading Test*   Comprehension and passage scores from the Gray Oral Reading Test were obtained from students in grades four to five.

In all cases, tests were administered by testers who were not affiliated with the project. Every attempt was made to keep testers unaware of whether a school was a Success for All or a control school. Testers were trained to a high degree of reliability and then observed on a sampling basis to be sure they were administering the tests properly.

The tests used were not keyed to the particular intervention, but they are widely used, standardized measures assessing a broad range of components of reading. Outcomes on district-administered standardized tests have been reported in district evaluations and generally conform to the patterns found in the individually administered data (see Slavin, Madden, and Wasik 1997).

Analyses of covariance with pretests as covariates were used to compare raw scores in all evaluations, and separate analyses were conducted for students in general and for students in the lowest 25 percent of their grades.

The figures presented in this chapter summarize student performance in grade equivalents (adjusted for covariates) and effect size (proportion of a standard deviation separating the experimental and control groups), averaging across individual measures. Neither grade equivalents nor averaged scores were used in the analyses, but they are presented here as a useful summary. Outcomes are presented for all students in the relevant grades in Success for All and control schools and also for students in the lowest 25 percent of their grades, who are most at risk. In most cases, the low 25 percent was determined based on Peabody Picture Vocabulary Test scores given as pretests. In Baltimore and Charleston, however, Peabody pretests were not given, and low 25 percent analyses involved the lowest-performing students after the test.

Each of the evaluations summarized here followed children who began in Success for All in first grade or earlier in comparison with children who had similarly attended the control school since first grade. Because Success for All is a prevention and early intervention program, students who start in it after first grade are not considered to have received the full treatment (although they are of course served within the schools). For more details on methods and findings, see Slavin and others (1996) and the full site reports.

READING OUTCOMES

The results of the multisite replicated experiment evaluating Success for All are summarized in figure 2.1 for each grade level, one through five. The results show statistically significant ($p = 0.05$ or better) positive effects of Success for All (compared to controls) on every measure at every grade level, one through five. For students in general, effect sizes ranged from +0.39 to +0.62. Effects were somewhat higher than this for the Woodcock Word Attack scale in first and second grades, but in grades three through five, effect sizes were more or less equivalent on all aspects of reading. Consistently, effect sizes for students in the lowest 25 percent of their grades were particularly positive, ranging from +1.03 in first grade to +1.68 in fourth grade. Again, cohort-level analyses found statistically significant differences favoring low achievers in Success for All on every measure at every grade level. A follow-up assessment of Baltimore schools found that a difference of approximately one grade equivalent (and an effect size still near half a standard deviation) maintained into grades six and seven, when children were no longer in the program schools.

The results summarized in figure 2.1 include all experimental-control comparisons in which children's reading performance was assessed on individually administered tests. Results on group-administered standardized tests were similar in magnitude, but more inconsistent from year to year and from school to school. However, districts have carried out their own successful evaluations of Success for All on standardized tests used for accountability in Baltimore, Charleston (West Virginia), Flint (Michigan), Ft. Wayne, Memphis, Miami, Modesto, San Antonio, West Palm Beach (Florida), and Wichita Falls (Texas) (see Slavin, Madden, and Wasik 1997).

Figure 2.1 Mean Reading Grade Equivalents and Effect Sizes for Students in Success for All and Control Schools, by Grade, 1988 to 1996

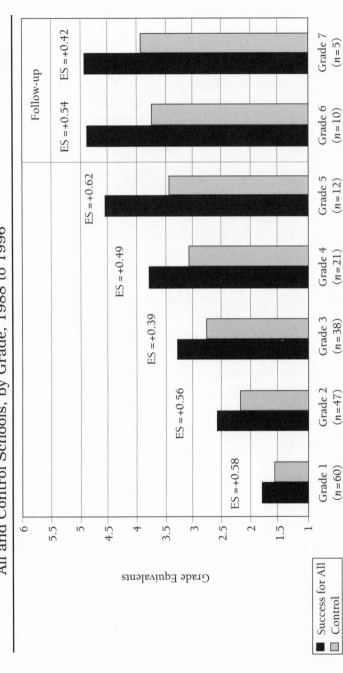

Notes: n equals number of cohorts (all students at the indicated grade level in a given year); only includes cohorts in Success for All or control schools since first grade.

CHANGES IN EFFECT SIZES OVER YEARS OF IMPLEMENTATION

One interesting trend in outcomes from comparisons of Success for All and control schools relates to changes in effects sizes according to the number of years a school has been implementing the program. Figure 2.2, which summarizes these data, was created by pooling effect sizes for all cohorts in their first year of implementation, all cohorts in their second year, and so on, regardless of calendar year.

Figure 2.2 shows that mean reading effect sizes progressively increased with each year of implementation. For example, Success for All first graders scored substantially better than control first graders at the end of the first year of implementation (+0.49). The experimental-control difference was even higher for first graders attending schools in the second year of program implementation (+0.53), increasing to an effect size of +0.73 for schools in the fourth year. A similar pattern is apparent for second- and third-grade cohorts.

There are two likely explanations for this gain in experimental-control differences. One is that as schools get better at implementing Success for All, outcomes improve. This is a logical outcome, which gives evidence of the degree to which ongoing professional development, coaching, and reflection enable school staff to improve student achievement progressively over time. However, while first-year first-grade cohorts started the program in first grade, second-year cohorts started in kindergarten, and most third- and fourth-year cohorts started in prekindergarten. Some or all of the gain in effect sizes could be due to a lasting effect of participation in the Success for All prekindergarten and kindergarten program.

Whatever the explanation, the data summarized in figure 2.2 show that while Success for All has an immediate impact on student reading achievement, this impact grows over successive years of implementation. Over time, schools may become increasingly able to provide effective instruction to all of their students.

PERFORMANCE ASSESSMENT

Recently released scores on the Maryland School Performance Assessment Program (MSPAP) from the four Roots and Wings pilot schools in St. Mary's County, Maryland, show remarkable gains at both the third- and fifth-grade levels.

Roots and Wings is a comprehensive restructuring program for elementary schools developed at Johns Hopkins University under fund-

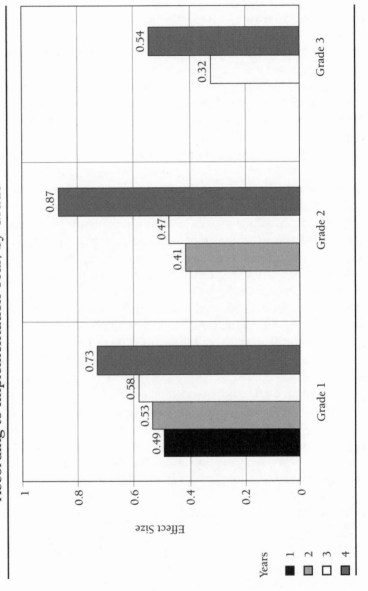

Figure 2.2 Effect Sizes for Students in Success for All and Control Schools According to Implementation Year, by Grade

ing from the New American Schools Development Corporation. The program includes innovative curricula and instructional methods emphasizing cooperative learning, simulations, experiments, and frequent assessment of student progress. Based on Success for All, Roots and Wings provides tutors and family support services to children who need them. Success for All is the reading, language arts, writing, and family support component of Roots and Wings, which provides new programs in math, science, and social studies. St. Mary's County served as the pilot site for Roots and Wings, starting in 1992.

As shown in figures 2.3 and 2.4, on average, Roots and Wings schools made substantially greater gains on MSPAP than did the state as a whole between 1993 and 1996. The Roots and Wings schools serve populations that are significantly more disadvantaged than state averages. On average, 48 percent of Roots and Wings students are eligible for the free and reduced-price lunch program, compared with 30 percent for the state; 21 percent of Roots and Wings students are eligible for Title I, in comparison with 7 percent for the state. Yet the Roots and Wings schools' MSPAP scores are now higher than state averages in third- and fifth-grade reading, writing, math, and science and are almost at the state mean in language and social studies.

ENGLISH LANGUAGE LEARNERS

The education of English language learners is at a crossroads. For many years, researchers, educators, and policymakers have debated questions of the appropriate language instruction for students who enter elementary school speaking languages other than English. Research on this topic has generally found that students taught to read in their home language and then transitioned to English ultimately become better readers in English than do students taught to read only in English (García 1991; Willig 1985; Wong-Fillmore and Valadez 1986). More recently, however, attention has shifted to another question. Given that students are taught to read in their home language, how can we ensure that they *succeed* in that language? See, for example, García (1994). There is no reason to expect that children failing to read well in Spanish, for example, will later become good readers and successful students in English. On the contrary, research consistently supports the common-sense expectation that the better that students in Spanish bilingual programs read Spanish, the better their English reading will be (García 1991; August and Hakuta 1997). Clearly, the quality of instruction in home-language reading is a key

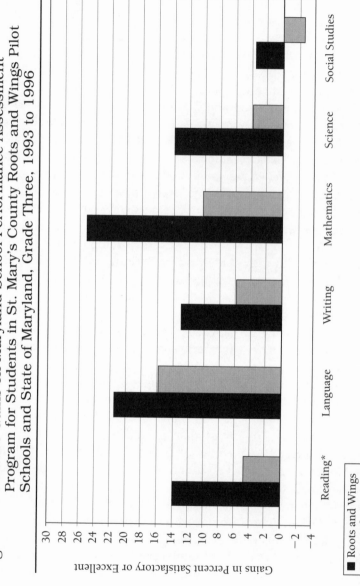

Figure 2.3 Relative Gains on Maryland School Performance Assessment Program for Students in St. Mary's County Roots and Wings Pilot Schools and State of Maryland, Grade Three, 1993 to 1996

Gains in Percent Satisfactory or Excellent

Reading* Language Writing Mathematics Science Social Studies

■ Roots and Wings
▨ State of Maryland

* 1993 reading scores were declared invalid. Gains are for 1994 to 1996.

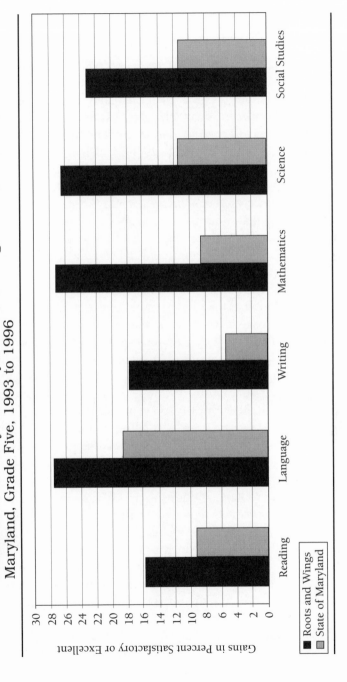

Figure 2.4 Relative Gains on Maryland School Performance Assessment Program for Students in St. Mary's County Roots and Wings Pilot Schools and State of Maryland, Grade Five, 1993 to 1996

factor in the ultimate school success of English language learners and must be a focus of research on the education of these children.

Even if all educators and policymakers accepted the evidence favoring bilingual over English-only instruction, there would still be large numbers of English language learners being taught to read in English. This is true because of the practical difficulties of providing instruction in languages other than English or Spanish; teachers fully proficient in Southeast Asian languages, Arabic, and other languages are in short supply, as are materials to teach in these languages. Speakers of languages other than English or Spanish are among the fastest-growing groups in our nation's schools (U.S. General Accounting Office 1994). Further, many Spanish-dominant students are taught to read in English, because of shortages of bilingual teachers, insufficient numbers of Spanish-dominant students in one school, parental desires to have their children taught in English, or other factors. For these reasons, a large percentage of English language learners will always be taught in English only, with instruction in ESL. As with bilingual programs, the quality of reading instruction and ESL instruction and the integration of the two are essential in determining the success of English language learners being taught in English only.

There is remarkably little research evaluating programs designed to increase the Spanish reading performance of students in bilingual programs. Hertz-Lazarowitz, Ivory, and Calderón (1993) have evaluated a bilingual adaptation of Cooperative Integrated Reading and Composition (BCIRC) in El Paso elementary schools starting in second grade. This program, an adaptation of the CIRC program that forms the basis of the upper-elementary reading program used in Success for All, has students work in small cooperative groups. Students read to each other, work together to identify characters, settings, problems, and problem solutions in narratives, summarize stories to each other, and work together on writing, reading comprehension, and vocabulary activities. Students in BCIRC classes scored significantly better than control students on the Spanish Texas Assessment of Academic Skills at the end of second grade, and as they transitioned to English in third and fourth grades, they performed significantly better than control students on standardized reading tests given in English.

An evaluation of Success for All with English language learners was carried out by Dianda and Flaherty (1995) at the Southwest Regional Laboratory in Southern California. This study involved three schools.

Fremont Elementary in Riverside and Orville Wright Elementary in Modesto have substantial Spanish bilingual programs. The third, El Vista Elementary, also in Modesto, uses an ESL approach to serve a highly diverse student body speaking seventeen languages. Students in all three schools were compared with matched students in matched schools. In each case, students were assessed in the language of instruction (English or Spanish).

Data from first graders in the three schools were analyzed together by Dianda and Flaherty (1995), pooling data across schools in four categories: English-dominant students, Spanish-dominant students taught in Spanish (*Lee Conmigo*), Spanish-dominant students taught in English (sheltered students), and speakers of languages other than English or Spanish taught in English. The pooled results are summarized in figure 2.5.

As is clear in figure 2.5, all categories of Success for All students scored substantially better than control students. The differences were greatest, however, for Spanish-dominant students taught in bilingual classes (effect size = +1.03) and in sheltered English programs (+1.02). The bilingual students scored at grade level and more than six months ahead of the control group. The sheltered students scored about two months below grade level but were still four months ahead of the control group. Both English-speaking students and speakers of languages other than English or Spanish scored above grade level and about two months ahead of the control group.

The effects of Success for All on the achievement of English language learners are substantially positive. Across three schools implementing *Lee Conmigo*, the average effect size for first graders on Spanish assessments was +0.88; for second graders (at Philadelphia's Fairhill Elementary) the average effect size was +1.77. For students in sheltered English instruction, effect sizes for all comparisons were also very positive, especially for Cambodian students in Philadelphia and Mexican American students in California.

SPECIAL EDUCATION

Perhaps the most important goal of Success for All is to place a floor under the reading achievement of all children. This goal has major implications for special education. If the program makes a substantial difference in the reading achievement of the lowest achievers, then it should reduce special education referrals and placements. Further, students whose Individual Education Plan indicates learn-

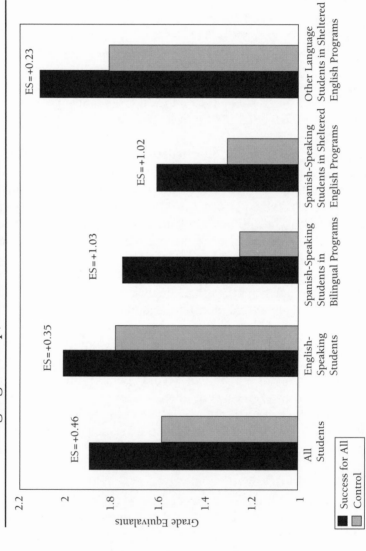

Figure 2.5 Achievement of Success for All and Control Students, by Language Group, Riverside and Modesto

ES=+0.46

ES=+0.35

ES=+1.03

ES=+1.02

ES=+0.23

All
Students

English-
Speaking
Students

Spanish-Speaking
Students in
Bilingual Programs

Spanish-Speaking
Students in Sheltered
English Programs

Other Language
Students in Sheltered
English Programs

Grade Equivalants

2.2

2

1.8

1.6

1.4

1.2

1

■ Success for All
□ Control

Source: Dianda and Flaherty 1995.

ing disabilities or related problems are typically treated the same as other students in Success for All. That is, they receive tutoring if they need it, participate in reading classes appropriate to their reading level, and spend the rest of the day in age-appropriate, heterogeneous homerooms. Their tutor or reading teacher is likely to be a special education teacher, but otherwise they are not treated differently. One-to-one tutoring in reading, plus high-quality reading instruction in the mainstream at the student's appropriate level, should be more effective than the small-group instruction provided in special education classes. For this reason, students who have been identified as being in need of special education services are expected to perform substantially better than similar students in traditional special education programs.

The philosophy behind the treatment of special education issues in Success for All is called "neverstreaming" (Slavin and others 1991). That is, rather than waiting until students fall far behind, then are assigned to special education, and then are eligible to be mainstreamed into regular classes, Success for All schools intervene early and intensively with students who are at risk to try to keep them out of the special education system. Once students are far behind, special education services are unlikely to bring them up to age-appropriate levels of performance. Students who have already failed in reading are likely to have an overlay of anxiety, poor motivation, poor behavior, low self-esteem, and ineffective learning strategies that will interfere with learning no matter how good special education services may be. Ensuring that all students succeed in the first place is a far better strategy if it can be accomplished. In Success for All, research-based preschool, kindergarten, and first-grade reading, one-to-one tutoring, and family support services give the most at-risk students a good chance to develop enough reading skills to remain out of special education or to perform better in special education than would otherwise be the case.

The data relating to special education outcomes clearly support these expectations. Several studies focused on questions related to special education. One of the most important outcomes in this area is the consistent finding of the program's particularly large effects for students in the lowest 25 percent of their classes. While effect sizes for students in general averaged around + 0.50 on individually administered reading measures, effect sizes for the lowest achievers averaged in the range of + 1.00 to + 1.50 across the grades. Across five

Baltimore schools, only 2.2 percent of third graders averaged two years behind grade level, a usual criterion for special education placement. In contrast, 8.8 percent of control third graders scored this poorly. Baltimore data also showed that special education placements for learning disabilities were cut in half (Slavin and others 1992). A recent study of two Success for All schools in Ft. Wayne, Indiana, found that over a two-year period 3.2 percent of Success for All students in grades kindergarten through one and one through two were referred to special education for learning disabilities or mild mental handicaps. In contrast, 14.3 percent of control students were referred in these categories (Smith, Ross, and Casey 1994).

Taken together, these findings support the conclusion that Success for All both reduces the need for special education services (by raising the reading achievement of very low achievers) and reduces special education referrals and placements.

Another important question concerns the effects of the program on students who have already been assigned to special education. Here again, there is evidence from different sources. In the study comparing Reading Recovery and Success for All, first graders in special education in the Reading Recovery group were not tutored but instead received traditional special education services in resource rooms. In the Success for All schools, first graders assigned to special education were tutored one-to-one (by their special education teachers) and otherwise participated in the program in the same way as all other students. Special education students in Success for All were reading substantially better (+0.77) than special education students in the comparison school (Ross and others 1995). In addition, Smith, Ross, and Casey (1994) combined first-grade reading data from special education students in Success for All and control schools in four districts: Memphis, Ft. Wayne, Montgomery, and Caldwell. Success for All special education students scored substantially better than controls (mean effect size = +0.59).

COSTS

Success for All is usually implemented in high-poverty Title I schoolwide projects, schools that have significant resources to devote to programs likely to benefit at-risk children. Most schools that implement the program do so by restructuring existing Title I resources and personnel (plus similar resources such as state compensatory education) rather than by seeking additional funding or personnel.

The first-year program cost for materials and training for a school of five hundred students is approximately sixty-five thousand dollars or one hundred thirty dollars per student, split roughly evenly between the cost of student materials and trainers (including travel). This drops to about twenty-five thousand dollars per year for additional training and replacement materials in the second and third years.

Personnel for the program, almost invariably reassigned from other functions in the school, include one full-time facilitator plus two to four tutors. Many schools use a mix of certified teachers and paraprofessionals as tutors. Existing staff are used to form family support teams and to perform other key functions.

Because of its requirements for facilitators, tutors, and extensive professional development and materials, Success for All is an expensive program, but it is within the capabilities of most Title I school-wide projects. In evaluations of the program, control groups had roughly the same resources and personnel as the Success for All schools. The program is not an add-on, but a restructuring of resources available to high-poverty schools.

CONCLUSIONS

The results of evaluations of twenty-three Success for All schools in nine districts in eight states clearly show that the program increases student reading performance. In every district, Success for All students learned significantly more than matched control students. Significant effects were not seen on every measure at every grade level, but the consistent direction and magnitude of the effects show unequivocal benefits for Success for All students. This chapter also shows particularly large impacts on the achievement of limited English proficient students in both bilingual and ESL programs and on both the number of special education referrals and the achievement of students assigned to special education. It compares the outcomes of Success for All with those of another early intervention program, Reading Recovery.

The Success for All evaluations have used reliable and valid measures and individually administered tests that are sensitive to all aspects of reading: comprehension, fluency, word attack, and word identification. Performance of Success for All students has been compared with that of matched students in matched control schools, who provide the best indication of what students would have received without the program. Replication of high-quality experiments in such a wide variety of schools and districts is extremely unusual.

An important indicator of the robustness of Success for All is the fact that of the more than four hundred eighty schools that have used the program for periods of one to eight years, fewer than twenty have dropped out (usully because of changes of principals). Many other Success for All schools have survived changes of superintendents, principals, facilitators, and other key staff, major cuts in funding, and other serious threats to program maintenance.

The research summarized here demonstrates that comprehensive, systemic, school-by-school change can take place on a broad scale in a way that maintains the integrity and effectiveness of the model. The twenty-three schools in nine districts that we are studying in depth are typical of the larger set of schools currently using Success for All in their quality of implementation, resources, demographic characteristics, and other factors. Program outcomes are not limited to the original home of the program; in fact, outcomes tend to be somewhat better outside of Baltimore. The widely held idea, based on the Rand Corporation study of innovation (Berman and McLaughlin 1978; McLaughlin 1990), that comprehensive school reform must be invented by school staff themselves is certainly not supported in research on Success for All. Although the program is adapted to the needs of each school and school staff must agree to implement the program by a vote of 80 percent or more, Success for All is developed externally with specific materials, manuals, and structures. The observation that this program can be implemented and maintained over considerable time periods and can be effective in each of its replication sites supports the idea that every school staff need not reinvent the wheel.

There is nothing magic about Success for All. None of its components is completely new or unique. Obviously, schools serving disadvantaged students can have great success without a special program if they have an outstanding staff, and other prevention and early intervention models, such as Reading Recovery (Pinnell 1989) and the School Development Program (Comer 1988) also have evidence of effectiveness with disadvantaged children. The main importance of the Success for All research is not in validating a particular model or in demonstrating that disadvantaged students can learn. Rather, its greatest contribution is in demonstrating that success for disadvantaged students can be routinely ensured in schools that are not exceptional or extraordinary (and were not producing great success before the program was introduced). We cannot ensure that every school has a charismatic principal or every student has a charismatic teacher. Nevertheless, we can ensure that every child, regardless of family background, has an opportunity to succeed in school.

The demonstration that an effective program can be replicated and can be effective in its replication sites removes one more excuse for the continuing low achievement of disadvantaged children. In order to ensure the success of disadvantaged students, we must have the political commitment to do so and the funds and policies to back up this commitment. Success for All requires a serious commitment to restructure elementary schools and to reconfigure uses of Title I, special education, and other funds to emphasize prevention and early intervention rather than remediation. These and other systemic changes in assessments, accountability, standards, and legislation can facilitate the implementation of Success for All and other school reform programs. However, we must also have methods that are known not only to be effective in their original sites but also to be replicable and effective in other sites. The evaluations presented in this chapter provide a practical demonstration of the effectiveness and replicability of one such program.

This chapter was adapted from Slavin and others 1996. This research was supported by grants from the Office of Educational Research and Improvement, U.S. Department of Education (OERI-R-117-R90002 and R-117-D40005), from the Carnegie Corporation, the Pew Charitable Trusts, and the Abell Foundation. However, any opinions expressed do not necessarily represent the positions or policies of our funders.

REFERENCES

Adams, Marilyn Jager. 1990. *Beginning to Read: Thinking and Learning About Print*. Cambridge, Mass.: MIT Press.

August, D., and K. Hakuta. 1997. *Improving Schooling for Language-Minority Children: A Research Agenda*. Washington, D.C.: National Research Council.

Berman, P. A., and Milbrey McLaughlin. 1978. *Federal Programs Supporting Educational Change: A Model of Education Change*. Vol. 8: *Implementing and Sustaining Innovations*. Santa Monica, Calif.: Rand Corporation.

Comer, J. 1988. "Educating Poor Minority Children." *Scientific American* 259(5): 42–48.

Dianda, Marcella R., and J. F. Flaherty. 1995. "Effects of Success for All on the Reading Achievement of First Graders in California Bilingual Programs." Paper presented to the American Educational Research Association, annual meeting. San Francisco (April 1995).

García, E. E. 1991. "Bilingualism, Second Language Acquisition, and the Education of Chicano Language Minority Students." In *Chicano School Failure and Success: Research and Policy Agendas for the 1990s*, edited by R. R. Valencia. New York: Falmer.

———. 1994. "The Impact of Linguistic and Cultural Diversity on America's Schools: A Need for New Policy." Paper presented to the American Educational Research Association, annual meeting. New Orleans (April 1994).

Glass, G. V., B. McGaw, and M. L. Smith. 1981. *Meta-Analysis in Social Research*. Beverly Hills, Calif.: Sage.

Hertz-Lazarowitz, R., G. Ivory, and Margarita Calderón. 1993. *The Bilingual Cooperative Integrated Reading and Composition (BCIRC) Project in the Ysleta Independent School District: Standardized Test Outcomes.* Baltimore, Md.: Johns Hopkins University, Center for Research on Effective Schooling for Disadvantaged Students.

Horwitz, R. I. 1987. "Complexity and Contradiction in Clinical Trial Research." *American Journal of Medicine* 82: 498–510.

Madden, Nancy A., Robert E. Slavin, Nancy L. Karweit, Lawrence J. Dolan, and Barbara A. Wasik. 1993. "Success for All: Longitudinal Effects of a Restructuring Program for Inner-City Elementary Schools." *American Educational Research Journal* 30(1): 123–48.

Matt, G. E., and T. D. Cook. 1994. "Threats to the Validity of Research and Synthesis." In *The Handbook of Research Synthesis*, edited by Harry Cooper and Larry V. Hedges. New York: Russell Sage.

McLaughlin, M. W. 1990. "The Rand Change Agent Study Revisited: Macro Perspectives and Micro Realities." *Educational Researcher* 19(9): 11–16.

Pinnell, Gay Su. 1989. "Reading Recovery: Helping At-Risk Children Learn to Read." *Elementary School Journal* 90(2): 161–82.

Pinnell, Gay Su, C. A. Lyons, D. E. DeFord, A. S. Bryk, and M. Seltzer. 1994. "Comparing Instructional Models for the Literacy Education of High-Risk First Graders." *Reading Research Quarterly* 29(1): 8–39.

Ross, Steven M., Lana J. Smith, Jason Casey, and Robert E. Slavin. 1995. "Increasing the Academic Success of Disadvantaged Children: An Examination of Alternative Early Intervention Programs." *American Educational Research Journal* 32: 773–800.

Slavin, Robert E. 1986. "Best-Evidence Synthesis: An Alternative to Meta-Analytic and Traditional Reviews." *Educational Researcher* 15(9): 5–11.

————. 1987. "Ability Grouping and Student Achievement in Elementary Schools: A Best-Evidence Synthesis." *Review of Educational Research* 57(3): 347–50.

————. 1995. *Cooperative Learning: Theory, Research, and Practice*, 2d ed. Boston: Allyn and Bacon.

Slavin, Robert E., and Nancy A. Madden. 1993. "Multisite Replicated Experiments: An Application to Success for All." Paper presented to the American Educational Research Association, annual meeting. Atlanta (April 1993).

Slavin, Robert E., Nancy A. Madden, Lawrence J. Dolan, Barbara A. Wasik, Steve Ross, Lana Smith, and Marcella Dianda. 1996. "Success for All: A Summary of Research." *Journal of Education for Students Placed at Risk* 1(1): 41–76.

Slavin, Robert E., Nancy A. Madden, Nancy L. Karweit, Lawrence Dolan, and Barbara A. Wasik. 1992. *Success for All: A Relentless Approach to Prevention and Early Intervention in Elementary Schools*. Arlington, Va.: Educational Research Service.

————. 1994. " 'Whenever and Wherever We Choose': The Replication of Success for All." *Phi Delta Kappan* 75(8): 639–47.

Slavin, Robert E., Nancy A. Madden, Nancy L. Karweit, Lawrence Dolan, Barbara A. Wasik, Alta Shaw, K. L. Mainzer, and Barbara Haxby. 1991. "Neverstreaming: Prevention and Early Intervention as Alternatives to Special Education." *Journal of Learning Disabilities* 24(6): 373–78.

Slavin, Robert E., Nancy A. Madden, Nancy L. Karweit, N. L. Livermon, and Lawrence Dolan. 1990. "Success for All: First-Year Outcomes of a Comprehensive Plan for Reforming Urban Education." *American Educational Research Journal* 27: 255–78.

Slavin, Robert E., Nancy A. Madden, and R. J. Stevens. 1989/90. "Cooperative Learning Models for the 3 R's." *Educational Leadership* 47(4): 22–28.

Slavin, Robert E., Nancy A. Madden, and Barbara A. Wasik. 1997. *Success for All and Roots and Wings: Summary of Research on Achievement Outcomes*. Baltimore, Md.: Johns Hopkins University, Center for Research on the Education of Students Placed at Risk.

Smith, Lana J., Steve M. Ross, and Jason P. Casey. 1994. *Special Education Analyses for Success for All in Four Cities*. Memphis: University of Memphis, Center for Research in Educational Policy.

Stevens, Robert J., Nancy A. Madden, Robert E. Slavin, and A. M. Farnish. 1987. "Cooperative Integrated Reading and Composition: Two Field Experiments." *Reading Research Quarterly* 22(4): 433–54.

U.S. General Accounting Office. 1994. *Limited English Proficiency: A Growing and Costly Educational Challenge Facing Many School Districts*. Washington, D.C.

Wasik, Barbara A., and Nancy A. Madden. 1995. *Success for All Tutoring Manual*. Baltimore, Md.: Johns Hopkins University, Center for Research on the Education of Students Placed at Risk.

Wasik, Barbara A., and Robert E. Slavin. 1993. "Preventing Early Reading Failure with One-to-One Tutoring: A Review of Five Programs." *Reading Research Quarterly* 28(2): 178–200.

Willig, A. C. 1985. "A Meta-Analysis of Selected Studies on the Effectiveness of Bilingual Education." *Review of Educational Research* 55(3): 269–317.

Wong-Fillmore, L., and C. Valadez. 1986. "Teaching Bilingual Learners." In *Handbook of Research on Teaching*, 3d ed., edited by M. C. Wittrock. New York: Macmillan.

CHAPTER 3

Reading One-to-One:
An Intensive Program Serving a
Great Many Students While
Still Achieving Large Effects

George Farkas

One of the untold stories in the loss of President Johnson's War on Poverty concerns the failure of the Title I/Chapter I Program to achieve its goals.[1] This is unfortunate, since program expenditure levels have been quite high, growing since 1965 to a 1997 annual level above $7 billion. This is about twice the size of the better-known Head Start program (which focuses on younger children). If Title I had been successful, or had at least proceeded via thoughtful and systematic planned variations—and appropriate evaluation—we might expect to know a great deal about what works for improving the reading skills of children from low-income households during the early elementary grades. (These children and skills have been the target of this program of federal aid to local school districts during most of its existence.) Instead, much of what we have learned from these program expenditures is *what does not work,* and these failed efforts continue to constitute the bulk of the program's service delivery. That is, much of the instruction provided by this program, both historically and currently, has been and continues to be ineffective (Slavin 1989; Natriello, McDill, and Pallas 1990; Arroyo and Zigler 1993). Indeed, a recently released report of the most comprehensive evaluation ever undertaken reconfirmed the general ineffectiveness of this program (*Education Week,* April 2, 1997).

Nevertheless, one noteworthy reform has operated under Title I funding—a tradition of service delivery built around one-to-one reading instruction with trained tutors. This tradition began with a program called Reading Recovery, which today exists in hundreds of school districts. The model was expanded and improved by a program called Success for All, which has, by now, been disseminated relatively widely across school districts. (For a more extensive treatment of Success for All, see chapter 2 in this volume.) As we shall see, both programs have achieved significant gains in student achievement. However, both programs use certified teachers as tutors, thereby incurring very high unit costs of service delivery. These costs are so high as to preclude serving the great majority of students in need of services.

This chapter focuses on Reading One-to-One, a program that, by spring 1997, had tutored more than six thousand students in more than seventy schools across more than ten school districts. This program uses trained and managed college students and community residents to deliver tutoring services similar to those of the other two programs. Most important, it produces student gains comparable to those of the other two programs, but at much lower unit cost. That is, this program model could serve many more children with the same budget as the other programs, while delivering similar reading gains. If widely disseminated, this model could accomplish the original goals of Title I and serve essentially all needy students within the current program budget.

The chapter is organized as follows. The first section provides a background for the discussion by briefly reviewing prior program innovations under Title I. The second section summarizes the history of Reading One-to-One program development and dissemination. The third section describes the program's curriculum, and the fourth describes procedures for recruiting, training, and managing tutors. The fifth section discusses our experiences and lessons learned regarding program implementation and dissemination, and the sixth summarizes the research evidence on the magnitude of the program's effects on student reading skills. The seventh section compares the per student benefits and costs of this program with those of its leading competitors. The chapter closes with a summary and discussion.

BACKGROUND

Traditionally, Title I service delivery has been organized as follows. To be certain that at-risk children receive add-on services, program regulations require that Title I expenditures be kept strictly separate from regular school district expenditures. That is, Title I money cannot substitute for funds that the local school district would spend anyway. Instead, Title I is required to provide services over and above those that the district would ordinarily provide.

The result has been to create a self-contained bureaucracy within the bureaucracy of our major urban school districts. The Title I director within each district controls her own budget, often involving millions of dollars, which she receives annually from Washington. With it, she hires, fires, and places Title I teachers and teacher aides in schools. Even within each school, the program has its own separate existence. The Title I director determines each school's Title I budget, based on the number of low-income (free and reduced-lunch) students enrolled there. She then assigns a lead Title I teacher, several other teachers, and (typically) several aides, to the school. These Title I staffers also have their own (often relatively large) budget for books and other materials. The lead Title I teacher assigned to the school is in charge of testing the children and determining which students qualify for Title I services. She and the other Title I staff typically pull these children out of their classes for special instruction in groups of five to ten students. Both within school districts as entities, and also within individual schools, the program is essentially self-contained.

It has also gained a poor reputation. The lowest-performing children, with the greatest psychological and medical problems, are pulled out of class. Although each student has a different problem and performance level, they are instructed together in groups of five to ten. The Title I teachers sometimes have low skill and are typically provided with little training or effective curriculum to address the needs of these children. Faced with an essentially impossible task, constantly getting nowhere with the most troubled children, they naturally have low morale. The children are stigmatized, the teachers are stigmatized, the entire program is stigmatized. Its failure to produce positive results for children is widely known (Slavin 1989; Arroyo and Zigler 1993; Natriello, McDill, and Pallas 1990; *Education Week*, April 2, 1997). This itself has created a negative feedback effect—the more skilled teachers have left, further driving down skill levels, student gains, and morale and making it more difficult to recruit skilled teachers. The regular staff of classroom teachers see little gains from the students they send to Title I instruction and form their own low opinion of the program. Meanwhile, however, program funds continue to flow from Washington without interruption, and the internal bureaucracy functions smoothly. To this day, most Title I add-on services are provided in the time-honored mode—a Title I teacher pulls five to ten children out of classes for one period of group instruction each day.

Eventually, a reform movement has sprung up. The best known and apparently most effective are Reading Recovery, from the Ohio State University School of Education, and Success for All, from a federally funded research center at Johns Hopkins University. Both focus on one-on-one tutoring, using certified teachers. Both have significantly raised the reading performance of at-risk children (Madden and others 1993; Wasik and Slavin 1993; Pinnell and others 1994, 1995; Rasinski 1995; Slavin and others 1995).

These results are not surprising. Common sense suggests that to reach, say, the five lowest performers in any particular first-grade class, the best strategy is to pull them out of the class and work intensively with each. Only in this way can instruction be focused on each student's specific starting point and instructional needs and also be keyed to building up the self-confidence and self-esteem that are typically depressed in these students. The approach follows that of Slavin and others (1990, 258):

> Students receive help early on, when their problems are small. This help is intensive and effective enough to catch students up with their classmates so that they can profit from their regular classroom instruction. Instead of letting students fall further and further behind until they need special or remedial education or are retained in grade, students . . . are given whatever help they need to keep up in their basic skills.

Most important, research studies using appropriate statistical techniques have begun appearing on a regular basis in the major journals, demonstrating that one-on-one instructional programs are effective with low-performing children. *Over the thirty years of experience with Title I, only one-on-one instructional programs have demonstrated such a record of success with at-risk children.*

At bottom, the success of one-on-one tutoring is based on the following unique characteristics. First, the instructional curriculum and feedback are custom-tailored and fine-tuned to the student's current level of performance. Second, bonding with an adult provides the encouragement necessary to maintain time-on-task and good concentration. And finally, the privacy of one-on-one allows the student to risk failing. At the same time, there is no other student to give the answer. The intensive personal interaction with a tutor who has bonded with the student and responds sensitively to his or her skills, personality, and moods functions as an "operating room" in which to repair the student's skills, habits, and styles.

Programs such as Success for All report positive experiences with cooperative learning techniques that place the students in paired-reading situations. For the weakest students within Success for All, this supplements, rather than replaces, one-on-one tutoring. Reading One-to-One has also experimented with having tutors work with two or more students at a time. Always the finding has been that a high-quality tutoring session is not sustainable in other than a one-on-one format.

As implemented by the two most widely known tutoring programs—Reading Recovery and Success for All—the tutoring intervention employs certified teachers and is thus quite expensive. Indeed, in their review of such programs, Wasik and Slavin (1993, 179) identify this high cost as their chief drawback: "The major drawback to tutoring is its cost. Providing tutoring to large numbers of students across the grade span would, of course, be prohibitive." *Yet such delivery of intensive services to large numbers of students is exactly what is needed.*

Unfortunately, using certified teachers on the regular payroll to perform this tutoring is prohibitively expensive. Reading One-to-One has attained results similar in magnitude to those of Reading Recovery and Success for All while operating at less than one-quarter of their cost. The history of this program is the subject of the following section.

PROGRAM HISTORY AND STRUCTURE

My academic research on school performance (Farkas and others 1990a, 1990b; Farkas 1993, 1996) was put to a practical test when, in 1990, school reformers from the business community challenged me to recommend an intervention. A review of my research results led me to several conclusions. First, the vocabulary and reading comprehension basic skills of far too many central-city children from low-income households, including relatively large numbers of African American and Hispanic students, are abysmally low. Second, higher skills in these areas are absolutely essential if these students are to succeed. Third, remediation to improve these skills must work directly and powerfully on the student's self-esteem and work habits, as well as on the skills themselves. Fourth, the intervention must occur in elementary school, where the skills are taught and a pattern of failure is typically established.

Surveying the literature in this area, it became obvious that two existing programs already accomplished these goals—Reading Recovery and Success for All. Accordingly, I set out to use my own university students to provide similar services within the Dallas public schools. During spring 1991, thirty undergraduate and graduate students from the University of Texas at Dallas were recruited to register for course credit and participate in the project. For three hours of credit, they were required to tutor two hours per day, on two separate days of the week, for a total of four hours per week. For six credit hours, they were required to tutor eight hours per week, preferably on at least three days, and for nine credit hours, they would have to tutor twelve hours per week, preferably on at least four days.

With the assistance of the staff of the Reading Recovery Program within the Richardson Independent School District and of Robert Slavin and Barbara Wasik of Success for All, the tutors were trained to implement half-hour one-on-one tutoring sessions with first, second, and third graders.[2] These sessions combined whole language and phonics approaches and were based on maximizing the time that the student spent actively reading to the tutor. Each session included the following elements: familiar rereading of two to three little books; reading of a new book (possibly with the tutor taking a "running record" for diagnostic purposes; Clay 1979); a drill of letters, sounds, and words; and a writing section in which the child dictated, wrote, and read back a short story (possibly only a sentence or two). Students worked from leveled books of the "Sunshine" series (Wright Publishing Co.) as well as from classroom-assigned basal readers (textbooks containing a collection of stories) and other materials provided by the teachers.

We began operating within one elementary school whose principal had invited us to implement the program. Logistics were organized as follows: school records were used to identify more than one hundred seventy first to third graders in this school who were in the bottom fortieth percentile on the Iowa Test of Basic Skills (ITBS) reading test administered in the fall of 1990. These were sorted by classroom (each of the first to third grades was divided into four or five classes of approximately twenty-two students each), and the classroom teachers were approached as to their willingness to let these children be pulled out of class for tutoring. The teachers each gave a schedule of times when they would permit such pullout.

Schedules of availability were collected from each of the tutors, and these were matched to those provided by the teachers. This matching was something of a nightmare, but it *did* provide an approximate random assignment—students were assigned to tutors (sometimes more than one) and to varying numbers of hours per week simply on the basis of our ability to make a match and work out everyone's schedule.

Tutors were trained in the reading instruction techniques pioneered by Reading Recovery (Clay 1979) and Success for All (Slavin and others 1990). In a two-hour period, they administered half-hour sessions to each of four students. After each session, the tutor was instructed to take a few minutes to complete a tutoring session report form. These reports formed the basis of the progress file kept on each student tutored. At the end of the term, tutors wrote a term paper summarizing their experiences and observations. These term papers and student progress files were retained to facilitate the research component of the project.

The program evolved from this beginning. During fall 1991, four new schools asked to join the program. The process was advanced through word of mouth among principals, but also through the decentralization that had just occurred within the district, in particular, the creation of areas and area directors and the increased authority given to individual schools to spend their Title I money. At the same time, schools were pressured to spend the money effectively to improve test scores.

The major opportunity for disseminating the program occurred during spring 1992, when I was permitted to describe the program at one of the monthly meetings of the superintendent and his area directors. At this meeting, one of the area directors stated that federal reform of the Chapter I guidelines permitted programs such as ours to be run with Chapter I funds. This area director invited us to speak at his next monthly meeting with his principals, as did other area directors.

The result of these presentations, combined with positive word of mouth from the principals and teachers of our operating schools, was that twelve schools signed up to use a portion of their Chapter I funds to hire paid tutors for the 1992 to 1993 school year. Central to this process was the establishment, via pressure from the area director, of the notion that under school-centered education, and for the first time, principals throughout the district could control how their Chapter I program moneys would be spent.

By spring 1993, twenty-six schools signed up for paid tutoring for the 1993 to 1994 school year. This was repeated again during the spring of 1994, so that thirty-two schools were signed up for the 1994 to 1995 school year. Across these thirty-two schools, we provided approximately one hundred forty-four thousand hours of one-to-one instruction to twenty-four hundred students at a total cost of 1.8 million dollars. During this period of program expansion, no school dropped the program due to dissatisfaction with our work. Instead, we collected twenty-five pages of (single-spaced) positive comments from the teachers and principals of the schools where we were operating. We also estimated the reading gains of tutored students statistically, concluding that they were relatively large—seventy sessions increased reading comprehension by half a grade level. These statistical results are discussed in detail here and in Farkas (1996).

Despite these positive outcomes, top school administrators took actions that drastically reduced the size of the tutoring program; in particular, they removed the discretion of principals over the bulk of Title I funds. (For a detailed description of these events, see Farkas 1996, chap. 12.) Reading One-to-One continues in Dallas through the present time (spring 1998), but in a much smaller number of schools. At the same time, however, the program has expanded to other locations.

As a result of the work of a University of Texas system task force, Aileen Johnson, a professor of reading in the School of Education at University of Texas at Brownsville, began a Reading One-to-One program in several local elementary schools in 1994, using her education students as tutors. These programs have continued and expanded to additional schools in the area, so that by spring 1998 eleven schools were operating programs in the greater Brownsville area.

In March 1995, the trade paper for the American Association of School Administrators ran an article about Reading One-to-One. As a consequence, a number of schools in the districts of Magna and Provo surrounding Salt Lake City elected to try the program, and programs are currently operating in seven schools. (An interesting feature of this implementation is that in some schools the majority of tutors are teacher aides.) In addition, when an area principal became a superintendent in Alaska, he brought the program there. During fall 1997, the program—translated into Spanish—also began operating in Guanajuato, Mexico.

In the summer of 1995, I and several coauthors prepared a paper for Jerry Junkins, chief executive officer of Texas Instruments. It was titled "Can All Children Learn to Read at Grade Level by the End of Third Grade?" (For a portion of the arguments in this paper, see Farkas 1996, chap. 10.) He showed the article to Governor Bush of Texas, and it formed one basis for the Texas Reading Initiative. I sent a copy to a friend at the U.S. Department of Education, and he shared it with Gene Sperling, a White House staffer. Sperling then used it as one of the bases for President Clinton's America Reads Initiative, announced in August 1996. In subsequent conversations, I convinced Sperling that for the intervention to be successful, tutors have to receive at least some compensation for their work. This led the staff to modify the president's program to its present form, which uses Americorps volunteers and college work-study students as tutors in a nationwide effort.

Our role in helping to formulate America Reads led to contact with a number of national reading experts. Some of them came to observe our program and were favorably impressed. Our growing reputation led to a number of other opportunities. During the winter of 1996 to 1997, we became an Americorps site, using Americorps members as tutors. We also trained a number of other Americorps sites to implement our program across various Texas school districts. In February 1997, the Houston School District asked us to implement a large-scale tutoring effort using local college students. Within four weeks, we had trained and placed more than two hundred college students to work with more than a thousand at-risk students in seventeen Houston schools. (During the fall 1997, the Houston program expanded to twenty-five schools.) On March 1, 1997, we presented our work to the Reading Panel of the National Academy of Sciences. Our curricular development, tutor manual and training procedures, management structures, and statistical research were well received.

CURRICULUM

Reading One-to-One curriculum and management also evolved over this time period. In curricular terms, we found that most first-graders, as well as many of the higher-grade students we tutored, did not yet know their letters and sounds and had not mastered sounding-out skills for unfamiliar words. They required this basic instruction before they could begin to progress through the curriculum of reading increasingly difficult little books. Accordingly, we created Alphabet and Word Families curricula for these sets of skills, adding these to the Reading Comprehension curriculum, which itself continued to evolve. By 1994 the Reading One-to-One tutor's manual had evolved beyond dependence on the Johns Hopkins manual and had become fully our own creation. In particular, it placed greater emphasis on phonemic awareness and phonological processing than do Reading Recovery or Success for All.

Children to be tutored are selected by their teachers and principal. Tutors follow a specific curriculum that combines elements of phonics and whole language. In particular, phonics are emphasized in the Alphabet and Word Families curricula, which explicitly teaches letter/sound relationships and phonological processing skills, and the students read from book series with a controlled (decodable) vocabulary. (For discussions of the importance of this research-based instructional strategy for children who are mastering beginning reading, see Adams 1990; Honig 1996.) This instructional material has been added to the Reading Recovery and Success for All curricula. However, the more advanced Reading Comprehension students *do* work from whole-language books, which provide much greater opportunities for tutors to work on building their comprehension and reading fluency skills.

For each child, the one-on-one forty-minute tutoring sessions are scheduled each day for either three or four days per week, depending on the plan selected by the individual school.[3] Detailed records concerning the child's progress are updated each session and kept on file in the school. Teachers receive progress reports on their students twice each semester.

During tutoring sessions, tutors seek to identify the strengths and weaknesses of each student's reading performance, provide lessons that teach unused reading skills, and encourage the continuation of productive reading behavior. Tutors are taught recommended strategies for implementing these actions. The goal is to give each student the reading time and guidance that he or she needs to achieve grade-level academic performance.

During each session, the tutor focuses on teaching letter/sound relationships, using sounds to read words in connected text, and understanding what is read. These are the key elements in the reading process. These elements are addressed in the three curricula designed for students of different skill levels. Each session is made up of four parts. Skills are assessed every fifth session. Students are advanced to a higher curriculum once they have scored high marks on these assessments.

ASSESSMENT

On the first day of tutoring, all students are given a series of tests to determine their placement. They are presented with shuffled flash cards containing the fifty-two upper- and lower-case letters and are asked to name each letter and tell the sound it makes. Students are also given a letter writing assessment and seven phonemic awareness (sound-sense) assessments. For the latter, they are asked to answer ten questions for each of the following: (a) rhyming (produce a rhyming word when prompted), (b) beginning sounds (detect the beginning sound in a spoken word), (c) ending sounds (detect the ending sounds in a spoken word), (d) blending sounds (blend individual sounds to produce a whole word), (e) segmenting words (segment a spoken word into its separate sounds), (f) deleting the beginning sound (delete the beginning sound of a spoken word and pronounce the remaining part of the word), and (g) substituting beginning sounds (substitute beginning sounds into a spoken word to create a new word).

Students are also given a Word Families assessment. The student is shown a list of words taken from eighteen sets of word families, comprising a total of seventy-two word families, and is asked to read them. A student who knows less than 65 percent of the letters or sounds is placed in the Alphabet curriculum. A score above 65 percent on the Alphabet assessment but below 90 percent on the Word Families assessment places the student in the Word Families curriculum. These students learn phonetically regular words, each associated with a "family" of words that contain a targeted sound or phonetic pattern. These word families are ordered and grouped by type of sound and level of difficulty.[4]

Students are classified into the Reading Comprehension curriculum when they have letter and sound identification scores greater than 65 percent *and* a Word Families test score greater than 90 percent. Once students are identified as Reading Comprehension students, they are given a series of "cloze" tests to determine their actual reading level. Students read a story that has every fifth word omitted. As they read the story, they are expected to fill in each blank with an appropriate word.

Students are tested on books of different levels until they score in the 60 to 80 percent range. They then begin instruction at this level.

TUTORING SESSION FOR ALPHABET STUDENTS

Students with weak letter/sound identification or phonemic awareness and phonological processing skills must be taught these skills explicitly if they are to learn to sound out and decode text. In the Alphabet curriculum, these skills are taught intensively and are applied to very beginning reading via "Bob Books," a commercially produced set of very simple, controlled-text, small books. The four basic parts of each session in this lesson plan are the following:

Part 1: Review of letters/sounds (ten minutes)

- Practice hearing sounds in words (sound-sense exercises)
- Review letter names and sounds studied in previous sessions using flash cards, plastic letters, or other manipulatives.

Part 2: Letter/sound instruction (fifteen minutes)

- Teach the name, shape, and sound of one or more letters
- Create flash cards of these letters and their code words for the letter or word bank and home study.

Part 3: Reading (five minutes)

- Have the student read a "Bob Book" keyed to specific letters, providing assistance and repetition as necessary
- As appropriate, create sentences for the student to read.

Part 4: Assisted writing (five minutes)

- Have the student write words and simple sentences using the letters and words they have already learned and are currently being taught.

Every session, the tutor works with the student on one of the phonological processing (sound-sense) activities that the student has not yet achieved a perfect score on, and every fifth session the student is assessed on letter/sound identification and letter writing. The students remain in the Alphabet curriculum until they have mastered both letter identification and basic letter sounds. A student is able to advance to the Word Families curriculum after he or she scores 90 percent or higher on both letter and sound identification assessments.

TUTORING SESSION FOR WORD FAMILY STUDENTS

Word Family students are taught word attack skills via eighteen groupings (seventy-two families) of phonetically regular words, each containing a targeted sound or phonetic pattern. Sight words (which cannot be sounded out) are also taught. These word families are ordered and grouped by type of sound and level of difficulty. Tutors have the students read from the Phonics Readers (Steck Vaughn Publishing Company), which use a controlled vocabulary keyed directly to each of the word families. The four basic parts of each session in this lesson plan are the following:

Part 1: Review (ten minutes)

- Review word families and sight words studied in previous sessions using flash cards created during those lessons

- If the student has not scored 100 percent on all sound-sense skills, teach those still lacking.

Part 2: Word family instruction (fifteen minutes)

- Teach the spelling and meaning of a word family lead word

- Identify the basic sound of the word family, introduce the other family members, and teach the sounding-out skills

- Make flash cards for the word bank and home study.

Part 3: Reading (five minutes)

- Have the student read the book that corresponds to the particular word family (or families) taught in the session.

Part 4: Assisted writing (five minutes)

- Have the student orally compose, then write, sentences using words from the book read in part 3

- Include previously learned word families in the composition.

Word Families are taught in the order listed below. There are seventy-two total word families, subdivided into eighteen groups:

Group 1: Short [a]. The short vowel sound for the letter [a] is the sound at the beginning of "apple."

Group 2: Short [i]. The short vowel sound for the letter [i] is the sound at the beginning of "itch."

Group 3: Short [u]. The short vowel sound for the letter [u] is the sound at the beginning of "up."

Group 4: Short [o]. The short vowel sound for the letter [o] is the sound at the beginning of "opposite."

Group 5: Short [e]. The short vowel sound for the letter [e] is the sound at the beginning of "empty."

Before teaching long vowel sounds, tutors familiarize themselves with the following information. When teaching long vowel families, they teach the student these rules:

- Magical [e]. When a word ends in a vowel / consonant / [e], generally, the vowel says its name (long vowel sound) and the [e] is silent. "The [e] casts a spell on the other vowel that makes the other vowel say its own name."

- Words with two vowels together. "When two vowels go walking, the first one does the talking and usually says its name." Sometimes when two vowels appear adjacent to each other in a word, the first vowel says its own name (long sound) and the second is silent. Many words in the specified books conform to this two-vowel guideline.

Group 6: Long [a]

Group 7: Long [i] and long [u]

Group 8: Long [o]

Group 9: Long [e]

Group 10: [s] blends

Group 11: [r] blends

Group 12: [l] blends

Group 13: Three-letter blends

Group 14: Final blends.

When the letter pairs [th], [sh], [ch], [wh], [ck], or [ng] appear in a word, they each represent a single sound. For instance, the [ch] in "chair" is not pronounced with the sound for [c] plus the sound for [h]. Instead, [ch] has its own sound. When teaching families sixty through sixty-nine, the tutors teach the sound represented by the *pair* of letters.

Group 15: [th] digraphs. There are two distinct sounds for [th].

Group 16: [wh] and [sh] digraphs

Group 17: [ch] digraphs

Group 18: [ck] and [ng] digraphs.

At the beginning of every fifth session progress is assessed by asking the student to read a random member of each previously introduced word family. The student advances to the Reading Comprehension curriculum when he or she is able to read randomly selected words from each of the families with 90 percent or better accuracy.

TUTORING SESSION FOR READING COMPREHENSION STUDENTS

Students who score 90 percent or better on the Word Families test have read a great many of the Steck-Vaughn phonics readers and can easily decode most phonetically regular words. They are ready to begin reading more challenging books containing less regular vocabulary and the complexity of real texts—principal and secondary themes and meanings and more complex information, plot, and characterization. These students read books from the Wright Group Publishing Co.'s Sunshine series. The first level is broken down into sublevels, increasing in difficulty from A to J. (Students who have scored 90 percent or higher on the Word Families assessment can typically begin with level G or higher.) After level J of the first level, there are levels two through eleven. These leveled books are the preferred material for taking rudimentary running records with which to measure student achievement and remaining deficits.[5] We have also prepared comprehension questions for all of these books and linked these to the specific skills targeted by the Texas standardized reading test. The four basic parts of each session in this lesson plan are the following:

Part 1: Review (five to ten minutes)

- Have the student read one or more books that are familiar or that are below his or her current reading level. The student need not read an entire book. He or she may read only a few pages or one chapter

- Provide some guidance on decoding strategies

- Provide sound-sense skills instruction (if still needed).

Part 2: New reading (fifteen minutes)

- Introduce a new book at the student's current reading level. The student's current reading level will be determined by the initial and subsequent cloze puzzles

- As the student reads the book, offer advice on using reading strategies

- Take a running record

- Check student comprehension.

Part 3: Word list instruction (five minutes)

- Teach words from the word bank

- Teach words from the word lists.

Part 4: Creative writing (five to ten minutes)

- Help the student compose a "story" or other written work

- Help the student read and edit the composition.

ASSESSMENT OF READING PROGRESS

We developed cloze tests for Wright Group books. These tests are administered at the first Reading Comprehension session and periodically thereafter to determine the student's correct reading level. A student progresses to the next level of books only after scoring in the 60 to 80 percent range for that level. The most informative measure of a student's reading performance is the collection of running records that reflect the student's reading experiences. Tutors take running records to record the number of correctly decoded words and to note the types of errors the student makes. Tutors repair each of the decoding deficits identified. In addition to the daily running record, tutors also use a list of comprehension questions we have developed for each book. As the student reads a new book, the tutor periodically stops and tests the student's knowledge of the material being read.

TUTOR RECRUITMENT, TRAINING, AND MANAGEMENT

Our systems and practices for recruiting, training, and managing tutors have evolved significantly during the seven years of program operation. Key issues have centered around the cognitive skills of tutors and the training and management of tutors.

Tutors may be college students, community residents, or teacher aides. However, we have learned that in order to be effective, their own language skills (including grammar, spelling, and punctuation) must be at or above the eighth-grade level. Accordingly, we developed an examination to test for this, and since 1994, all Reading One-to-One tutors have been required to pass this exam. (Recently, this exam was administered to 360 tutor applicants in Houston, many of them college students, and 297 passed.) Applicants who pass this test then complete an application and receive a personal interview and are given a criminal background check.

Those applicants selected are given a detailed tutor's manual and receive seven hours of training over two days (with at least one evening between the sessions to study the manual). The training culminates in a written examination. Those who pass are then placed in a school, with the understanding that their training is incomplete; the remainder occurs in conjunction with their "learning by doing" as active tutors. Experienced staff then sit with each tutor during tutoring sessions. The staff fill out an assessment form and provide feedback on strengths and weaknesses and tips for improvement. This occurs several times until the tutor's performance has reached a sufficiently high level that she or he can be "certified" as a Reading One-to-One tutor.

Daily management is the responsibility of a full-time Reading One-to-One coordinator within each school. The coordinator monitors the tutors' attendance and performance. In addition, an area supervisor (central staff member) circulates among the schools, sitting with each tutor during a session, grading his or her performance, and providing feedback. When the tutor's performance achieves a certain level, she or he becomes a certified Reading One-to-One tutor.

PROGRAM IMPLEMENTATION AND DISSEMINATION

The mechanisms employed for implementing and disseminating the program are crucial. In particular, we have sought to systematize the steps necessary to implement the program properly and have insisted that dissemination to new locations include both initial training and set-up *as well as* periodic monitoring and retraining by our staff. Finally, we collect data on student performance and program implementation and prepare a report on our findings.

Implementation begins when a locality identifies one or more individuals to manage the program. When possible, these individuals come to Dallas (or another location where Reading One-to-One is operating) to observe the program in its fully operational state. At this time, they are introduced to a variety of systems and procedures, including the testing and training of tutors, curriculum, student folders, record-keeping, assessment and measurement of student progress, materials (books as well as the cloze puzzles and comprehension questions that accompany them), and the manuals that spell out tasks, behaviors, and responsibilities both for the on-site managers (coordinators) of individual sites and for the area supervisors who oversee these managers across multiple sites.

This introduction is followed by a start-up procedure in which a team of Reading One-to-One staff visits the locality. Site coordinators are trained both in their management responsibilities and in the reading curriculum itself. Each school site is visited, and principals and teachers are informed about the program. The physical location of the program, the necessary materials and their layout, and other issues are discussed. Typically, Reading One-to-One staff also assist with the screening and hiring of tutors. They train the tutors and test them on this training. They assist local staff in placing and scheduling tutors in a fashion compatible with locational and time-of-day preferences and with the times that students are available for tutoring in each school. They then begin the process of sitting with each tutor, rating his or her performance, and providing feedback on how to tutor more effectively.

Several times during the year, Reading One-to-One staff return to each school. They examine the full range of issues associated with program implementation and rate each site coordinator on the quality of this implementation. They also provide further rating of, and assistance to, the tutors as well as retrain current tutors and train new tutors. In all of these activities, the goal is to train local staff members to run the program completely by themselves. However, it is our belief that full attainment of this goal requires continued involvement by Reading One-to-One staff, which can typically phase out after a two-year period of assistance and monitoring.

Over time, monitoring of each site's implementation is particularly important where the program operates across many schools or where the program's start-up is rapid. An extreme instance of this occurred in spring 1997, when the Houston School District asked us to implement a program immediately using more than two hundred paid tutors in seventeen elementary schools. Many of these schools had been oper-ating the Success for All program for some time, and program coordinators at each school were typically counselors, special education teachers, or Title I teachers, some of whom were also the site's Success for All coordinator. In this case we made ninety-six separate school monitoring visits during a six-week period and were told that the great success of our program was at least partly attributable to this implementation effort (for further discussion, see Farkas 1997).

PROGRAM EFFECTS

The central issue remains the standard program evaluation question: what are the effects of this intervention, and what is the mechanism by which they operate? It is to this subject that we now turn.

DATA AND METHODS FOR STUDYING PROGRAM EFFECTS

The best way to evaluate a program intervention is to assign subjects randomly to the treatment and to a comparison group. Then, the two groups are identical on all causal variables, including unmeasured ones, so that any difference in cognitive score gains can be attributed to the intervention. Unfortunately, such random assignment is rarely possible in compensatory programs such as Reading One-to-One. In such cases, it is common to compare outcomes between a group who receives the treatment and an appropriately selected comparison group. But this strategy is fraught with problems because the treatment and comparison groups are likely to be different on key variables other than the treatment itself (that is, they are poorly matched). This situation is typically at its worst in evaluating compensatory education programs such as Reading One-to-One for three reasons. First, students are assigned to the group receiving tutoring in a highly non-random manner. That is, teachers typically assign those students who "need tutoring most." This includes students with troubled home lives, difficulty concentrating in class, and emotional or behavioral problems. These are the students who would have progressed least in the absence of the program. Second, measures of these variables that teachers use implicitly to assign students to the program are not available on the school district's database. Thus, they cannot be entered into a regression analysis and be statistically controlled (adjusted for) when using the treatment and comparison group to estimate the program's effect. Finally, Texas excludes large numbers of (mostly English as a Second Language) students from testing in the early elementary grades. Since students are nonrandomly excluded, with the lowest performers most likely to be missing from the data set, biases introduced by the first two problems are likely to be magnified.

The program dealt with these problems as follows. First, instead of attempting to construct a (poorly matched) comparison group of students who were not tutored, a "comparison group" was found from within the tutored students. This was accomplished by comparing outcomes for tutored students who received more sessions with those who received fewer. That is, the program treatment variable was the number of tutoring sessions that the student received. This restricted the attention to students who were selected by their teachers for tutoring and compares students within this group who are relatively similar in most ways other than the number of tutoring sessions they received. Students received more or fewer sessions in a "quasi-random" fashion determined by accidents of scheduling (teacher decisions about when students would be available for pullout combined with when tutors were available for tutoring) and whether or not the school contracted for three or four sessions per week. (The latter is further controlled by school dummy variables in the analysis.) But what about the possibility that for some unknown reason, the "better" students were assigned more tutoring sessions? This possibility was investigated by using regression analysis to predict the total number of tutoring sessions a student received. No statistically significant tendency was found for the "better students" (those who had higher scores on reading comprehension prior to tutoring or those who were more attentive during tutoring) to receive more tutoring sessions. In fact, the opposite was the case, since limited English proficient (LEP) students tended to receive more tutoring sessions. Thus, if any bias was introduced by using the number of sessions variable to estimate the program effect, it was in a conservative direction. That is, the estimates of program effect are likely to be *smaller* than the true effect.

The second problem—the nonrandom assignment of students to tutoring on the basis of unmeasured causal variables—was largely solved by using the number of tutoring sessions, with its "quasi-random assignment," to measure the treatment. However, going one step further, a variable was created that *does* measure the student's ability to concentrate, namely the "attentiveness during tutoring" variable. Because this is based on direct observation by the tutor, averaged over many sessions, it is a very accurate measure of a student's emotional and behavioral functioning. Our ability to hold this variable (which is not available on standard district databases) constant when estimating program effects further guarantees that our estimates of program effect are unbiased and efficient.

Finally, we dealt with the issue of large numbers of cases nonrandomly missing due to students being excused from ITBS testing by administering our own tests to all tutored students, both before and after tutoring. The resulting Reading Achievement Scale (table 3.1) is a curriculum-referenced test in the sense that it directly embodies the instructional goals of Reading One-to-One. The Woodcock-Johnson reading comprehension test is the most widely used instrument for evaluating reading interventions. (See, for example, Madden and others 1993; Pinnell and others 1994.) And we have both of these (one-on-one administered) measures for all students tutored, with none excluded from the study. Thus, this third problem, too, is fully resolved. In no sense does the program "teach to" the Woodcock-Johnson test. Rather, program curriculum and training were developed completely independently of the material on this test.

In this analysis we examine program effects for children who were tutored during 1994 to 1995, the fifth year of program operations. We restrict attention to those students who received a reasonable "dose" of the program treatment—at least twenty-five sessions. As mentioned, program effects are estimated from a regression analysis in which the key independent variable is the number of tutoring sessions a student received. An attractive feature of this analysis is that it controls for the student's attentiveness during tutoring. This is the average across all tutoring sessions of the tutor's rating (one, two, or three) of the student's ability to concen-

Table 3.1 Reading One-to-One Achievement Scale, 1994 to 1995

Score	Reading Level
1	Knows the name of, and sound made by, less than 25 percent of the fifty-two lower- and upper-case letters
2	Knows the name of, and sound made by, 25 to 50 percent of the fifty-two lower- and upper-case letters
3	Knows the name of, and sound made by, 50 to 75 percent of the fifty-two lower- and upper-case letters
4	Knows the name of, and sound made by, more than 75 percent of the fifty-two lower- and upper-case letters
5	Word family group 1, short [a] sound
6	Word family group 2, short [e] sound
7	Word family group 3, short [o] sound
8	Word family group 4, short [u] sound
9	Word family group 5, short [i] sound
10	Word family group 6, "magical [e]"
11	Word family group 7, words with two different vowels together
12	Reads level 1 books, sublevel A to C
13	Reads level 1 books, sublevel D to F
14	Reads level 1 books, sublevel G to J
15	Reads level 2 books
16	Reads level 3 books
17	Reads level 4 books
18	Reads level 5 books
19	Reads level 6 books
20	Reads level 7 books
21	Reads level 8 books
22	Reads level 9 books
23	Reads level 10 books
24	Reads level 11 books
25	Reads library books

trate during the session. Further, for the Reading Achievement Scale and for the Woodcock Reading Comprehension Test score, we have measures for all students tutored, both before and after tutoring. This is a much better situation than occurs for the Iowa Test of Basic Skills, because more than half of tutored elementary students are typically exempted from this test and thus would have to be excluded from an evaluation based solely on it. This would be particularly worrisome, because these students are far from randomly chosen. Instead, they are typically from families who speak Spanish at home and who thus experience the greatest difficulties in English reading comprehension.

Finally, the methodology we are using is somewhat unusual within this subfield of educational program evaluation. It is much more common to use a "matched comparison schools" design (see, for example, the program effect estimates reported for Success for All in chapter 2). However, our design may be superior to that using matched comparison schools because the "matching" is often poor, so that the schools and children who receive the program are often systematically different from the "comparison schools" who do not. These differences are rarely accounted for (that is, they are not "controlled" or adjusted for) in the ensuing analysis. Of course, the best procedure is the classic experimental design in which students are randomly assigned either to receive or not to receive the "treatment." In its absence, knowledge of the true impact of these programs remains less certain than we would prefer.

PROGRAM EFFECTS

Table 3.2 shows the means of the variables for students who received at least twenty-five tutoring sessions. Across first, second, and third grade, between 54 and 58 percent of these students are male. They are also overwhelmingly Hispanic—75 percent among first graders, 72 percent among second graders, and 68 percent among third graders. This is largely due to political and bureaucratic features of program growth—Hispanic administrators over majority Hispanic areas of the school district seemed most open to, and interested in, the program. It is also influenced by the fact that Hispanic children from Spanish-speaking homes were often perceived by their teachers as being most in need of tutoring. This also varies by grade level—African American children constituted 8 percent of tutored first graders, 19 percent of tutored second graders, and 25 percent of tutored third graders. (Recall that we allowed classroom teachers to select those students they wanted tutored.)

For all three grades, the average student received about sixty tutoring sessions. On a scale of one to three, the attentiveness of the average first grader was 2.6. Second and third graders averaged 2.7. Clearly, most children are quite attentive in the one-on-one format. Children who received fewer than thirty-five tutoring sessions were typically "alternates," who were tutored only when a regularly scheduled student was absent; 5 percent of first graders, 4 percent of second graders, and 8 percent of third graders fell into this category.

Table 3.2 Means of Variables for Full-Time Reading One-to-One Students, 1994 to 1995

Indicator	First Grade	Second Grade	Third Grade
Male	0.543	0.546	0.584
Hispanic	0.748	0.717	0.684
African American	0.084	0.190	0.249
Number of sessions	61.40	61.39	60.52
Average attentiveness	2.59	2.67	2.71
Alternate[a]	0.054	0.035	0.084
Limited English proficiency	0.600	0.576	0.540
Receives free lunch	0.867	0.859	0.844
Receives reduced-price lunch	0.032	0.061	0.058
Has repeated this grade	0.069	0.033	0.021
Reading Scale score			
Before	3.27	7.65	10.29
After	10.48	14.30	17.24
Woodcock Reading Comprehension			
Before	0.713	1.564	2.467
After	1.494	2.317	3.123
Number	405	538	430

[a]Tutored only when a regularly scheduled student was absent.

Tutored students are seriously at risk of school failure: 60 percent of tutored first graders were LEP, as were 58 percent of second graders and 54 percent of third graders. Across all three grades, approximately 90 percent of tutored students received a free or reduced lunch (the great majority received a free lunch).

The two reading measures available for all tutored students are the Reading Achievement Scale score and the Woodcock Reading Comprehension score (in grade equivalents). The program Reading Achievement Scale score is detailed in table 3.1. The lowest level, one, indicates that a student knows fewer than 25 percent of his or her letters or sounds; the highest level, twenty-five, indicates that a student can read books proficiently at approximately the fifth-grade level. (This scale differs from the program curriculum in that it is based on the curriculum in place during 1994 to 1995, when there were seven groups of word families instead of the current eighteen.)

Table 3.2 shows that tutored first graders began with an average Reading Achievement Scale score of 3.3 and ended with an average score of 10.5. This means that at the beginning of tutoring, the average first grader knew fewer than 75 percent of his or her letters and sounds. By the end of tutoring, the average first grader had learned the letters and sounds and five word family groupings and was working on word family group six (magical [e]). Tutored second graders began at level 7.7, word family group three. These students ended, on average, at level 14.3, reading level-one books, G through J. Finally, tutored third graders began at level 10.3 (word family group six) and ended at level 17.2, reading level-four books. These are substantial average gains, particularly because they have been achieved by the very lowest-performing students. However, they fall short of bringing the average student all the way up to reading at grade level.

Another view of these students' average reading abilities before and after tutoring is provided by their Woodcock Reading Comprehension scores, measured in grade equivalents. First graders begin at 0.7 grade equivalents, ending at 1.5 grade equivalents. (By comparison, the average U.S. first grader begins at 1.0 and ends at 1.9.) Tutored second graders begin at 1.6 grade equivalents and end at 2.3 grade equivalents. Tutored third graders begin at 2.5 grade equivalents and end at 3.1 grade equivalents. The overall finding is similar to that indicated by the Reading Scale scores—tutored students make substantial progress in one year but do not, on average, move all the way up to grade level. Of course, the issue is the incremental gains that can be attributed to the one-on-one tutoring the students receive. That is, other things being equal, what extra gains are due to each additional tutoring session received by the typical student?

This question is answered using the Reading Achievement Scale score by the regression analyses reported in table 3.3. Moving across the second row of this table, we see that, across each of grades one, two, and three, the effect of more tutoring sessions is positive and statistically significant. Among first graders, one hundred tutoring sessions (the high end of what students typically receive) raises reading by 8.4 levels. For second graders, the gain is 5.1 levels, and for third graders, it is 7.4 levels. These substantial gains show that tutoring exerts a substantial, positive effect on students' reading levels. Of course, the average student received only sixty sessions. Our estimates suggest that after this many sessions, first graders gain 5.0 levels, second graders gain 3.1 levels, and third graders gain 4.4 levels. One goal for the future is to manage our relationships with the schools so that more students can receive closer to one hundred sessions during the school year. A second goal is to provide tutoring for students over the sum-

Table 3.3 Regression Analysis of Reading Achievement Scale, by Grade

Indicator	First Grade	Second Grade	Third Grade
Intercept	5.418	−15.765	−12.765
Number of tutoring sessions	0.084***	0.051***	0.074***
	(6.26)	(5.19)	(6.31)
Average attentiveness	2.426***	2.372***	1.808***
	(5.11)	(5.99)	(3.43)
Reading achievement before	0.980***	0.573***	0.526***
	(13.52)	(21.34)	(17.57)
Alternate[a]	−0.511	−0.932	−0.636
	(0.72)	(1.47)	(1.20)
Male	−0.284	−0.113	0.065
	(1.02)	(0.56)	(0.26)
African American	−0.279	0.615	−0.204
	(0.45)	(1.32)	(0.33)
Hispanic	0.400	−0.053	−0.950*
	(0.80)	(0.14)	(1.71)
Has repeated this grade	−0.768	1.512**	−1.084
	(1.13)	(2.55)	(1.25)
Limited English proficiency	−0.196	−0.827***	−0.291
	(0.53)	(2.90)	(0.81)
Receives free lunch	−0.447	0.749*	−0.466
	(0.93)	(1.95)	(1.08)
Receives reduced-price lunch	1.322	0.826	−0.707
	(1.51)	(1.55)	(1.10)
R^2	0.519	0.607	0.618
Mean of dependent variable	10.494	14.301	17.244
Number	405	538	430

Notes: All regressions include dummy variables for each of the different schools and a variable for the child's age. The absolute value of the t-statistic is in parentheses.
[a]Tutored only when a regularly scheduled student was absent.
*10 percent significance.
**5 percent significance.
***1 percent significance.

mer, so that, for example, with the school year and summer combined, a student might receive as many as one hundred and fifty sessions.

Other predictor variables also show interesting effects. In particular, the students' attentiveness during tutoring and their reading achievement level before tutoring began are also strong positive predictors of the final reading achievement level.

Table 3.4 repeats these calculations using the Woodcock-Johnson reading comprehension test score. We administered this instrument

Table 3.4 Regression Analysis of Woodcock Reading Comprehension Score, by Grade

Indicator	First Grade	Second Grade	Third Grade
Intercept	3.987	−3.063	−4.236
Number of tutoring sessions	0.0073**	0.0078***	0.0067*
	(2.40)	(5.19)	(1.68)
Average attentiveness	0.255**	0.642***	0.605***
	(2.37)	(5.38)	(3.38)
Woodcock Comprehension, before	0.317***	0.643***	0.674***
	(5.32)	(15.62)	(15.05)
Alternate[a]	0.062	0.282	−0.205
	(0.38)	(1.49)	(1.14)
Male	0.008	0.039	−0.104
	(0.12)	(0.64)	(1.22)
African American	−0.221	0.094	−0.126
	(1.55)	(0.68)	(0.59)
Hispanic	−0.131	−0.067	0.077
	(1.16)	(0.59)	(0.41)
Has repeated this grade	−0.183	−0.107	−0.250
	(1.19)	(0.60)	(0.85)
Limited English proficiency	−0.219***	−0.258***	−0.330***
	(2.66)	(3.08)	(2.78)
Receives free lunch	0.108	−0.102	−0.107
	(0.99)	(0.88)	(0.73)
Receives reduced-price lunch	0.784***	−0.113	−0.328
	(3.94)	(0.71)	(1.52)
R^2	0.194	0.464	0.469
Mean of dependent variable	1.494	2.317	3.123
Number	405	538	430

Notes: All regressions include dummy variables for each of the different schools and a variable for the child's age. The absolute value of the t-statistic is in parentheses.
[a]Tutored only when a regularly scheduled student was absent.
*10 percent significance.
**5 percent significance.
***1 percent significance.

to all students before and after tutoring, so no cases are excluded. The Woodcock, which is administered one-on-one, is the research instrument most commonly used in published evaluations of compensatory reading programs (see, for example, Madden and others 1993; Pinnell and others 1994).

Looking across the second row of table 3.4 we see that the effect of more tutoring sessions is always positive and statistically significant. The estimated effects for one hundred tutoring sessions are 7.3

months of gain for first grade, 7.8 months for second grade, and 6.7 months for third grade. For sixty sessions, estimated effects are 4.4 months of gain for first grade, 4.7 months for second grade, and 4.0 months for third grade. These are large effects and, as we shall see, are quite competitive with those reported in published studies of Reading Recovery and Success for All. These results constitute the strongest evidence that Reading One-to-One is a successful intervention for tutored students.

Once again, other variables also show interesting effects. Both student attentiveness and the student's Woodcock score before tutoring began are positively related to Woodcock reading comprehension at the end of tutoring. There is also a tendency for LEP students to score lower in reading comprehension.

Table 3.5 repeats these calculations using ITBS scores (scaled in grade equivalents) administered by the district. The chief problem is that a large number of students must be deleted from the calculation because they were not administered the ITBS both before and after tutoring. Among first graders, so many are missing the "before" score (measured by a test administered when they would have been in kindergarten) that only eleven students have both scores. This is too few for the calculation, so the first column of this table is empty.

Columns two and three report the results for second and third graders for whom the ITBS reading comprehension test score was available. Among second graders, these represent 214 of the 538 tutored students studied in tables 3.3 and 3.4. Among third graders, they represent 218 of the 430 third graders studied. The second row of table 3.4 shows that even with this restricted sample, the program effects are similar to those estimated in tables 3.3 and 3.4. Sixty tutoring sessions increased the reading comprehension of second graders by 4.6 months and that of third graders by 4.8 months. As before, positive effects are also found for student attentiveness and student reading comprehension prior to the beginning of tutoring.

In sum, all three reading comprehension measures show positive effects of Reading One-to-One tutoring, with magnitudes of effect on the order of four to five months of gain for sixty tutoring sessions. These effects are on an order of magnitude similar to those reported for the more expensive programs—Reading Recovery and Success for All. Two other observations are similar to findings reported by Success for All. First, Slavin and others (1995) report that their largest effects occurred for LEP students. Since a majority of Reading One-to-One

Table 3.5 Regression Analysis of ITBS Reading Comprehension Score, by Grade

Indicator	First Grade	Second Grade	Third Grade
Intercept		−5.031	−0.017
Number of tutoring sessions		0.0077*	0.0080
		(1.78)	(1.42)
Average attentiveness		0.563***	0.333
		(3.83)	(1.42)
ITBS Comprehension, before		0.245	0.569***
		(1.61)	(4.26)
Alternate[a]		0.450*	0.075
		(1.79)	(0.35)
Male		0.098	−0.028
		(1.10)	(0.25)
African American		−0.111	−0.385
		(0.75)	(1.62)
Hispanic		−0.114	0.087
		(0.88)	(0.37)
Has repeated this grade		0.369	0.320
		(1.46)	(1.00)
Limited English proficiency		−0.403***	0.172
		(3.01)	(0.93)
Receives free lunch		0.295**	−0.178
		(2.08)	(1.04)
Receives reduced-price lunch		0.095	0.155
		(0.46)	(0.63)
R^2, adjusted		0.184	0.148
Mean of dependent variable		2.178	2.639
Number	11	214	218

Notes: All regressions include dummy variables for each of the different schools and a variable for the child's age. The absolute value of the *t*-statistic is in parentheses.
[a]Tutored only when a regularly scheduled student was absent.
*10 percent signficance.
**5 percent significance.
***1 percent significance.

tutored students are LEP, this may at least partially account for the relatively large effects reported here. Second, Slavin and others (1995) find that as a school gains experience operating the program, the annual effects increase. They attribute this to a positive learning curve. We have observed a similar phenomenon, with the effects reported above for 1994 to 1995 being significantly larger than those observed for the previous year (Farkas and others 1994). We attribute these gains to management activities accompanying program maturation. In particular, we instituted much stricter controls on the cognitive skills of tutors during 1994 to 1995. To be hired, they had to pass a general English skills test and then an examination on the training they received. Further, their tutoring was monitored closely, and they were shown how to improve their instructional skills. Those who still did not meet the required standard were let go. Further, student assessment procedures were improved: "cloze" tests were introduced to ensure that students were moved up to the next reading level only when they had fully mastered the comprehension skills required by the current level.

The qualitative evidence of program success has also been substantial. Teachers and principals have praised the positive outcomes they observed for tutored children. Some of these comments are quoted in Farkas (1996, chap. 11). Similar responses are associated with almost all program implementations (for an example from our large-scale, no-advance-warning startup in Houston, see Farkas 1997). In addition, a number of nationally recognized reading experts have made site visits in which they sat with tutors and observed their work. In all cases, they commented very favorably on the quality of the work they saw.

BENEFIT-COST COMPARISONS WITH OTHER PROGRAMS

Of course, the most important evidence regarding the effectiveness of hourly paid tutors is the magnitude of the gains achieved by the students they tutor. *During 1994 to 1995, these gains were approximately the same order of magnitude as those reported by Reading Recovery and Success for All.* This is shown in table 3.6, where we see that all three programs report gains of approximately 0.3 to 0.7 grade equivalent (three to seven months of instruction) above what students would have attained without tutoring.[6] This is particularly remarkable for Reading One-to-One, which achieved these gains while serving more than four times as many students as the other programs for each dollar spent. The research community is coming to realize that successful assistance for at-risk students needs to be continuous throughout the elementary years. This makes effective, low-unit-cost programs particularly attractive.

The per-unit costs of Reading One-to-One continue to be rock-bottom. For some years now in Dallas, we have paid tutors approximately seven dollars per hour, which, with fringe benefits, comes to about eight dollars per hour. We have covered all our management and

Table 3.6 School-Year Gains Achievable via Quality
One-to-One Tutoring (in Grade Equivalents)

Grade, Program, and Source	Average Gain	Average Gain from	
		60 Sessions	100 Sessions
First grade			
Success For All			
Madden and others (1993)	0.2		
Slavin and others (1994)	0.3		
Reading recovery			
Pinnell and others (1994)	0.3[a]		
Reading One-to-One (table 3.4)		0.4	0.7
Second grade			
Success For All			
Madden and others (1993)	0.5		
Slavin and others (1994)	0.3		
Reading One-to-One (table 3.4)		0.5	0.8
Third grade			
Success For All			
Madden and others (1993)	0.5		
Slavin and others (1994)	0.7		
Reading One-to-One (table 3.4)		0.4	0.7

Notes: The reported standardized effect estimates were translated into grade equivalents by relying on the correspondence reported in Slavin and others, 1994.
[a]Estimated from the Woodcock-Johnson Reading Inventory.

program development costs by billing local school districts $12.50 per hour for the complete tutoring service. This charge has included all materials, an on-site manager, and central administrative management by the Reading One-to-One program. We have hired, trained, and paid for all personnel. At this rate, the cost for a student receiving three tutoring sessions per week for twenty-three weeks (the largest number of usable instructional weeks we have found to be feasible within local school districts) is $578 for the school year.[7] Of course, where the local wage scale is lower than in Dallas (as is the case, for example, in Brownsville), an even lower cost can be achieved. Further, in 1997 we became an Americorps site, utilizing Americorps members and college work-study students as tutors. With these tutors, the annual cost of tutoring can be reduced by more than half, to less than $250 per student.

By contrast, programs that use certified teachers as tutors are typically many times more expensive. For example, in Texas, Reading Recovery teachers typically earn approximately forty thousand dollars a year, or, with fringes and benefits at 40 percent, approximately fifty-six thousand dollars per year. Overhead, training, management, and materials are typically substantial for these programs, because their top district administrators are usually quite well paid. Even assuming only 10 percent additional for these costs, the result is more than sixty thousand dollars a year per teacher. If this teacher tutors six students during the school year, the per student cost is ten thousand dollars. Were she to tutor twenty students during the year (an unlikely extreme), the cost per student would still be three thousand dollars. Clearly, the estimate that Reading One-to-One is less than one-quarter of the cost of such programs is quite conservative. And also clearly, the per student cost of these other programs is so high that this service delivery mechanism will never serve the very large number of at-risk students who so desperately need assistance.

SUMMARY AND DISCUSSION

The social technology we have developed lies halfway between the high-end programs that use teachers as tutors and the low-end programs that use volunteers. We have demonstrated that with an appropriate curriculum, training, and management, one can achieve most of the gains of the high-end programs at a cost that is much closer to that of the low-end programs. Perhaps most important, one-to-one is the most powerful form of instruction because it is the only one that provides all three of the following: (a) instruction exactly on the student's current level of performance (as opposed to aiming for a "class average"), (b) complete privacy to try and thus risk failure combined with no other student present to give the answer, and (c) immediate, appropriate feedback from a caring adult with whom the student has bonded.

As contrasted with many other educational innovations, Reading One-to-One begins immediately to affect large numbers of children and puts the money directly into the delivery of services to children. It immediately begins to repair the reading-related skills, habits, and styles of at-risk students. We have demonstrated that even though tutors are paraprofessionals rather than certified teachers, this form of intervention can be effective if (a) the tutors are first tested for their own cognitive skills, then trained in a serious and detailed curriculum, and then tested on this training, (b) the tutors receive feedback to improve their skills, (c) each tutor sees each student several times a week, and (d) regular measures of student progress are maintained.

Now is an exciting time, as the Clinton White House seeks to expand the use of paraprofessional tutors nationwide. Our experience with Reading One-to-One suggests that if these tutors are provided appropriate curriculum, training, and management they will make a great difference in the school lives of at-risk students.

The author thanks Paul Jargowsky, John Kain, and Royce Hanson for comments and suggestions. Keven Vicknair, Mary Warren, and other staff of the Center for Education and Social Policy at the University of Texas at Dallas made major contributions to the work reported here.

NOTES

1. When originally passed by Congress in 1965, this program was typically referred to as Title I (of the Elementary and Secondary Education Act). However, when reauthorized in more recent times, its name was changed to the Chapter I Program. When it was reauthorized again by Congress in 1994, the name was changed back to Title I. It is referred to as Title I throughout this chapter.

2. I am grateful to Jane Grigsby of Richardson Independent School District Reading Recovery for providing written materials as well as videotape of "Behind the Glass" sessions, for conducting training sessions for tutors, and for permitting me to attend the regular teacher training class meetings with "Behind the Glass" sessions. I am also grateful to Bob Slavin and Barbara Wasik of Johns Hopkins University for providing a copy of the (draft) tutor training manual that Wasik had written. Without the assistance of these individuals, this project would have been much more difficult to get under way.

3. Each child is scheduled for a forty-minute time period. "Pickup" and "return" travel times typically allow thirty to thirty-five minutes for instruction.

4. Much additional discussion would be necessary to explain and justify the program details summarized here. Many pedagogical issues would have to be addressed. Readers interested in this subject may contact the author directly (farkas@utdallas.edu).

5. A running record is a technique for providing a visual representation of the student's reading behavior. As the student reads, the tutor makes check marks on a blank piece of paper for each word read correctly. If a word is not read correctly, the tutor writes what the child said and then comes back later and writes next to this what the child should have read. The percentage of words read correctly can then be calculated, and—as we use the technique—the words missed show what decoding instruction the student still requires. This instruction is provided immediately.

6. Robert Slavin (personal communication) points out that these Reading One-to-One results are based on only one study, using a research design and statistical methodology that is somewhat unusual within this sub-field of program evaluation. By contrast, the Success for All results have been replicated several times, using a matched comparison-group methodology that is common within this subfield. More studies of the impacts of Reading One-to-One are desirable, and I hope to undertake these in the future. I also believe that without the ability to assign students randomly to treatment versus control groups, our knowledge of the true magnitude of programs' impacts is likely to be somewhat uncertain. Finally, in the absence of random assignment, research designs and statistical methodologies of the sort employed here may well be superior to the matched comparison-group design employed by Slavin. For a discussion of random assignment, econometric modeling techniques such as we have used and issues related to these, see Heckman and Smith (1995).

7. This is calculated as follows: 69 sessions $\times$ 0.67 hours per session $\times$ \$12.50 per hour = \$578.

REFERENCES

Adams, Marilyn Jager. 1990. *Beginning to Read*. Cambridge, Mass.: MIT Press.

Arroyo, Carmen G., and Edward Zigler. 1993. "America's Title I/Chapter I Programs: Why the Promise Has Not Been Met." In *From Head Start and Beyond: A National Plan for Extended Childhood Intervention*, edited by Edward Zigler and Sally J. Styfco. New Haven, Conn.: Yale University Press.

Clay, Marie M. 1979. *The Early Detection of Reading Difficulties*. Auckland, New Zealand: Heinemann.

Farkas, George. 1993. "Structured Tutoring for At-Risk Children in the Early Years." *Applied Behavioral Science Review* 1(1): 69–92.

———. 1994. "Reforming Compensatory Education with Reading One-to-One." Paper presented to the Annual Research Conference of the Association for Public Policy Analysis and Management. Chicago, Ill.(October 1994).

———. 1996. *Human Capital or Cultural Capital? Ethnicity and Poverty Groups in an Urban School District*. New York: Aldine de Gruyter.

———. 1997. *Reading One-to-One Implementation in Houston, Spring 1997*. Dallas: Center for Education and Social Policy, University of Texas at Dallas (June 13, 1997).

Farkas, George, Robert Grobe, Daniel Sheehan, and Yuan Shuan. 1990a. "Coursework Mastery and School Success: Gender, Ethnicity, and Poverty Groups within an Urban School District." *American Educational Research Journal* 27(4): 807–27.

————. 1990b. "Cultural Resources and School Success: Gender, Ethnicity, and Poverty Groups within an Urban School District." *American Sociological Review* 55(1): 127–42.

Heckman, James J., and Jeffrey A. Smith. 1995. "Assessing the Case for Social Experiments." *Journal of Economic Perspectives* 9(2): 85–110.

Honig, Bill. 1996. *Teaching Our Children to Read*. Thousand Oaks, Calif.: Corwin Press.

Madden, Nancy A., Robert E. Slavin, Nancy L. Karweit, Lawrence J. Dolan, and Barbara A. Wasik. 1993. "Success for All: Longitudinal Effects of a Restructuring Program for Inner-City Elementary Schools." *American Educational Research Journal* 30(1): 123–48.

Natriello, Gary, E. L. McDill, and A. M. Pallas. 1990. *Schooling Disadvantaged Children*. New York: Teachers College Press.

Pinnell, Gay Su, C. A. Lyons, D. E. DeFord, A. S. Bryk, and Michael Seltzer. 1994. "Comparing Instructional Models for the Literacy Education of High-Risk First Graders." *Reading Research Quarterly* 29(1): 8–39.

————. 1995. "Response to Rasinski." *Reading Research Quarterly* 30(2): 272–75.

Rasinski, Timothy. 1995. "Commentary: On the Effects of Reading Recovery." *Reading Research Quarterly* 30(2): 264–71.

Slavin, Robert. 1989. *Effective Programs for Students at Risk*. Needham Heights, Mass.: Allyn and Bacon.

Slavin, Robert, Nancy Madden, Lawrence Dolan, and Barbara Wasik. 1994. "Success for All: Longitudinal Effects of Systemic School-by-School Reform in Seven Districts." Paper presented at the annual meeting of the American Educational Research Association. New Orleans, La. (April 1994).

Slavin, Robert, Nancy Madden, Lawrence Dolan, Barbara Wasik, Steven Ross, Lana Smith, and Marcella Dianda. 1995. "Success for All: A Summary of Research." Paper presented to the American Educational Research Association, annual conference. San Francisco (April 1995).

Slavin, Robert, Nancy Madden, Nancy Karweit, Lawrence Dolan, and Barbara Wasik. 1990. "Success for All: First-Year Outcomes of a Comprehensive Plan for Reforming Urban Education." *American Educational Research Journal* 27(2): 255–78.

Wasik, Barbara A., and Robert E. Slavin. 1993. "Preventing Early Reading Failure with One-to-One Tutoring: A Review of Five Programs." *Reading Research Quarterly* 28(2): 178–200.

CHAPTER 4

The Chicago Child-Parent Center and Expansion Program: A Study of Extended Early Childhood Intervention

Arthur J. Reynolds

Given the widespread concerns about academic underachievement, school failure, and other problematic behavior in our nation's schools, policymakers and the public at-large are increasingly turning to early childhood intervention as a preventative approach to these and other social problems. Support for early childhood programs has been expressed in a number of ways. The first national education goal is that all children will start school ready to learn (National Education Goals Panel 1994). The Head Start preschool program for economically disadvantaged children has nearly universal support and funding priority (Rovner 1990; Zigler and Muenchow 1992; National Head Start Organization 1990). Preschool education programs are expanding at the state and local levels in the belief that children will develop a good foundation for school success. Because the proportion of young children who are poor is 25 percent and growing, the number of children likely to need early intervention also is growing (Natriello, McDill, and Pallas 1990).

In this chapter, the effects of the Child-Parent Center (CPC) and Expansion Program on scholastic development up to age fourteen are reported for a large sample of minority (95 percent African American, 5 percent Hispanic) children from low-income families. The CPC program is a federally and state funded early childhood educational intervention for children in the Chicago public schools who are at risk for academic underachievement and school failure due to poverty and associated factors. Created in 1967, the CPCs provide comprehensive educational and family support services for children ages three to nine for up to six years of continuous intervention. It is the second oldest (after Head Start) federally funded early childhood intervention for economically disadvantaged children and is the oldest continuously funded extended intervention program in the United States. Study children are participants in the Chicago Longitudinal Study, an ongoing investigation of the 1989 graduating cohort of the CPCs and a comparison group of non-CPC participants who participated in a less-extensive intervention.[1] The CPC program is specific to Chicago and is unrelated to the Parent-Child Development Centers, a federally funded family support program for children under the age of three.

This chapter discusses the research and policy context of early childhood intervention, describes the development of the CPCs and the Chicago Longitudinal Study, and reports short- and long-term effects of the program implemented between 1983 and 1989. Special attention is given to age-fourteen (eighth-grade) findings for reading and mathematics achievement, incidence of grade retention and special education placement, and a measure of consumer life skills competency.

RESEARCH AND POLICY CONTEXT

Studies of model and large-scale programs over the past two decades have demonstrated that good-quality early childhood interventions for economically disadvantaged children improve their cognitive and affective readiness for school and can promote longer-term school success such as greater school achievement, lower incidence of grade retention and special education placement, and less problematic behavior (Barnett 1992; Berrueta-Clement and others 1984; Consortium for Longitudinal Studies 1983; McKey and others 1985; Campbell and Ramey 1994). Effective programs vary considerably in their timing, duration, and targets of intervention. Center-based educational support programs that focus on cognitive enrichment, family support programs that focus on home-based parenting education, and combination programs all have been shown to promote children's development during the sensitive period before they enter school (Seitz 1990; Yoshikawa 1994), although program intensity appears to be a key ingredient of success (Ramey and Ramey 1992).

While these findings have enriched the base of educational and policy research in human development and education, three important substantive issues have not been adequately addressed. First, the amount and quality of existing evidence concerning the long-term effects of large-scale government-funded programs are inadequate to in-form public policy. As repeated often but forgotten frequently, most of the evidence on long-term effects into high school comes from small-scale model programs that differ in significant ways from large-scale established programs like Head Start (Crum 1993; Haskins 1989; White 1985; Woodhead 1988; Zigler and Styfco 1993). Model programs are usually more expensive to operate than large-scale programs, have larger and better trained staff, and are rarely implemented in inner-city communities. Studies of large-scale programs typically rely on retrospective quasi-experimental designs and are more likely to suffer from problems regarding noncomparability of groups, attrition, and limited data after the program (Barnett 1992; Haskins 1989). Such problems make findings difficult to interpret. On the positive side, however, large-scale programs have longer implementation histories than model programs and include larger samples that increase the statistical power and generalizability of findings. Although studies of model programs indicate how effective early interventions *can be*, policymakers and the public are most interested in knowing how effective current large-scale programs *are*. In a time of intensive fiscal accountability at all levels of government, research on the effects of large-scale programs is needed now more than ever.

A second substantive issue is that research has not determined the optimal timing and duration of intervention exposure. Although it is increasingly believed that a one- or two-year preschool program cannot immunize children from school failure, the optimal length of intervention is not clear (Zigler and Styfco 1993). Do two or three years of intervention beginning at age three yield the same effect as two or three years beginning at age five? Do programs that extend into the primary grades yield more long-lasting effects than programs that stop in kindergarten? Unfortunately, most studies confound the effects of timing and duration of intervention (Seitz and others 1983; Fuerst and Fuerst 1993; Madden and others 1993). One exception is the Abecedarian project (Campbell and Ramey 1994, 1995), which traced ninety-three children who participated to varying degrees in a model intervention in Chapel Hill, North Carolina, from birth to age eight. Investigators found that participation in the five-year preschool program was positively associated with higher cognitive ability and school achievement as well as lower grade retention and special education placement up to age fifteen. The three-year school-age program was found to have limited independent effects and was associated only with reading achievement at age fifteen. Certainly, more evidence is needed, especially given recent proposals to extend programs into the primary grades (Zigler and Muenchow 1993).

A final question that has not been addressed adequately by previous research concerns the factors and processes that mediate (account for) long-term effects of early childhood intervention. Once a direct relationship has been established between program participation and the outcome variable of interest, the causal mechanisms or pathways that produce this main effect must be identified (Wachs and Gruen 1982; Woodhead 1988). Two hypotheses have been postulated to explain longer-term effects of early childhood intervention. In the cognitive advantage hypothesis, the immediate positive effect of program participation on cognitive development at school entry initiates a positive cycle of scholastic development and commitment that culminates in improved developmental outcomes in adolescence and beyond (see Berrueta-Clement and others 1984; Schweinhart, Barnes, and Weikart 1993). In the family support hypothesis, the longer-term effects of intervention occur to the extent that family functioning has been improved. Because early intervention programs often involve parents, it is believed that family processes must be affected to produce longer-term effects (Seitz 1990). This focus is consistent with a confirmatory approach to program evaluation (Reynolds 1997a).

Knowledge about the pathways of effects of early childhood intervention has significant implications for research and practice. First, it adds to basic theoretical knowledge of how early interventions exert their effects over time in conjunction with other influences. Second, the pathways that are identified can be used to help design and modify intervention programs for children and families. These hypotheses, for example, direct attention to different intervention approaches, one being child-centered and another parent-focused. Finally, investigation of pathways of effectiveness provide confirmatory evidence of program impact: Are the identified processes consistent with the theory of the program?

PROGRAM BACKGROUND

The CPC program is a center-based intervention that provides comprehensive educational and family support services to economically disadvantaged children and their parents. The CPCs were established in 1967 through Title I of the landmark Elementary and Secondary Education Act (ESEA) of 1965. Starting with four centers on the west side of the city, the program was designed to serve families in high-poverty neighborhoods that were *not* being served by Head Start or other early childhood programs. Currently, the CPCs are funded through Title I of the ESEA. Since 1978, the primary-grade portion of the program (expansion program) has been funded by Title I through the State of Illinois. The Chicago public schools currently operate twenty-four CPCs; twenty have services from preschool to third grade, and four have services only in preschool and first and second grades. The rationale of the program is that healthy scholastic and social development is more likely to occur in a stable-school learning environment in which parents are active participants in their children's education.

To be eligible, children must reside in school neighborhoods that receive Title I funds. Title I funds are given to schools serving high percentages of low-income families. As with many early childhood programs, children must demonstrate educational need, and parents must agree to participate in the program. To enroll children most-in-need, and reduce self-selection, the centers conduct outreach activities such as distributing program descriptions in the community, visiting families door-to-door, and advertising locally. The CPCs are located in the most economically disadvantaged neighborhoods in Chicago. Centers are located in five of the six poorest neighborhoods in the city: Grand Boulevard, Near West Side, Oakland, Riverdale, and Washington Park (according to the 1990 census). On average, 66 percent of the children in the school communities served are low-income. The average neighborhood poverty rate for the Chicago public schools is 42 percent (Chicago Public Schools 1986b).

CHICAGO LONGITUDINAL STUDY

The Chicago Longitudinal Study includes all children ($n = 1,150$) who enrolled in the twenty CPCs with preschool and kindergarten programs beginning in fall of 1983 and graduated from kindergarten in spring of 1986. Children enrolled at ages three or four and could participate up to age nine in the spring of 1989 (end of third grade). Among this group were 176 children who received services from the CPCs in kindergarten (but not preschool) and had the opportunity to participate in the primary-grade component. Because children entered and exited the program at different ages, there was significant natural variation in the duration of participation (from one to six years). Also six of the twenty centers offered the intervention through third grade (the original CPCs), while the other centers offered it through second grade (later CPCs). Consequently, the relationship between duration of participation and adjustment can be investigated. Another study of the CPC program follows the progress of the 1967 cohort of graduates from the original CPCs (Fuerst and Fuerst 1993). Table 4.1 shows the attributes of the different program groups. See appendix 4B for a brief history of the Chicago Longitudinal Study.

The non-CPC comparison group included 389 children who graduated in 1986 from government-funded all-day kindergarten programs in six randomly selected schools that serve large proportions of low-income families. The schools participated in the Chicago Effective Schools Project, a school system program to meet the needs of high-risk children. These schools matched the poverty characteristics of the CPCs and, like CPC participants, children were eligible for and participated in government-funded programs. They had no systematic intervention experiences from preschool to third grade, although some enrolled in Head Start as well as the CPC expansion program.

The sample characteristics of the original CPC program and comparison groups are displayed in table 4.2. The CPC program group includes children with any participation in the program from preschool to grade three. At the beginning of the study, the groups were similar on several characteristics including school poverty, sex, race (both included almost all black children), and socioeconomic status (SES) as proxied by eligibility for free lunch. Program participants had parents with a higher rate of high school graduation and fewer of brothers and sisters than nonparticipants. These differences were taken into account in estimating program effects. Of the original sample of 1,539 children, 1,164 (76.5 percent) were active in the Chicago public schools in eighth grade (77 percent of the program group and 72 percent of the comparison group). No selective attrition was found between the program and comparison groups (see Reynolds 1994, 1995). In the eighth-grade study sample, 762 had CPC preschool and kindergarten participation (402 did not) and 544 had CPC extended program participation (620 did not). Sample sizes for number of years of participation were as follows: zero years = 275, one year = 21, two years = 140, three years = 223, four years = 168, five years = 265, and six years = 72.

Children in the comparison group of this quasi-experimental study did not enroll in the CPCs primarily because they did not live in a neighborhood of the center. Thus geographic location rather than family motivation determined nonparticipation. Some

Table 4.1 Kindergarten Cohort in the Chicago Longitudinal Study, 1985 to 1986

Program Group	Sample Size	Number of Sites	Program Start Date	Years of Preschool Exposure	Kindergarten	School Age	Range of Years
1. Original Child-Parent Centers		6	1967–1969	1 or 2	Full day	3	3–6
1986	325						
1994	238						
2. Later Child-Parent Centers		14	1970–1978	1 or 2	Full day or half day	2	3–5
1986	649						
1994	524						
3. No preschool Child-Parent Center (comparison 1)		6	—	0	Full day	3	1–4
1986	176						
1994	116						
4. No Child-Parent Centers (comparison 2)		7	—	0	Full day	0	0
1986	389						
1994	286						
Total		25	—	—	—	—	
1986	1,539						
1994	1,164						

— Not available.

Notes: School-age (expansion) component included first, second, and third grades. The total number of different sites was twenty-five because groups one and three enrolled in the same sites, and groups two and four overlapped by two sites.

Table 4.2 Original Sample Characteristics of CPC Program and Comparison Groups

Characteristic	Program Group ($n = 1,150$)	Comparison Group ($n = 389$)	F	p
Girls (percent)	50.7	50.6	0.00	0.974
Black (percent)	95.6	94.8	0.36	0.548
Age in kindergarten	63.3	63.8	3.08	0.079
	(3.7)	(4.0)		
High school graduate (percent)	59.7	50.9	5.36	0.021
With free lunch (percent)	84.2	82.1	0.58	0.447
School poverty (percent of children who are poor)	66.5 (8.7)	67.5 (11.6)	3.29	0.070
Number of children	2.4	2.7	4.13	0.043
	(1.6)	(1.8)		
Years of program participation	3.68 (1.32)	—		

Notes: Numbers vary from 947 (high school graduates) for family background to 1,539 (years of program participation) for program participation and school poverty. Sample sizes are listed in parentheses.

comparison-group children, for example, participated in Head Start. Reynolds and Temple (1995) found that preschool participation can be predicted with 86 percent accuracy from child, family, and school-level information.

Why did children who enrolled in the CPCs leave before the end of the program? Some parents preferred to send their children to regular school programs. They enrolled their children in preschool and kindergarten with the intention of moving afterwards. Other parents moved out of the school neighborhood for professional (job change) or personal reasons.

PROGRAM COMPONENTS

Like the Head Start program, the CPCs provide comprehensive services, require parent participation, and implement child-centered approaches to social and cognitive development for economically disadvantaged children. Child-Parent Centers have three distinguishing features. As part of the school system, they are administrative centers housed in separate buildings or in wings of their parent elementary school. They also staff a parent room. Head Start programs typically contract with social service or community agencies, not with school systems. They do not have staffed parent rooms in addition to classrooms, although they do provide extensive health screening services on-site. Second, eligibility for the CPCs is based primarily on neighborhood poverty; for Head Start it is based primarily on family-level poverty. Since both programs give preference to children most-in-need, this distinction is more illusory than real in practice. Both programs expect or require parent involvement. A third and most important difference is that the CPCs provide up to six years of intervention services from ages three to nine, while Head Start is primarily a preschool program. Thus the CPC program combines Head Start and follow-through programs to provide the opportunity of a school-stable environment during preschool and the early primary-grade years.

The organizational components of the CPCs are shown in figure 4.1. Each center has a head teacher who coordinates the curriculum and parent involvement components, outreach, and physical health services. The head teacher reports to the principal of the parent elementary school. The CPC program has been consistently implemented with success based on classroom observations, interviews, and school records (Chicago Public Schools 1986a, 1987; Reynolds 1994; Conrad and Eash 1983).

HEAD TEACHER

The head teacher is the program coordinator with overall responsibility for organizing and implementing program services. This primarily involves teaming up with the parent-resource teacher, the school-community representative, and the classroom teachers and aides. The full-time head teacher also organizes in-service training and workshops for classroom staff. Administrative support staff, including a clerk and secretary, help the head teacher administer the program.

CHILD DEVELOPMENT CURRICULUM COMPONENT

The CPCs offer a half-day preschool program (three hours), full-day kindergarten program at most sites (six hours), and full-day primary-grade services (six hours). Although no uniform curriculum is provided, the relatively structured classroom activities are designed to

Figure 4.1 Child-Parent Center Program

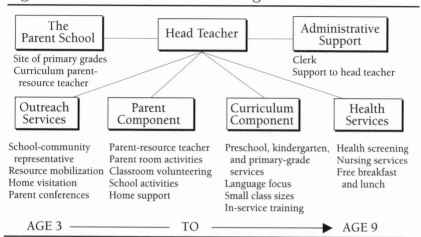

promote basic skills in language and reading as well as social and psychological development. To implement individualized learning activities, class sizes are small, and each classroom has a teacher aide. Inservice training is provided on a regular basis in conjunction with the Department of Early Childhood Programs. The curriculum approach is a mixture of teacher-directed activities and social interactions synonymous with the developmental-interactionist instructional approaches. The philosophy is that learning is best facilitated by a structured but diverse set of learning experiences (large groups, small groups, field trips). The curriculum materials include Bank Street readers, Peabody language development kits, a variety of formal language programs (for example, basal readers), and instructional kits and activities developed by the Department of Early Childhood Programs called the Early Assessment and Remediation Laboratory.

In preschool, class sizes are, on average, seventeen children per teacher. With a teacher aide for each class, the teacher-to-child ratio is one to eight. In kindergarten and the primary grades, class sizes average twenty-five children per teacher with a teacher aide, for a staff to child ratio of approximately one to twelve. Typical class sizes in the regular school program are thirty, with no teacher aides. Parent volunteers may further reduce these ratios, especially in preschool and kindergarten. The smaller class sizes allow for child-centered approaches to language and cognitive development as well as social relations. Children learn to read and write through a broad spectrum of experiences such as small group activities, shared reading, and journal writing. In this process, teachers provide frequent feedback and positive reinforcement as well as emphasize task accomplishment. Also teachers frequently read stories to the class to develop the idea that reading is enjoyable and to demonstrate literacy skills. Classes also go on field trips to, for example, the Museum of Science and Industry and the zoo. Being certified in early childhood education, classroom teachers provide developmentally appropriate activities. In preschool and kindergarten, the focus is on foundations of language development such as recognizing letters and numbers, oral communication, listening, and an appreciation for reading and drawing. In the primary grades, the focus is on the acquisition and reinforcement of basic skills in reading and mathematics.

PARENT INVOLVEMENT COMPONENT

The centers make substantial efforts to involve parents in the center and in the education of their children. At least one half-day per week of parent involvement in the center is required. The full-time parent-resource teacher organizes a parent room within the center to implement parent educational activities, initiate interactions among parents, and foster parent-child interactions.

As shown in table 4.3, a wide range of activities are encouraged in the program, including parent room activities, classroom volunteering, participation in school activities, and opportunities for further education and training. The diversity of activities is designed to accommodate parents' daily schedules and different needs. As the program's title indicates, parent involvement is a critical force in children's social development. Direct parent involvement in the program is expected to enhance parent-child interactions as well as attachment to school, thus promoting school readiness and social adjustment.

SCHOOL-COMMUNITY OUTREACH SERVICES

The full-time noninstructional school-community representative in each center provides outreach services to families in three related areas. First, they identify families in the neighborhood who are in most educational need. They make door-to-door visits of likely participants, distribute brochures and advertisements of enrollment, and communicate in formal and informal ways. Second, the school-community representative conducts a home or school visit with all enrolling fam-

Table 4.3 Types of Parent Involvement in the Child-Parent Centers

Parent Involvement Examples	Relative Focus
Volunteer in the classroom	Medium
Read to small groups	
Go on field trips	
Supervise play activities	
Play games with small groups	
Participate in parent room activities	High
Participate in parent reading groups	
Complete craft projects	
Attend in-services in child development, financial	
management, cooking, and home economics	
Participate in school activities	High
Attend meetings and programs	
Attend parent-teacher conferences	
Attend social events	
Enroll in educational courses	Low
Enroll in parent education courses	
Complete high school coursework	
Home support activities	High
Receive home visits	
Interact with child through reading and playing	
Go to library with child	

Note: Ratings are based on teacher interviews, classroom observations, and the program theory.

ilies. One visit on enrollment in the program is required. Additional visits occur on a most-in-need basis. Moreover, informal conferences are held between the parent and the school-community representative. Finally, the school-community representative mobilizes resources by referring families to community and social service agencies such as employment training, mental health services, and welfare services. Transportation services are provided to children as well as parents.

PHYSICAL HEALTH AND MEDICAL SERVICES

On entering the program, children undergo an on-site health screening from a registered nurse. Tests are given for vision and hearing. Parents are expected to provide records of their child's immunization history. Special medical and educational services such as speech therapy also are available. All children in the morning or all-day programs receive free breakfasts and lunches; otherwise they just receive free lunches.

DIFFERENCES BETWEEN PRESCHOOL / KINDERGARTEN AND PRIMARY-GRADE COMPONENTS

Although the continuity of program services from preschool to second or third grade distinguishes the Child-Parent Centers, there are two differences between the preschool and school-age components. First, the primary-grade (expansion) program is implemented in the parent elementary school rather than in the Child-Parent Center. At least half of each classroom is composed of children from the CPCs. Second, program coordination is streamlined. The head teacher and the parent-resource teacher are combined into one position (curriculum parent-resource teacher), although the parent involvement component does not change. Moreover, the school-community representative serves the whole school, not just children from the CPCs. As with the preschool and kindergarten program, extra instructional supplies and staff training are provided.

COSTS

Expenditures for the CPC program (in 1996 dollars) are estimated at $4,180 per year for each of the half-day preschool and kindergarten programs and at $1,500 per year for the primary-grade component (over and above the regular school program). These amounts do not include expenditures for providing the free breakfast and lunch program (funded by the U. S. Department of Agriculture) and for implementing full-day kindergarten programs in fourteen centers (funded by Title II of ESEA).

DATABASE IN THE CHICAGO LONGITUDINAL STUDY

Since 1986, the Chicago Longitudinal Study of the Child-Parent Centers has investigated the impact of participation in early childhood intervention on children and families as well as the contribution of individual, family, and school-related factors to school adjustment. Yearly data on children's progress have been collected from school system records, including standardized test scores. Beginning in kindergarten, teachers, parents, and children have been surveyed and interviewed about children's scholastic, social, and psychological development. These and other data are compiled in the project codebook (Reynolds and others 1996). This longitudinal study provides a rare opportunity to investigate the long-term effects of a large-scale program for different levels of participation as well as the possible sources of intervention effects.

Table 4.4 reports the variables that have been used to investigate the effects of the CPC program. For brevity, only findings for the child outcomes reading and math achievement, cumulative grade retention, special education placement, and life skills competence are reported here because they are the most connected theoretically to program enrollment. Reading and math achievement test scores are from

Table 4.4 Measures Used to Investigate Program Effects

Measure	Grade in Which Collected
Demographic factors	
Children's sex, race, age in months	Kindergarten
Parents' educational background, eligibility for free lunch, family structure, and size	Two to six
School socioeconomic status	Kindergarten
Program participation	
Participation in preschool and kindergarten, grades one to three	Prekindergarten to three
Duration of participation (zero to six years)	Prekindergarten to three
Child outcomes	
Reading comprehension and mathematics: Total scores on the Iowa Tests of Basic Skills (1988 norms, standard scores)	Kindergarten to eight
Life skills competence (raw scores on the 63-item Minimum Proficiency Skills Test); sample item: Mary wishes to buy a new car and needs a loan from the bank to buy the car. What is a loan?	Eight and nine
Grade retention (cumulative incidence)	Kindergarten to eight
Special education placement (cumulative incidence)	Kindergarten to eight
Parent participation in school (teacher and parent ratings)	One to six
Delinquency behavior (school records)	Seven and eight
Self-perceptions of competence (ratings on items such as "I am smart" and "school is important")	Three to six
Teacher ratings of school adjustment (ratings on classroom adjustment and social and emotional development)	Kindergarten to seven

Notes: Sample sizes vary by measure. They are smallest for parent education and lunch eligibility ($n = 947$) and highest for children's school records and kindergarten achievement ($n > 1,530$).

the Iowa Tests of Basic Skills (1988 norms; Hieronymus and Hoover 1990). Life skills competence is measured by the Chicago Minimum Proficiency Skills Test. The test is taken in eighth grade and includes sixty-three items assessing consumer life skills in the areas of computation, language arts, and problem-solving (see Reynolds and Bezruczko 1989). Special education placement and grade retention are indicators of school competence and were taken from school records. For reports on other outcomes, including family outcomes, see Reynolds, Mehana, and Temple (1995) and Reynolds (1994, 1995).

RESEARCH FINDINGS

Findings are reported here for four questions that have been a major focus of the study. Outcome data in eighth grade (age fourteen in spring 1994) are emphasized, including the newly reported measure of life skills competence. In the age-fourteen study sample of 1,164 students, 878 were CPC program participants and 286 were non-CPC participants.

IS ANY PARTICIPATION IN THE PROGRAM ASSOCIATED WITH SCHOOL PERFORMANCE?

To obtain conservative estimates of the impact of the CPC program, the performance of CPC participants was compared to that of comparison-group participants without regard to the extent of participation in the program. Results of the multiple regression analyses are presented in tables 4.5 and 4.6. The explanatory variables included the dichotomous program variable, the demographic factors in table 4.3, plus a composite indicator for missing demographic data.[2] In these and other analyses reported here, inclusion of the demographic variables generally reduced the size of the program effect 10–15 percent.

At the end of the program in third grade (one year after the program, for second-grade graduates), CPC graduates had significantly higher scores than comparison-group peers in reading and math achievement. The program group's 5.7 and 4.2 point advantage in reading and math achievement (about four to five months of performance), respectively, correspond to effect sizes of 0.34 and 0.32 standard deviations. An effect size is the mean difference between groups divided by the pooled standard deviation of the outcome variable. These significant differences remained stable up to the end of

Table 4.5 Adjusted Means of CPC Program and Comparison Groups for Reading and Math Achievement over Time

Groups	Reading Achievement (Grade)			Math Achievement (Grade)		
	Three	Five	Eight	Three	Five	Eight
Any CPC participation	98.6	112.8	146.1	101.8	118.5	148.4
No participation	92.9	109.8	142.3	97.6	114.7	144.9
Difference	5.7**	3.0*	3.8*	4.2**	3.8**	3.5*
Effect size	0.34	0.17	0.17	0.32	0.24	0.19
Sample size	1,289	1,234	1,158	1,289	1,234	1,158

Note: Iowa Tests of Basic Skills (ITBS) standard scores are based on a moving average (ranging from 40 to 250).
* $p < 0.01$.
** $p < 0.001$.

eighth grade. The magnitude of the effect sizes declined over time, however.

CPC participants were significantly less likely to be retained in grade and to receive special education services than their comparison-group peers. The program group had a 31 percent lower rate of grade retention (25.3 versus 36.5 percent) of grade retention and spent 0.30 fewer years in special education than the comparison group after accounting for differences in child and family background. The magni-

Table 4.6 Eighth-Grade Adjusted Means of CPC Program and Comparison Groups for Life Skills Competence, Grade Retention, and Special Education Placement

Group	Life Skills Competence	Percent Ever Retained	Years in Special Education
Any CPC participation	40.7	25.3	0.6
No participation	37.7	36.5	0.9
Difference	3.0**	−11.2**	−0.3**
Effect size	0.28	n.a.	0.16
Sample size	1,158	1,164	1,164

n.a. Not applicable.
Note: Iowa Tests of Basic Skills (ITBS) standard scores are based on a moving average (ranging from 40 to 250).
* $p < 0.01$.
** $p < 0.001$.

tude of the estimated effects on grade retention and special education placement increased over time. Reynolds (1994) reported a 27 percent lower rate of grade retention between groups in third grade (19.2 versus 26.2 percent) and no significant differences for special education placement.

Adjusted means also are reported for life skills competence. No other studies of early intervention have used such an indicator of social competence. This test measures consumer life skills in seven domains, including personal finance, health, transportation, occupations, communication, government, and community resources. It is administered in eighth grade, and students are required to obtain a passing score (answering correctly more than 60 percent of items) before graduating from high school. CPC graduates answered, on average, three more items correctly than did the non-CPC comparison group (40.7 and 37.7 percent), for an effect size of 0.28 standard deviations. Program participants also had a 20 percent higher rate of passing than nonparticipants in the program (63 and 50 percent).

A related question concerns the effect of preschool participation. Table 4.6 shows the adjusted means of children who participated in the CPC program in preschool and kindergarten and that of all other sample participants. The latter participated in kindergarten programs in the CPCs at age five or in the comparison group schools but did not participate in preschool.

After controlling for demographic variables plus program participation in the primary grades, preschool participation was associated with a 5.4 point gain in reading achievement, a 4.3 gain in math achievement, and a 2.7 point gain in life skills competence. Respective effect sizes were 0.24, 0.23, and 0.26. Any preschool participation was associated with a 25 percent reduction in grade retention (24 versus 31.8 percent) and 0.40 fewer years in special education.[3] Group differences for primary-grade participation also were estimated. Any participation in a primary-grade program was significantly but modestly associated with higher life skills competence (effect size = 0.14) and a lower rate of grade retention (24 versus 31 percent, or a 23 percent decline). Because these results do not take duration of participation into account, findings should be interpreted cautiously.

The preschool findings are consistent with those reported in grades five and six (Reynolds 1995) and with findings based on alternative methodologies for detecting selection bias. Using the Heckman two-stage econometric technique and the latent covariance psychometric technique, Reynolds and Temple (1995) found preschool effect sizes of 0.32 in sixth grade. These effects were similar to ordinary regression analysis and did not differ across model specification.

IS DURATION OF PARTICIPATION ASSOCIATED WITH CHILDREN'S SCHOLASTIC PERFORMANCE?

Because children participated in the program up to six years, the relationship between years of participation and school performance was investigated. If a dosage-response relationship is established between years of participation and school adjustment, then the likelihood is enhanced that program participation improves school performance. Table 4.7 charts the relationship between the number of years of participation and five outcomes at the end of eighth grade for 1,164 children. The value of zero is for the non-CPC comparison group. The means are adjusted for differences in sex of child, parent education, eligibility for a free lunch, age at kindergarten entry, number of siblings, race, and school SES in kindergarten (given in table 4.2).

Duration of CPC program participation was significantly associated with better performance on all measures of competence, including higher reading and math achievement, greater life skills competence, and lower rates of special education placement and grade retention.[4] School performance increased noticeably after four years of intervention. Five or six years of participation yielded the best performance, and the six-year group was above the Chicago public school average in reading achievement. Relative to the no-participation group, the six-year group had a one-year advantage in reading achievement, and the five-year group had a seven-month advantage. Most impressive was the cumulative rate of grade retention for the six-year group (11 percent) and the five-year group (19 percent), which were at or below the national average of 18 percent. Moreover, 74 percent of the six-year group earned a passing score (thirty-eight or more items answered correctly) on the life skills competence test compared with 57 percent of the comparison group, a 30 percent increase.

A large proportion of program children, however, were performing well below the national average in school achievement. In grade-equivalent scores, whereby the national average is 8.8 years, the six-year group was 1.1 years below the national average (eight months for never-retained children), the five-year and four-year groups were 1.4 and 1.9 years below the national average, respectively.

Table 4.7 Eighth-Grade Adjusted Means of CPC Preschool and Comparison Groups for Five Outcomes

Group	Reading Achievement	Mathematics Achievement	Life Skills	Percent Retained	Years in Special Education
Preschool participation	147.4	149.4	41.2	24.0	0.51
No preschool participation	142.0	145.1	38.5	31.8	0.87
Difference	5.4**	4.3**	2.7**	−7.8**	−0.36**
Effect size	0.24	0.23	0.26	n.a.	0.23
Sample size	1,158	1,158	1,159	1,164	1,164

n.a. Not applicable.
Note: Iowa Tests of Basic Skills (ITBS) standard scores are based on a moving average (ranging from 40 to 250).
* $p < 0.01$.
** $p < 0.001$.

In a multiple regression analysis with five dummy variables (one for each of the years in table 4.8 except that years one and two were combined), participation for four, five, or six years yielded significantly higher math achievement and life skills competence, and lower rates of grade retention and special education placement, than no participation. Only children with five and six years of participation performed significantly better than the non-CPC comparison group in reading achievement. All the three- through six-year groups had significantly lower rates of grade retention. Children with one and two years of participation were not distinguishable from the non-CPC comparison group on any outcome. See appendix 4A for all regression coefficients associated with program participation.

These findings also can be used to estimate the effect of participation in the extensive program. Six years of participation yielded effect sizes in standard deviations of 0.52 (11.4 points), 0.47 (8.6 points), and 0.50 (5.2 points) for reading achievement, math achievement, and life skills competence. Six years also were associated with an 80 percent reduction in grade retention (34.7 to 6.9 percent) and 0.4 fewer years of special education. For five years of participation, effect sizes were 0.33 (7.2 points) for reading achievement, 0.39 (7.1 points) for math achievement, and 0.35 (3.7 points) for life skills competence; grade retention was reduced 51 percent (34.7 percent to 16.9 percent); and 0.6 fewer years were spent in spe-

Table 4.8 Scholastic Adjustment in Eighth Grade (Age Fourteen) by Duration of CPC Participation

Years of Intervention	Reading Achievement	Percent Passing Life Skills	Percent Retained in Grade	Years in Special Education
Zero	6.7	57	34	0.9
One	6.5	57	39	1.1
Two	6.7	58	32	1.0
Three	7.0	62	27	0.7
Four	6.9	68	23	0.6
Five	7.4	72	19	0.3
Six	7.7	74	11	0.4

Notes: Mean values were adjusted for the child and family background factors in table 4.2. Numbers from zero to six years of intervention were 275, 21, 140, 223, 168, 265, and 72.

cial education. When years of preschool or kindergarten and years of primary-grade intervention are included, both contribute significantly to the total impact of the program. This impact of duration is similar to results in the third and fifth grades (Reynolds 1994). Thus both the timing and duration of program participation are key ingredients of intervention.

DOES PARTICIPATION IN EXTENDED INTERVENTION LEAD TO BETTER SCHOOL PERFORMANCE THAN LESS-EXTENSIVE INTERVENTION?

This question considers the influence of primary-grade intervention above and beyond the influence of preschool and kindergarten intervention. It addresses the potential value of extending intervention into the primary grades. The analysis of this question included only children who participated in the CPC program in at least preschool and kindergarten and were active in the study in eighth grade. Table 4.9 reports the performance of children who participated for the maximum of six years compared to those whose participation ended in kindergarten. In addition to the demographic factors, both reading and math achievement scores at the end of kindergarten were included as covariates.

Extended intervention from preschool to third grade was significantly but moderately associated with all outcomes except special education placement. The differences in reading and math achievement equal six and four months of performance, respectively. Especially

Table 4.9 Eighth-Grade Adjusted Means for Extended Program Participation and Less Extended Participation

Group	Reading Achievement	Mathematics Achievement	Life Skills	Percent Retained	Years in Special Education
Prekindergarten plus kindergarten plus primary through third grade	154.9	154.3	44.6	6.9	0.35
Prekindergarten plus kindergarten only	147.7	142.7	40.6	32.1	0.61
Mean difference	7.2**	5.2**	4.0**	−18.6***	−0.26
Effect size	0.33	0.29	0.39	n.a.	0.19
Sample size	649	649	650	654	654

n.a. Not applicable.

Notes: Reading and math achievement are developmental standard scores on the Iowa Tests of Basic Skills (ITBS). Sample size includes all children with extended intervention not just the two groups shown. Kindergarten reading and math achievement test scores are included as covariates. Effect sizes are in standard deviations.

* $p < 0.05$.
** $p < 0.01$.
*** $p < 0.001$.

large were the differences in grade retention between groups. In the extended intervention group, 6.9 percent were retained compared with 32.6 for the comparison group, a 79 percent reduction.[5] Part of the reduction in grade retention could be due to school-specific factors.

Also investigated were the effects of extended intervention up to second grade rather than third grade (four or five years of participation). Although children with extended participation through second grade had consistently better performance than the preschool and kindergarten group, only the difference for special education placement was significant. The extended intervention group spent 0.44 fewer years in special education than the preschool and kindergarten group.

These findings are consistent with a seventh-grade analysis by Temple and Reynolds (1995), in which 426 children participated from preschool through the third grade and 191 children only participated in kindergarten, but also change schools only once up to second or third grade. After controlling for demographic variables, kindergarten achievement, achievement growth, attrition, and later school mobility, regression results indicated that children participating up to second or third grade scored five points higher in reading and six points higher in math achievement. However, children who participated up to third grade had, on average, the highest achievement.

These findings support the positive influence of duration of program participation, controlling for the timing of program entry. Does the timing of entry into intervention influence school performance, controlling for duration of participation? To address this question, the performance of 158 children who participated in the program for four years beginning in preschool was compared with that of 60 children who participated for four years beginning in kindergarten. School performance consistently favored the early-entry group, but differences were not statistically significant. The effect size for reading achievement was 0.21 standard deviation (four standard-score points), however. These findings are different from those at the two-year follow-up (Reynolds 1994). Of course, results are limited to children with four years of participation. For example, table 4.8 clearly shows the positive influence of early and extensive participation in the program.

WHICH FACTORS MEDIATE THE EFFECTS OF PARTICIPATION?

A major question raised by these findings is how these observed positive effects of the CPC program come about. In other words, what are the pathways through which long-term effects are achieved? These pathways not only identify additional targets of intervention after the program but also provide a rationale for explaining observed program effects, which is critical for quasi-experimental findings. If the estimated program effects are explained by processes predicted by the program theory, causal inference is strengthened. This approach is called confirmatory program evaluation (Reynolds 1997a). The emphasis of the approach is to establish developmental mechanisms through which the program affects long-term outcomes. If the identified pathways are consistent with the program theory, causal inference is strengthened.

Figure 4.2 presents the findings of a latent-variable structural model of intervention effects up to sixth grade for a subsample of CPC children. The coefficients are standardized regression coefficients.

Figure 4.2 Mediated Effects of Preschool Intervention

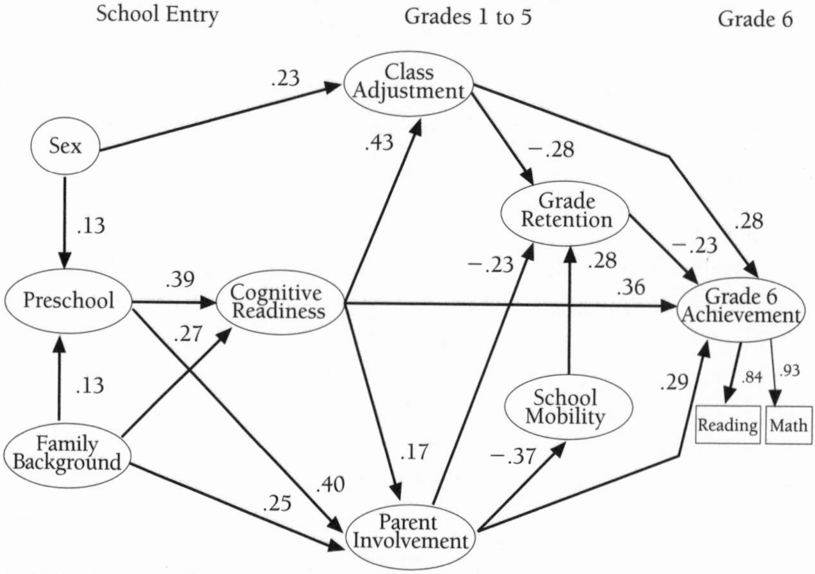

This confirmatory model includes five factors as mediators of the effects of preschool intervention: (a) cognitive readiness at kindergarten entry, (b) teacher ratings of school adjustment, (c) parent involvement in school, (d) school mobility (number of school moves), and (e) grade retention. Parent involvement was measured by parent ratings of parent involvement in school and teacher ratings of parent involvement in school up to fourth grade. Sixth-grade achievement included both reading and math achievement test scores (see Reynolds and others 1996 for details). The model was estimated for three hundred sixty children who participated in the six CPCs that provided services to third grade (two hundred forty participated in preschool, and one hundred twenty did not). For parsimony, paths involving participation in the primary-grade component are not shown.

This confirmatory model supports both the cognitive-advantage and family support hypotheses discussed in the introduction. One primary path of influence to sixth-grade school achievement was through cognitive readiness at kindergarten entry ($b = 0.140$ or 0.39×0.36). Preschool participants start school more ready to learn, and this readiness is reflected in sixth-grade school achievement. Another primary path of influence on sixth-grade school achievement was through parent involvement in school (b = 0.116 or 0.40 × 0.29). Preschool participation was positively associated with parental school involvement, which in turn significantly influenced later school achievement. However, as with the cognitive-advantage hypothesis, the family support hypothesis appears to be an incomplete explanation of preschool effectiveness. The model fits better than several alternative models and suggests that the pathways of influence of early childhood intervention are complex and involve several alterable variables. Grade retention and school mobility appear to inhibit the transmission of preschool effects. They also negatively influence school achievement in sixth grade. Although not shown, participation in the primary-grade portion of the CPCs was associated with higher teacher ratings of school adjustment (b = 0.10) and parent involvement in school (b = 0.33). Recent analysis of the full study sample largely supports these findings (Reynolds 1997b).

DISCUSSION

The Child-Parent Center program was designed to promote children's school success by providing comprehensive educational and family support services spanning two important periods of development: the preschool years and the transition to formal schooling in the primary grades. Tracing the development of the 1989 graduates of the program up to age fourteen, findings indicate that large-scale programs can be successful in promoting the school success of economically disadvantaged children. Specifically, (a) any participation in the program was significantly associated with school performance up to eighth grade, (b) duration of participation was significantly associated with school performance, especially for children who participated for five or six years, (c) participation in extended childhood intervention to second and third grade yielded significantly better school performance than participation ending in kindergarten. Finally, longer-term effects of the program can be explained by cognitive-advantage and family support hypotheses, both of which are theoretically linked to the program. The pathways of effects are complex, however.

Overall, findings in the Chicago Longitudinal Study demonstrate that established large-scale early childhood programs can be successful for economically disadvantaged children. They can promote positive school adjustment beyond second and third grade, as has been shown for other programs (Consortium for Longitudinal Studies 1983). These findings mollify the growing pessimism about the longer-term effects of early intervention. Unique to the Child-Parent Centers, however, are the integration of preschool, kindergarten, and primary-grade services. Participation in early childhood intervention also has indirect effects (see figure 4.2), and they often are not measured, which means that the total impact of the program is underestimated.

A second conclusion is that the duration of intervention is significantly associated with all indicators of school performance. Participation in primary-grade intervention positively influences performance above and beyond earlier intervention, even after taking into account kindergarten achievement in reading and math. Longer-lasting interventions, which provide an array of services such as smaller class sizes, teacher training, and parent involvement activities, allow children greater opportunities to develop the scholastic and social skills necessary for sustained effects. Studies by Alexander and Entwisle (1988) and Reynolds (1989, 1991) support the value of intervening school-based and family support factors in promoting successful adjustment to the primary grades. Of course, the positive influence of extensive participation also indicates that early entry into the program at age three (timing) contributes to later school performance. Thus the findings of similar school performance of four-year participants who began in preschool and four-year participants who began in kindergarten should be interpreted with caution.

Why does the Child-Parent Center and Expansion Program lead to such persistent improvements in school performance? The beneficial effects of duration of participation indicate that program continuity is a key ingredient. Unlike almost all early childhood programs, the CPCs integrate preschool and kindergarten components and coordinate the primary-grade component with the parent elementary school, all within a single administrative system of a public school. Second, the program begins prior to formal schooling (ages three or four) so that a strong foundation for learning can be formed. School performance beginning in kindergarten presages later performance. Third, parent involvement is a major focus of the program. A multifaceted array of support services are provided, from basic parent education to volunteer activities in and out of the center. Compared with Head Start and other government-funded programs, the parent program in the CPCs is intense. Each center employs a full-time noninstructional parent-resource teacher who runs a separate parent-resource room. The fourth key ingredient associated with persistent effects is the curriculum's emphasis on basic skills. Although curricula vary across centers, all staff seek to facilitate school achievement. Viewed in the context of the parent program and other learning experiences (field trips), such an approach can provide a strong foundation for educational success. Nevertheless, as shown in table 4.8, the school achievement of CPC graduates, even those with five or six years of participation, is still considerably below the national average. Thus early childhood intervention is not a panacea for all challenges facing low-income children and families. Other approaches are needed as well.

These reasons dovetail with findings from the structural analysis in figure 4.2 of the pathways through which program participation affects later adjustment. Two explanations are apparent. Both are consistent with the program's theory as well as the findings in figure 4.2. One is the cognitive-advantage hypothesis, which is that program participation enhances children's early cognitive and language development so that they are more likely to begin school ready to learn and that this greater readiness provides advantages in adjusting to school. A second explanation for longer-term program effects is the family support hypothesis. The intervention encourages parent involvement in school and in children's education such that when the intervention ends parents are more likely to continue to provide the nurturance necessary for their children to maintain the gains made in the program. While cognitive functioning at school entry and parent involvement foster the program's longer-term effectiveness, two other factors appear to inhibit the transmission of long-term gains: (a) frequent school mobility and (b) grade retention. Avoiding these two life events after the intervention ends helps maintain learning gains. Continued follow-up of these pathways and others will be necessary, as will analyses examining the total study sample of children. Other plausible hypotheses that explain long-term effects may include school support, social adjustment, and motivational advantage. These should be studied further.

Although the quasi-experimental design of the study means that findings should be interpreted with caution, several strengths substantially enhance the validity of findings. First, the internal validity of findings has been investigated extensively through analysis of attrition, selection bias, alternative comparison groups, multiple outcome variables, and consideration of the duration of treatment participation (for example, Reynolds 1994, 1995; Reynolds and Temple in press). Findings have been largely consistent across these analytic approaches. Such in-depth sensitivity analyses are rare in intervention research. A second strength of the study is the prospective longitudinal design and comprehensive data collection of the project, which enable investigation of year-to-year changes in outcomes and comparisons among outcomes. For example, program effects are stronger in the scholastic domain than in the social domain. This is consistent with the theory of the program. Without extensive ongoing data collection, this distinction would not have been possible. A third strength of the study is that pathways of effects of the program have been investigated to explain how the program could produce long-term effects. Findings of alternative model specifications indicate that the pathways involving cognitive development and parent involvement are plausible. This finding confirms the efficacy of the program. Finally, the investigation of a large-scale established program and relatively large sample increases the generalizability of findings to typical programs and there is ample statistical power to detect difference across groups and among subgroups in the sample. Very few studies of early interventions have these attributes.

RECOMMENDATIONS

Collection and analyses of follow-up data in high school are currently being undertaken to investigate the longitudinal relationships between program participation and scholastic adjustment. Relationships with juvenile delinquency and high school completion also will be pursued. Based on the available findings, however, three recommendations are warranted.

First, the Child-Parent Center program should be fully funded and implemented in target schools. Unfortunately, in the past few years a number of schools have decided not to continue funding the primary-grade portion of the program, which uses Title I funding from the

State of Illinois. Unlike federal Title I funding, local schools have much latitude over state funds. Although schools have the authority to make their own decisions, and not all worthy programs can be implemented, funding decisions should favor programs that have demonstrated effects.

The reason that extended early childhood programs may be more effective is not just because they are longer in duration. They also encourage stability in school and home learning environments, and they occur at a very important time in children's development—the transition to formal schooling. School reform initiatives should take these issues into account.

A second recommendation is that parent involvement in the program should be enhanced. Although parent involvement is a primary source of effects, previous analysis indicates that parent involvement varies considerably across sites. Active involvement of parents in the full array of activities sponsored by the center is critical to the program's continued success. Since parent involvement in school appears to be a primary pathway for promoting long-term success, program and schoolwide efforts to involve parents in their children's education will benefit not only the early childhood interventions but also the general development of families and children.

Finally, extended intervention programs like the Child-Parent Centers should be implemented on a larger scale. Program implementation has been exclusive to Chicago. Replication of the program in other schools and cities would be valuable in determining its impact within other contexts. One impediment to expansion is that the Child-Parent Center program model is comprehensive and requires that preschool programs be physically as well as conceptually connected to a public elementary school in a school-within-a-school framework. Thus a strong commitment of financial and human resources to integrating preschool, kindergarten, and school-age programs is needed. The long-term benefits of implementing such an approach, however, are worth the investment.

APPENDIX 4A   ESTIMATED MODELS FOR YEARS OF PROGRAM PARTICIPATION

Table 4A.1 Eighth-Grade Reading Achievement

Variable	B	SE B	Sig T
NMISS[a]	−1.734	0.436	0.0001
4YEARS	2.855	2.006	0.1548
INCOME[b]	−0.039	0.067	0.5629
SEX[c]	8.099	1.252	0.0000
LUNCH[d]	−7.795	2.017	0.0001
EKAGE[e]	0.044	0.174	0.8020
6YEARS	11.402	2.818	0.0001
BLACK[f]	−11.043	3.033	0.0003
PARED	7.708	1.529	0.0000
NCHILD	−0.416	0.442	0.3468
1&2YEARS	−1.022	2.064	0.6207
3YEARS	2.332	1.910	0.2223
5YEARS	7.288	1.858	0.0001
(Constant)	153.488	12.502	0.0000

[a]Number of missing family-background variables
[b] School low-income
[c]1 = girls, 0 = boys
[d]Eligible for a free lunch
[e]Age at kindergarten entry (N months)
[f]1 = black, 0 = Hispanic

Table 4A.2 Eighth-Grade Math Achievement

Variable	B	SE B	Sig T
NMISS[a]	−1.537	0.367	0.0000
FOREYR	3.453	1.689	0.0411
INCOME[b]	−0.067	0.056	0.2334
SEX[c]	5.585	1.054	0.0000
LUNCH[d]	−6.467	1.698	0.0001
EKAGE[e]	−0.037	0.146	0.8031
SIXYR	8.486	2.373	0.0004
BLACK[f]	−8.403	2.554	0.0010
PARED	5.307	1.287	0.0000
NCHILD	−0.279	0.373	0.4548
ONTWYR	−0.509	1.738	0.7698
THREYR	1.435	1.608	0.3725
FIVEYR	7.015	1.564	0.0000
(Constant)	161.457	10.527	0.0000

[a]Number of missing family-background variables
[b] School low-income
[c]1 = girls, 0 = boys
[d]Eligible for a free lunch
[e]Age at kindergarten entry (N months)
[f]1 = black, 0 = Hispanic

Table 4A.3 Eighth-Grade Life Skills Competence

Variable	B	SE B	Sig T
NMISS[a]	−0.508	0.214	0.0175
FOREYR	2.887	0.982	0.0034
INCOME[b]	−0.032	0.033	0.3192
SEX[c]	2.094	0.613	0.0007
LUNCH[d]	−2.493	0.988	0.0117
EKAGE[e]	−0.017	0.085	0.8414
SIXYR	6.319	1.380	0.0000
BLACK[f]	−5.644	1.485	0.0002
PARED	2.709	0.749	0.0003
NCHILD	−0.498	0.217	0.0218
ONTWYR	0.525	1.011	0.6036
THREYR	2.109	0.935	0.0243
FIVEYR	4.553	0.910	0.0000
(Constant)	47.627	6.123	0.0000

[a]Number of missing family-background variables
[b] School low-income
[c]1 = girls, 0 = boys
[d]Eligible for a free lunch
[e]Age at kindergarten entry (N months)
[f]1 = black, 0 = Hispanic

Table 4A.4 Eighth-Grade Cumulative Grade Retention

Variable	B	SE B	Sig T
NMISS[a]	0.027	0.009	0.0029
FOREYR	−0.103	0.041	0.0123
INCOME[b]	−4.240	0.001	0.7548
SEX[c]	−0.164	0.026	0.0000
LUNCH[d]	0.108	0.041	0.0089
EKAGE[e]	−0.010	0.004	0.0048
SIXYR	−0.278	0.057	0.0000
BLACK[f]	0.088	0.062	0.1537
PARED	−0.081	0.031	0.0093
NCHILD	0.006	0.009	0.5311
ONTWYR	−0.002	0.042	0.9660
THREYR	−0.093	0.039	0.0174
FIVEYR	−0.169	0.038	0.0000
(Constant)	0.943	0.255	0.0002

[a]Number of missing family-background variables
[b] School low-income
[c]1 = girls, 0 = boys
[d]Eligible for a free lunch
[e]Age at kindergarten entry (N months)
[f]1 = black, 0 = Hispanic

Table 4A.5 Eighth-Grade Years in Special Education

Variable	B	SE B	Sig T
NMISS[a]	0.020	0.034	0.5584
FOREYR	−0.297	0.157	0.0583
INCOME[b]	0.006	0.005	0.2697
SEX[c]	−0.499	0.098	0.0000
LUNCH[d]	0.140	0.158	0.3752
EKAGE[e]	0.012	0.014	0.3660
SIXYR	−0.437	0.220	0.0476
BLACK[f]	0.187	0.237	0.4295
PARED	−0.248	0.119	0.0382
NCHILD	−0.005	0.035	0.8828
ONTWYR	0.202	0.161	0.2112
THREYR	−0.252	0.149	0.0919
FIVEYR	−0.547	0.145	0.0002
(Constant)	−0.215	0.977	0.8260

[a]Number of missing family-background variables
[b] School low-income
[c]1 = girls, 0 = boys
[d]Eligible for a free lunch
[e]Age at kindergarten entry (N months)
[f]1 = black, 0 = Hispanic

APPENDIX 4B   THE CHICAGO CHILD-PARENT CENTERS: A STUDY OF EXTENDED EARLY CHILDHOOD INTERVENTION

The Chicago Longitudinal Study began in 1986 as an evaluation of government-funded kindergarten programs for children at risk of school failure (due to poverty and associated factors) in the Chicago public schools. Because the study focused on the comparison of large-scale and established nonmodel programs and included a large sample size ($n = 1{,}539$), it was anticipated that the study would provide a unique opportunity to assess the efficacy of more typical early childhood interventions. The principal investigator and two colleagues in early childhood education evaluated this program. We began to trace children's development over time (a) to investigate the longitudinal effects of early childhood intervention and (b) to improve our understanding of the multiple and complex influences on social and scholastic adjustment. Beginning in 1987 (grade one) yearly follow-up data were collected from children, school records, standardized test scores, parents, and teachers with the financial and resource support of the Department of Research, Evaluation, and Planning of the Chicago public schools. Since this time, a wealth of information has been collected from children, parents, teachers, and school records, analyzed with multiple methodologies and disseminated in professional conferences and peer-review journals.

EARLY SHORT-TERM STUDIES

Early studies focused on the Child-Parent Center (CPC) preschool program, a Head Start–type program for economically disadvantaged children. The major components of the program are comprehensive support services, parent involvement, and a child-centered focus on language development. Children were selected on a most-in-need basis; 69 percent attended preschool, and 31 percent began school in kindergarten. The quasi-experimental design of the study, of course, necessitates cautious interpretations. Reynolds (1989) tested a social context model of scholastic adjustment for the original sample of 1,539 low-income minority children and found that preschool intervention was a significant contributor to first-grade academic achievement and teacher-rated classroom adjustment. Parent participation in school activities, school stability between kindergarten and grade one, and teacher ratings of motivation in kindergarten also significantly contributed to first-grade adjustment. The effect of preschool participation (controlling for school socioeconomic status and gender) were mediated by these factors. A follow-up analysis at grade two (Reynolds 1991) supported the pattern of effects found in the initial study as well as the overall fit of the model. Preschool participation was a notable contributor to the model. It had significant direct effects on kindergarten school achievement and parent involvement in first grade and significant indirect effects on second-grade outcomes. Teacher ratings of motivation, kindergarten achievement, and school mobility also contributed significantly to adjustment.

LONGER-TERM STUDIES

These earlier studies supported the immediate and short-term effects of preschool intervention as well as the importance of the social contexts immediately after preschool. Reynolds (1995) tested the effects of preschool intervention for several child outcomes through grade six for 887 black children entering the Child Parent Centers in preschool (age three or four; $n = 757$) or kindergarten (age five; $n = 130$). Two contrast groups were investigated: (a) children with any preschool enrollment (one or two years) versus those with no enrollment (zero years) and (b) children with two years of preschool versus those with one year. In the multiple regression analyses, the following theoretically relevant variables were taken into account: sex, parent education, parent expectations, age, eligibility for free lunch, school socioeconomic status, and number of siblings. The influence of any participation versus no participation was consistently significant in the expected direction up to and including grade six for reading and math achievement, teacher ratings, parental school involvement, and the incidence of grade retention and special education placement (overall mean effect size = 0.34 standard deviation). However, the influence of a second year of preschool intervention was not significant after kindergarten, although the direction of influence was consistently positive (overall mean effect size = 0.15). These results indicate that the effects of preschool intervention are not limited to short-term or indirect effects but are significant seven years after the program.

Reynolds (1994) investigated the relationship between the duration of total intervention and child outcomes at the end of the program (grade three) and at the two-year follow-up assessment (grade five). Results indicate that the duration of intervention was significantly associated, in the expected direction, with reading achievement, mathematics achievement, teacher ratings of school adjustment, parental involvement in school, and grade retention, controlling for socioeconomic status. Children in extended intervention (preschool to grades two or three) had better school adjustment than children with less intervention. Reynolds and Temple (in press) presented follow-up evidence through seventh grade.

Preparation of this chapter was made possible by grants from the National Institute of Child Health and Human Development (HD34294) and the Foundation for Child Development. The author thanks the Department of Research, Analysis, and Assessment in the Chicago public schools for cooperation in data collection and management and the Department of Early Childhood Programs in the Chicago public schools for helpful information about the Child-Parent Center program.

NOTES

1. Although the year of graduation from the Child-Parent Center and Expansion Program depended on the number of years the program was available at the school (two or three years), 1989 (third grade) was the last possible year of participation in the program. Consequently, 1989 rather than 1988 was used as the sample identifier.

2. The missing-data indicator is the number of family background variables with missing responses. They include parent education, lunch subsidy, number of children, and age in kindergarten. The missing-data indicator was included in the model after plugging each missing value with an estimate (see Cohen and Cohen 1983).

3. The magnitude of the effects of preschool is larger when it included only children who attended kindergarten programs in the CPCs but had no preschool experience. Effect sizes were 0.39, 0.36, 0.33, and 0.35, respectively, for reading achievement, math achievement, life skills competence, and years in special education. The rate of grade retention was 24.0 for the program group and 30.9 for the comparison group. Although not officially in CPC kindergartens, these 115 children received services in the centers, and many were in the same kindergarten classrooms as their CPC peers. They also participated in the primary-grade component.

4. The Pearson zero-order correlations were, respectively, 0.18, 0.19, 0.21, −0.20, and −0.15 for reading achievement, math achievement, life skills competence, grade retention, and special education placement. These correlations assume linearity and do not take range restriction into account.

5. Analyses including children who participated in the program for either five or six years up to third grade indicated significant mean differences (in favor of the program group) of 4.7 for reading achievement, 4.1 for math achievement, and 2.6 for life skills competence. Participation also was significantly associated with a 63 percent reduction in grade retention and 0.3 fewer years in special education.

REFERENCES

Alexander, K. L., and D. R. Entwisle. 1988. "Achievement in the First Two Years of School: Patterns and Processes." *Monographs of the Society for Research in Child Development* 53(2, serial no. 218).

Barnett, W. S. 1992. "Benefits of Compensatory Preschool Education." *Journal of Human Resources* 27(2): 279–312.

Berrueta-Clement, J. R., Lawrence J. Schweinhart, W. S. Barnett, A. S. Epstein, and David P. Weikart. 1984. *Changed Lives: The Effects of the Perry Preschool Program on Youths through Age Nineteen*. Ypsilanti, Mich.: High/Scope Press.

Campbell, F. A., and C. T. Ramey. 1994. "Effects of Early Intervention on Intellectual and Academic Achievement: A Follow-up Study of Children from Low-Income Families." *Child Development* 65(2): 684–98.

———. 1995. "Cognitive and School Outcomes for High-Risk African American Students at Middle Adolescence: Positive Effects of Early Intervention." *American Educational Research Journal* 32(4): 743–72.

Chicago Public Schools. 1986a. *Chapter II All-Day Kindergarten Program Final Evaluation Report: Fiscal 1985*. Chicago, Ill.: Department of Research and Evaluation.

———. 1986b. *ECIA Chapter II Application: Fiscal 1985*. Chicago, Ill.: Department of Research and Evaluation.

———. 1987. *Chapter II All-Day Kindergarten Program Final Evaluation Report: Fiscal 1986*. Chicago, Ill.: Department of Research and Evaluation.

Cohen, Jacob, and Patricia Cohen. 1983. *Applied Multiple Correlation/ Regression Analysis for the Behavioral Sciences*. Hillsdale, N.J.: Erlbaum.

Conrad, K. J., and M. J. Eash. 1983. "Measuring Implementation and Multiple Outcomes in a Child-Parent Center Compensatory Education Program." *American Educational Research Journal* 20(2): 221–36.

Consortium for Longitudinal Studies. 1983. *As the Twig Is Bent*. Hillsdale, N.J.: Erlbaum.

Crum, Daniel. 1993. "A Summary of the Empirical Studies of the Long-Term Effects of Head Start." Pennsylvania State University, Pennsylvania Park. Unpublished manuscript.

Fuerst, J. S., and Dorothy Fuerst. 1993. "Chicago Experience with an Early Childhood Program: The Special Case of the Child-Parent Center Program." *Urban Education* 28(1): 69–96.

Haskins, Ronald. 1989. "Beyond Metaphor: The Efficacy of Early Childhood Education." *American Psychologist* 44(2): 274–82.

Hieronymus, A. N., and H. D. Hoover. 1990. *Iowa Tests of Basic Skills: Manual for School Administrators*. Supplement. Chicago, Ill.: Riverside.

Madden, Nancy A., Robert E. Slavin, Nancy L. Karweit, Lawrence J. Dolan, and Barbara A. Wasik. 1993. "Success for All: Longitudinal Effects of a Restructuring Program for Inner-City Elementary Schools." *American Educational Research Journal* 30(1): 123–48.

McKey, R. H., Larry Condelli, Harriet Ganson, B. J. Barrett, Catherine McConkey, and M. C. Plantz. 1985. *The Impact of Head Start on Children, Families, and Communities*. DHHS Publication OHDS 85-31193. Washington: U.S. Government Printing Office.

National Education Goals Panel. 1994. *The National Education Goals Report: Building a Nation of Learners*. Washington: U.S. Government Printing Office.

National Head Start Association. 1990. *Head Start: The Nation's Pride, a Nation's Challenge*. Alexandria, Va.: National Head Start Association.

Natriello, Gary, E. L. McDill, and A. M. Pallas. 1990. *Schooling Disadvantaged Children: Racing against Catastrophe*. New York: Teachers College Press.

Ramey, S. L., and C. T. Ramey. 1992. "Early Educational Interventions with Disadvantaged Children—To What Effect?" *Applied and Preventive Psychology* 1(3): 131–40.

Reynolds, Arthur J. 1989. "A Structural Model of First-Grade Outcomes for an Urban, Low Socioeconomic Status, Minority Population." *Journal of Educational Psychology* 81(4): 594–603.

———. 1991. "Early Schooling of Children at Risk." *American Educational Research Journal* 28(2): 392–22.

———. 1994. "Effects of a Preschool plus Follow-on Intervention for Children at Risk." *Developmental Psychology* 30(6): 787–804.

———. 1995. "One Year of Preschool Intervention or Two: Does It Matter?" *Early Childhood Research Quarterly* 10(1): 1–31.

———. 1997a. "Confirmatory Program Evaluation: A Methodological Approach for Enhancing Causal Inferences in Social Experiments." Unpublished manuscript. Madison, Wisc.: University of Wisconsin, Madison.

———. 1997b. "Long-term Effects of the Chicago Child-Parent Center Program Through Age 15." Paper presented at the biennial meeting of the Society for Research in Child Development, Washington D.C. (April 1997.)

Reynolds, Arthur J., and Nikolaus Bezruczko. 1989. "Assessing the Construct Validity of a Life Skills Competency Test." *Educational and Psychological Measurement* 49(1): 183–93.

Reynolds, Arthur J., N. A. Mavrogenes, Nikolaus Bezruczko, and Mavis Hagemann. 1996. "Cognitive and Family Support Mediators of Preschool Effectiveness: A Confirmatory Analysis." *Child Development* 67(3): 1119–40.

Reynolds, Arthur J., N. A. Mavrogenes, Mavis Hagemann, and Nikolaus Bezruczko. 1993. *Schools, Families, and Children: Sixth-Year Results from the Longitudinal Study of Children at Risk.* Chicago, Ill.: Department of Research, Evaluation and Planning, Chicago Public Schools.

Reynolds, Arthur J., Majida Mehana, and J. A. Temple. 1995. "Does Preschool Intervention Affect Children's Perceived Competence?" *Journal of Applied Developmental Psychology* 16(2): 211–30.

Reynolds, Arthur J., and J. A. Temple. 1995. "Quasi-Experimental Estimates of the Effects of a Preschool Intervention: Psychometric and Econometric Comparisons." *Evaluation Review* 19(4): 347–73.

———. In press. "Extended Early Childhood Intervention and School Achievement: Age Thirteen Findings from the Chicago Longitudinal Study." *Child Development.*

Rovner, J. 1990. "Head Start is One Program Everyone Wants to Help." *Congressional Quarterly* 48(16): 1191–95.

Schweinhart, Lawrence J., H. V. Barnes, and David P. Weikart. 1993. *Significant Benefits: The High/Scope Perry Preschool Study through Age Twenty-seven.* Ypsilanti, Mich.: High/Scope Press.

Seitz, Victoria. 1990. "Intervention Programs for Impoverished Children: A Comparison of Educational and Family Support Models." *Annals of Child Development* 7: 73–103.

Seitz, Victoria, Nancy Apfel, L. Rosenbaum, and Edward Zigler. 1983. "Long-Term Effects of Projects Head Start and Follow Through: The New Haven Project." In *As the Twig Is Bent: Lasting Effects of Preschool Programs*, edited by Consortium for Longitudinal Studies. Hillsdale, N.J.: Erlbaum.

Temple, J. A., and Arthur J. Reynolds. 1995. "Extending Compensatory Intervention into the Primary Grades: Evidence from the Chicago Longitudinal Study." Paper presented to the American Economic Association, annual meeting. Washington, D.C.(1995).

Wachs, T. D., and G. E. Gruen. 1982. *Early Experience and Human Development.* New York: Plenum.

White, K. R. 1985. "Efficacy of Early Intervention." *Journal of Special Education* 19(4): 401–16.

Woodhead, Martin. 1988. "When Psychology Informs Public Policy: The Case of Early Childhood Intervention." *American Psychologist* 43(6): 443–54.

Yoshikawa, Hirokazu. 1994. "Prevention as Cumulative Protection: Effects of Early Family Support and Education on Chronic Delinquency and Its Risks." *Psychological Bulletin* 115(1): 27–54.

Zigler, Edward, and Susan Muenchow. 1992. *Head Start: The Inside Story of America's Most Successful Educational Experiment*. New York: Basic Books.

Zigler, Edward, and Sally Styfco, eds. 1993. *Head Start and Beyond: A National Plan for Extended Childhood Intervention*. New Haven, Conn.: Yale University Press.

CHAPTER 5

High/Scope Perry Preschool Program Effects at Age Twenty-Seven

Lawrence J. Schweinhart and David P. Weikart

Evidence gathered over twenty-two years indicates that the High/Scope Perry Preschool Program cut crime in half, reduced high school dropout and demand for welfare assistance, increased participants' adult earnings and property wealth, and provided taxpayers with a return of $7.16 for every dollar invested in the program (Schweinhart and others 1993). This chapter describes the scientific design that identified these remarkable effects and the preschool program that produced them. It describes the evidence from this study for preschool program effects and identifies similar findings from other studies. It interprets the meaning of this research and examines its implications for the development of public policies.

STUDY DESIGN

The 123 participants in the High/Scope Perry Preschool study lived in poverty and were at risk of school failure. From the African Americans who lived in the Perry Elementary School attendance area on the south side of Ypsilanti, Michigan, participants were selected for the study who met three criteria:

- They became three or four years old in 1962 or three years old in 1963 through 1965 (a selection strategy that permitted the program to serve three- and four-year-olds in the same classroom each year)

- Their families scored low on a socioeconomic status measure that combined parents' highest year of schooling and employment status and the number of persons per room in the household, an indicator that they lived in poverty

- The children of these families scored below ninety on the Stanford-Binet Intelligence Scale (Terman and Merrill 1960), an indicator that they were then at risk of school failure.

Fifty-eight study participants who attended the High/Scope Perry Preschool Program were assigned randomly to a "program group," and sixty-five study participants who did not attend a preschool program were assigned to a "no-program group." Each year from 1962 through 1965, incoming study participants were assigned by the following procedure:

- First, individuals were matched by their Stanford-Binet IQs (intelligence quotients) at study entry, and the pairs were split into two groups.

- Next the groups were matched on mean Stanford-Binet IQ, mean socioeconomic status, and boy-girl ratio by switching pairs of individuals with similar Stanford-Binet IQs between groups until the groups were alike. By a coin toss, one group was designated the program group and the other was designated the no-program group.

- Pairs of similar individuals were switched further so that twenty-three younger siblings were assigned to the same group as their older siblings. This procedure was a practical necessity to keep the program from affecting no-program group members through their families. In effect, it changed the sampling unit from child to family.

- Two children originally in the program group who could not participate in the program because their single mothers were employed were reassigned to the no-program group. This minor departure from random assignment led to the program group members having significantly fewer employed single mothers than the no-program group members (4 versus 22 percent, $n = 123$, $p = 0.018$, effect size $= 0.44$; all p-levels reported in this article are two-tailed). This difference slightly attenuated the group differences in outcomes because the children of employed single mothers achieved greater success than did the children of single mothers who were not in the work force.

Apart from this one difference, the program group and the no-program group were quite similar at study entry, with no statistically significant differences (at $p < 0.05$) in socioeconomic status, welfare status, father's employment or presence in the home, mother's or father's schooling or age, number of siblings, household density, birth order, gender, or Stanford-Binet score at study entry.

Because of the random assignment to groups and the similar group characteristics at study entry, this study has high internal validity; that is to say, it is highly probable that group differences in program outcomes are, in fact, effects of the preschool program.

PRESCHOOL PROGRAM

The program operated from October through May beginning with the 1962 to 1963 school year through the 1966 to 1967 school year. Developing and using the High/Scope curriculum, four teachers spent five mornings a week with a class of twenty to twenty-five three- and four-year-olds and made weekly ninety-minute home visits to each child and mother. The teachers were all certified in both early childhood and special education and received compensation according to the school district's salary schedule. At least one of the four teachers at any time was African American; of the ten women who served as teachers in the program, three were African American and seven were white.

In the High/Scope curriculum, children plan, carry out, and review their own learning activities (Weikart and others 1971; Hohmann and Weikart 1995). Teachers arrange the classroom in distinct activity areas and follow a daily routine that balances teacher and child initiative and control of activities. Teachers support children's development and learning by focusing on key experiences of logic and mathematics, language and literacy, creative representation, music and movement, social relations, and initiative. Key experiences in logic and mathematics involve sorting and ranking items in space and time, as elaborated in the work of Piaget (summarized by Piaget and Inhelder 1969). Teachers work with parents as partners, whose expertise regarding their individual children complements the teachers' expertise regarding the early childhood curriculum. Although the curriculum used in the High/Scope Perry Preschool Program was not so well-delineated in its early years, it always centered on children taking initiative for their own learning activities.

FINDINGS

Over the years, the evidence has accumulated that the High/Scope Perry Preschool Program contributed substantially to the lives of participants—in educational performance, economic productivity, and social responsibility. As shown in figure 5.1, by age twenty-seven significantly fewer members of the program group than the no-program group had experienced five or more arrests or received welfare assistance as adults; and significantly more of them had graduated from high school on time, earned two thousand dollars or more per month, or owned their own homes.

EDUCATIONAL PERFORMANCE

By age twenty-seven, the program group had completed a significantly higher level of schooling than the no-program group, with means of 11.9 versus 11.0 for the highest year of schooling ($n = 123, p = 0.016$, effect size $= 0.43$); 71 percent of the program group, but only 54 percent of the no-program group, had graduated from regular or adult high school or received General Educational Development certification ($n = 123, p = 0.055$, effect size $= 0.35$).[1] The finding of a preschool program effect on the high school graduation rate is important because it is a gateway to other long-term effects and because it has been corroborated in three other studies of preschool program effects (Fuerst and Fuerst 1993; Gotts 1989; Monroe and McDonald 1981). In this study, this finding was solely due to females: 84 percent of program females but only 35 percent of no-program females graduated from high school or the equivalent ($n = 51, p = 0.000$, effect size $= 1.14$), whereas 61 percent of program males and 67 percent of no-program males did so ($n = 72, p = 0.594$, effect size $= -0.12$). High school graduation was linked to commitment to schooling and school achievement for females, but not for males (Schweinhart and others 1993). Gender-program interaction effects were not found for test scores, earnings, or arrests.

Previous findings for educational performance indicate that, compared with the no-program group, the program group spent less time in programs for educable mental impairment; scored significantly higher on tests of educational performance at ages four through seven, fourteen, and nineteen; had a stronger commitment to schooling at age nineteen; and inspired their parents to have higher educational aspirations for them at age fifteen. The program group had only 39 percent as many years in programs for educable mental impairment as did the no-program group (group means of 1.1 versus 2.8 years, $n = 112, p = 0.009$, effect size $= 0.49$). From ages four through seven, but not afterward, the program group scored significantly better than the no-program group on the Stanford-Binet (Terman and Merrill 1960) and similar tests of intellectual performance—an ex-

Figure 5.1 Major Findings at Age Twenty-Seven

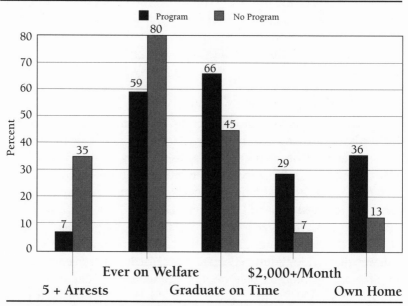

Source: Schweinhart and others 1993, 190. Adapted with permission.

ample of the infamous fade-out of the preschool program effect on intellectual performance. But not only did the program have a variety of other effects, thereby negating the generality of an effect fade-out; it also had its strongest effect on school achievement when study participants were fourteen years old, seven years after the cessation of the intellectual performance effect (mean raw scores on the California Achievement Test of 122.2 versus 94.5, $n = 95$, $p = 0.001$, effect size $= 0.68$; Tiegs and Clark 1963). The program group scored significantly higher than the no-program group on general literacy as measured by the Adult Performance Level Survey (American College Testing Program 1976) at age nineteen (24.6 versus 21.8 items correct out of 40, $p = 0.025$, effect size $= 0.43$), but not at age twenty-seven. At age nineteen, the program group had a better attitude toward high school than the no-program group (means of 22.3 versus 18.9; on a sixteen-item scale each scored one to three, $n = 121$, $p = 0.026$, effect size $= 0.40$). At age fifteen, 68 percent of the program group, but only 40 percent of the no-program group, reported that their schoolwork required home preparation ($n = 99$, $p = 0.010$, effect size

= 0.54). When children were fifteen years old, 55 percent of program group parents, but only 35 percent of no-program group parents, hoped that their children would get a college degree ($n = 94$, $p = 0.027$, effect size = 0.45).

Arrests

Police and court records showed that program group members averaged 2.3 arrests, half as many as the 4.6 arrests averaged by no-program group members; only 7 percent of the program group had been arrested five or more times, compared with 35 percent of the no-program group ($n = 123$, $p = 0.004$, effect size = 0.54). Only 12 percent of the program males had been arrested five or more times, compared with 49 percent of the no-program males, one-fourth as many (means of 3.8 versus 6.1, $n = 72$, $p = 0.018$, effect size = 0.58). Program group members spent significantly less time on probation than did no-program group members (means of 3.2 versus 6.6 months, $n = 123$, $p = 0.046$, effect size = 0.34). Similarly, in the Syracuse University Family Development Research Program (Lally, Mangione, and Honig 1988), a study of the effects of a program of high-quality day care and weekly home visits, significantly fewer program group than no-program group members were placed on probation for delinquent offenses as teens (6 versus 22 percent).

Economic Productivity

At age twenty-seven, 29 percent of the program group reported monthly earnings of $2,000 or more, significantly more than the 7 percent of the no-program group who reported earnings of this amount (means of $1,219 versus $766, $n = 115$, $p = 0.007$, effect size = 0.51). The difference for males was in better-paying jobs: 42 percent of program males compared with only 6 percent of no-program males reported monthly earnings of $2,000 or more (means of $1,368 versus $830, $n = 68$, $p = 0.035$, effect size = 0.53). The difference for females was in employment rates: 80 percent of program females but only 55 percent of no-program females were employed at the time of the age-twenty-seven interview ($n = 47$, $p = 0.062$, effect size = 0.56). Significantly more of the program group than the no-program group owned their own homes (36 versus 13 percent, $n = 117$, $p = 0.010$, effect size = 0.65) and owned two cars (30 versus 13 percent, $n = 117$, $p = 0.023$, effect size = 0.43). According to welfare assistance records and interviews at age twenty-seven, significantly fewer program group members than no-program group members received welfare assistance as adults (59 versus 80 percent, $n = 123, p = 0.010$, effect size $= 0.44$); "welfare assistance" involved mostly Aid to Families with Dependent Children, Food Stamps, and General Assistance, with a few cases of protective services, Medicaid, and public housing.

Commitment to Marriage

Forty percent of program females, but only 8 percent of no-program females, were married at age twenty-seven ($n = 49, p = 0.036$, effect size $= 0.71$). While 83 percent of the births to no-program females were out of wedlock (forty-three of fifty-two), only 57 percent of the births to program females (twenty-six of forty-six) were out of wedlock ($p = 0.005$). Although the same percentages of program males and no-program males were married (26 percent), the married program males were married an average of 6.2 years, while the married no-program males were married an average of only 3.3 years ($n = 20$, $p = 0.031$, effect size $= 1.01$).

Return on Investment

A benefit-cost analysis, conducted by W. Steven Barnett of Rutgers University, estimated the monetary value of the program and its effects, in constant 1992 dollars discounted annually at 3 percent. Although the analysis included economic benefits to program participants, only the economic benefits to the public, as taxpayers and as potential crime victims, are presented here. The average annual cost of the program was $7,252 per participant; forty-five of the program participants attended for two years and thirteen attended for one year. Thus the discounted, weighted average cost of the program, as shown in figure 5.2, was $12,356 per participant.

Also shown in figure 5.2, the average amount of economic benefits was $88,433 per participant, from the following sources:

- Savings in schooling, due primarily to reduced need for special education services and despite increased college costs for preschool-program participants

- The higher taxes paid by preschool-program participants because they had higher earnings

- Savings in welfare assistance

- Savings to the criminal justice system

Figure 5.2 Return to Taxpayers on Investment per Participant

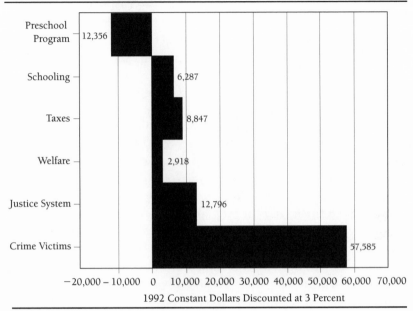

1992 Constant Dollars Discounted at 3 Percent

Source: From Schweinhart and others (1993). Adapted with permission.

- Savings to the potential victims of crimes never committed, based on in-court and out-of-court settlements for such crimes.

The $88,433 in benefits divided by the $12,356 in cost per participant results in a benefit-cost ratio of $7.16 returned to the public for every dollar invested in the High/Scope Perry program. Four-fifths of the economic benefits were due to savings to the criminal justice system and to potential crime victims.

Ignoring the extraordinary financial return on investment—an illogical but nonetheless common thing to do—the $7,252 per child per year seems high compared with what is typically spent on such programs. In 1994 Head Start spent $4,491 per child per year, less than two-thirds as much; and state prekindergarten programs usually spend less than Head Start. Fully 83 percent of the cost per child was due to teaching staff. Teaching staff were paid public school teacher salaries with a 10 percent bonus for their involvement in a special project; and the ratio of teaching staff to children averaged 1 to 5.7. It is reasonable to believe that the ratio could have been increased to one teacher for every eight children with no loss in quality or effectiveness. Had this been done, the cost per child per year would have been reduced to $5,522. Other efficiencies might have reduced the cost still lower. But an "efficiency" is a less expensive way to achieve the same results. Cost-cutting that strips away essentials and does not achieve the same results is false efficiency.

Figure 5.3 depicts a causal model based on the study's data (Schweinhart and others 1993). Statistically significant paths were identified from preschool experience and family socioeconomic status to intellectual performance after one preschool year. Intellectual performance after one preschool year predicted early elementary school motivation; both of them predicted years in programs for educable mental impairment (EMI); intellectual performance after one preschool year and years in EMI programs predicted literacy at age nineteen. Early elementary school motivation also predicted highest year of schooling, which in turn predicted monthly earnings at age twenty-seven and lifetime arrests. This model has three "gateway" variables: intellectual performance after one preschool year, motivation in early elementary school, and highest year of schooling. However, psychological constructs like intellectual performance and motivation are not as time-specific as events like highest year of schooling; they are more like currents in a temporal flow. Thus the immediate "gateway" outcomes of the High/Scope Perry Preschool Program might best be identified as intellectual performance and educational motivation.

DISCUSSION

The High/Scope Perry Preschool Program was a highly successful prevention program. Most prevention programs are designed to prevent a problem just before it happens; for example, almost all high school dropout prevention programs take place in high school. This common approach ignores the likelihood that problems have their roots much earlier in life. To continue with the same example, it is likely that the roots of high school dropout lie in experiences of school failure that begin in the first years of schooling. The rootedness of problems early in life offers an explanation not only for the great success of the High/Scope Perry Preschool Program but also for the relative lack of success of prevention programs that begin later in life, closer to the onset of manifest problems. The causal model depicted in figure 5.3 demonstrates the rootedness of adult status in earlier behavior.

Figure 5.3 A Causal Model of the High/Scope Perry Preschool Project Data

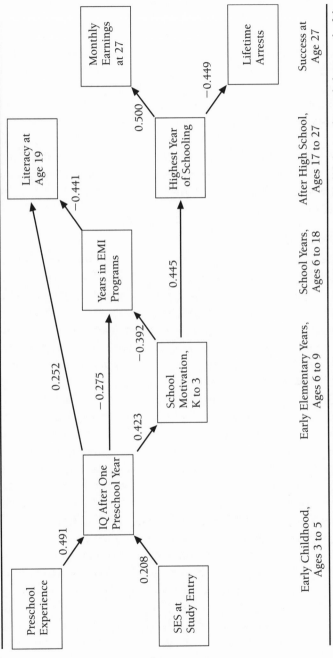

Source: From Schweinhart and others (1993), 190. Reprinted with permission. Each line presents a path of likely causality, with the strength of the association between the two variables represented by the beta weight.

The causal model suggests that both intellectual performance and educational motivation are appropriate objectives for early childhood education. Another reason to identify both intellectual performance and educational motivation as objectives is that identifying one or the other as the exclusive objective can distort early childhood education. A single-minded focus on improving children's intellectual performance ignores their social development and can lead to more cases of emotional disturbance or impairment during schooling, increased misconduct in the teen years, and three times as many felony arrests (Schweinhart, Weikart, and Larner 1986; Schweinhart and Weikart 1997). A single-minded focus on increasing children's motivation in the absence of improvement in performance can lead to a false sense of self-esteem that is not grounded in genuine accomplishment (Sachs 1981).

DEFINING QUALITY

One reasonable approach to replicating its results is to replicate the program just as it has been described in this chapter and elsewhere. Or, one might discard the peripheral elements of the program that are unrelated to long-term effects and focus on the essential elements that are related to long-term effects. It is also reasonable to insist not on perfect replication of those essential elements, but rather on the degree of replication necessary to achieve long-term effects. For example, it is probably peripheral whether classes took place in the morning or in the afternoon, but it is essential that classes met at least part-day, five days a week. It would probably not detract from the effectiveness of the program if classes met full-day or if they met part-day only four days a week. Similarly, as suggested, one teacher could serve eight children rather than the program's average of 5.7 children and still achieve long-term effects. Three general elements of the program are essential to its long-term success: its empowerment of children, parents, and teachers (Schweinhart and Weikart 1993).

The program empowered children by enabling them to initiate, plan, and carry out their own learning activities and thereby to become self-sufficient problem-solvers. This was the key to improving their intellectual performance and educational motivation. They did not merely learn the content of age-four tests; rather they learned how to solve the problems posed on tests in general. Although this problem-solving ability did not extend to permanently improved intellectual performance as measured by intelligence tests beyond age seven, it did extend to better performance on school achievement tests in middle school and literacy tests at the end of the high school years and, indeed, to greater lifetime educational and economic success. Children's accomplishment and their greater ability to solve educational problems strengthened their educational motivation or commitment to schooling. In turn, their commitment to schooling strengthened their subsequent educational and economic achievement.

The program empowered parents by making them full partners with teachers in contributing to their children's development. Through weekly home visits and group meetings, the staff functioned as experts in principles of child development and treated parents as experts on their own children. The staff made it clear to the parents that each child's development and progress in the program were of great importance; and they shared with parents how these activities were carried out in the classroom and showed how to carry them out at home. Weekly home visits have never become a widespread practice in early childhood education, but the Perry program's intensive focus on parents was probably essential to its long-term effectiveness.

The program empowered teachers by giving them full support for the program they were carrying out. They worked as a team to develop the High/Scope curriculum, and they received supervisory support in the implementation of this curriculum approach. They were qualified professionals and were paid public school teacher salaries. The project director, other teachers, and other school administrators respected them as contributing colleagues.

THE IMPORTANCE OF THE EXPERIMENTAL DESIGN

Had it not been for the study's experimental design, the program's long-term effects would not have been unambiguously detected. The scientific methodology of measuring differences in variables is designed to identify quantitative changes that could otherwise be almost undetectable. Program participants had no basis from which to judge the magnitude of the effects or what their lives would have been like if they had not attended the preschool program. It is doubtful that an interviewer, even using the age-twenty-seven questionnaire, could reliably distinguish between the characteristics of those who did and did not attend the preschool program, in the absence of the analytic methodology.

The experimental design gives the study high internal validity, generating considerable scientific confidence that group differences represent genuine program effects. But, because the study focused on 123 participants born in poverty, it is difficult to generalize it to the general population. In addition, the analytic identification of essential program elements means that the study only generalizes to programs that have these essential elements; it is not known how many existing preschool programs qualify. The next steps for early childhood research are to identify the essential characteristics of effective preschool programs and to assess the prevalence of these characteristics among existing programs. To achieve this goal, the U.S. Administration on Children, Youth, and Families has provided five years of funding for four Head Start Quality Research Centers, including one at the High/Scope Foundation.

THE PUBLIC POLICY MANDATE

Meanwhile, the mandate for public policy is to provide high-quality preschool programs for all three- and four-year-old children living in poverty. Existing Head Start and state prekindergarten programs serve only 53 percent of the nation's three- and four-year-olds living in poverty.[2] This is an illogical, unfair public policy—a lottery on whether eligible children receive a public service. In all the proposals for Medicare reform, for example, no one has proposed the draconian approach of serving only every other eligible recipient.

The second part of the mandate is that only high-quality preschool programs should be provided. In accord with this mandate, the Michigan State Board of Education in the late 1980s turned down state legislative funding for state prekindergarten programs until standards for these programs could be developed. But maintaining the quality of preschool programs is a constant struggle, because competing political priorities are pressing policymakers for financial attention.

A current example of such competition is the role of early childhood programs in welfare reform. One of the goals of welfare reform is to require families to transition from welfare to work. Thus welfare reform must assist families in the transition from welfare to work, a goal that generates a need for child care. Yet even as the need for quality in Head Start and state prekindergarten programs is widely acknowledged, there is virtually no recognition of the need for quality in the child care associated with welfare reform. Indeed, because welfare reform is sold as a cost-saving measure, support costs, such as child care, are minimized. The cost-saving goal in welfare reform runs directly counter to the mandate to support high quality in preschool programs for young children living in poverty.

High-quality preschool programs for young children living in poverty are no panacea; but, then, nothing is. These programs can lead to an extraordinary variety of important effects later in life. They are worth doing well for all young children living in poverty. To do less is to shortchange not just our children but ourselves.

NOTES

1. The effect size reported here is the quotient obtained by dividing the difference between the program group mean or percentages and the no-program group mean or percentages by the standard deviation of the whole sample.

2. The Current Population Survey estimated in 1994 that one-fourth of the nation's three- and four-year-olds were living in poverty—an estimated 1,957,000 children. Head Start and state prekindergarten programs served an estimated 1,030,593 children, with Head Start spending 3.3 billion dollars on 740,593 children (U.S. Administration on Children, Youth, and Families 1995) and states spending about $665 million on nearly 290,000 children (assuming the same numbers as in 1991/92; Adams and Sandfort 1994).

REFERENCES

Adams, Gina, and Jodi Sandfort. 1994. *First Steps, Promising Futures: State Prekindergarten Initiatives in the Early 1990s.* Washington, D.C.: Children's Defense Fund.

American College Testing Program. 1976. *User's Guide: Adult APL Survey.* Iowa City, Iowa: American College Testing Program.

Fuerst, J. S., and Dorothy Fuerst. 1993. "Chicago Experience with Early Childhood Program: The Special Case of the Child-Parent Center Programs." *Urban Education* 28(1, April): 69–96.

Gotts, E. E. 1989. *HOPE, Preschool to Graduation: Contributions to Parenting and School-Family Relations Theory and Practice.* Charleston, W. Va.: Appalachia Educational Laboratory.

Hohmann, Mary, Bernard Banet, and David P. Weikart. 1979. *Young Children in Action: A Manual for Preschool Educators.* Ypsilanti, Mich.: High/Scope Press.

Hohmann, Mary, and David P. Weikart. 1995. *Educating Young Children: Active Learning Practices for Preschool and Child Care Programs.* Ypsilanti, Mich.: High/Scope Press.

Lally, J. R., P. L. Mangione, and A. S. Honig. 1988. "The Syracuse University Family Development Research Program: Long-Range Impact of an Early Intervention with Low-Income Children and Their Families." In *Parent Education as Early Childhood Intervention: Emerging Directions in Theory, Research, and Practice,* edited by D. R. Powell. Norwood, N.J.: Ablex.

Monroe, Eleanor, and M. S. McDonald. 1981. "Follow-up Study of the 1966 Head Start Program, Rome City Schools, Rome, Georgia." Unpublished manuscript. Rome, Georgia: Head Start Program, Rome City Schools.

Piaget, Jean, and Barbel Inhelder. 1969. *The Psychology of the Child.* New York: Basic Books.

Sachs, David. 1981. "How to Distinguish Self-Respect from Self-Esteem." *Philosophy and Public Affairs* 10: 346–60.

Schweinhart, Lawrence J., Helen V. Barnes, and David P. Weikart, with W. S. Barnett and A. S. Epstein. 1993. *Significant Benefits: The High/Scope Perry Preschool Study Through Age Twenty-Seven.* Monograph 10 of the High/Scope Educational Research Foundation. Ypsilanti, Mich.: High/Scope Press.

Schweinhart, Lawrence J., and David P. Weikart. 1993. "Success by Empowerment: The High/Scope Perry Preschool Study through Age Twenty-seven." *Young Children* 48(7, November): 54–58.

———. 1997. *Lasting Differences: The High/Scope Preschool Curriculum Comparison Study through Age Twenty-three.* Monograph 12 of the High/Scope Educational Research Foundation. Ypsilanti, Mich.: High/Scope Press.

Schweinhart, Lawrence J., David P. Weikart, and M. B. Larner. 1986. "Consequences of Three Preschool Curriculum Models through Age Fifteen." *Early Childhood Research Quarterly* 1(1): 15–45.

Terman, L. M., and M. A. Merrill. 1960. *Stanford-Binet Intelligence Scale Form L-M: Manual for the Third Revision.* Boston: Houghton-Mifflin.

Tiegs, E. W., and W. W. Clark. 1963. *California Achievement Tests: Complete Battery, 1957 Edition.* Monterey Park: California Test Bureau (McGraw-Hill).

U.S. Administration on Children, Youth, and Families. 1995. *Project Head Start Statistical Fact Sheet.* Washington, D.C.

Weikart, David P., Linda Rogers, Cardyn Adcock, and Donna McClelland. 1971. *The Cognitively Oriented Curriculum: A Framework for Preschool Teachers.* Urbana, Ill.: University of Illinois.

CHAPTER 6

Enhancing the Life Course for High-Risk Children: Results from the Abecedarian Project

*Craig T. Ramey, Frances A. Campbell,
and Clancy Blair*

This chapter describes the lasting effects of an intensive early childhood intervention program on the intellectual development and academic achievement of a sample of African American adolescents born into poverty. The belief that early childhood education can positively influence the life success of poor children goes at least as far back as the eighteenth-century writings of Jean-Jacques Rousseau. Today that belief is manifested through the allocation of more than ten billion state and federal dollars for early childhood programs such as Head Start, Follow Through, and Title I, all initiatives designed to prevent academic failure among children of low-income families.

There can be no doubt that educators and policymakers are facing extremely serious problems of student underachievement. Despite universal free education, too many students from low-income minority families drop out of school unprepared to compete in the workplace (see, for example, Hill and Duncan 1987). African Americans have particularly high dropout rates and are three times more likely than whites to be poor (Duncan 1991). In her book *Children of Color*, Jewell Gibbs noted that, in 1980, nearly one-quarter of African Americans between the ages of eighteen and twenty-one were out of school but had not graduated (Gibbs 1989). Similarly, poverty is associated with an increased likelihood of teenage pregnancy (Sullivan 1993) and of juvenile delinquency and subsequent crime (Garmezy 1985). All these factors perpetuate impoverishment and social pathology.

Experiences very early in the life span are thought to provide a critical foundation for subsequent cognitive development (Hunt 1961; Bloom 1964), but the early environment of the poor or socially disadvantaged child may not support optimal cognitive development

(Scarr 1981). Early educational intervention can potentially enhance cognitive development, leading to a greater transfer of cognitive and academic skills to later settings, such as school (Ceci 1991). Early academic success in school can lead to higher levels of academic confidence and motivation (Zigler and others 1982), which may in turn help to prevent school dropout, leading to better vocational preparation, subsequent higher rates of employment, and ultimately greater economic power and social contribution. Despite this compelling logic, there are few long-term studies of the efficacy of early educational programs, with subjects randomly assigned to treatment and control conditions, and periodic long-term assessments of educational outcomes.

Many analysts have assessed outcomes of the most widespread early childhood program, Project Head Start (Cicirelli 1969; McKey and others 1985); however, Head Start has never been evaluated in a randomized, controlled trial. A meta-analysis of Head Start's benefits indicated that, despite some exceptions, by the end of the second year in public school educationally meaningful differences between Head Start participants and comparison children were no longer apparent (McKey and others 1985). This finding, however, may be spurious due to the poor matching of Head Start children and comparison cases. Another important source of information about the effects of early intervention derives from the Consortium for Longitudinal Studies in which eleven early childhood programs (not Head Start programs) assessed their graduates several years after the programs ended. The consortium found no lasting program effects on intelligence quotient (IQ) scores or academic test performance but did find robust, enduring benefits in the form of fewer retentions in grade, fewer placements into special education, and improved attitudes toward education (Lazar and others 1982).

Also supporting the value of early education, investigators studying long-term outcomes from one of the consortium programs, the Perry Preschool project, found greater educational gains, better employment records, and fewer instances of lawbreaking among nineteen-year-olds who had preschool treatment in their program (Berrueta-Clement and others 1984). Benefits through age twenty-seven have now been reported for Perry Preschool participants in the form of increased rates of high school graduation for females and better records of employment for males (Schweinhart, Barnes, and Weikart 1993).

There are many unanswered questions about the timing, duration, and service delivery models of such programs as well as unanswered questions about program and participant characteristics, and their interactions, as mediators or moderators of intervention effectiveness (Blair and Ramey 1997). Investigation of the effectiveness of early intervention has proceeded beyond questions about overall effectiveness ("did the intervention work—yes or no?") to more specific questions about who does, or does not, do well when receiving intervention services (Guralnick 1997). For example, in its program characteristics, Head Start is neither as intense, in number of hours per day, nor as long-lasting a program as might be provided for poor children. It began as a limited summer program and, even when expanded to the full school year, typically has been provided only for four-year-olds and often for only half days. Similarly, most of the programs included in the Consortium for Longitudinal Studies enrolled youngsters ages two years or older; many began treatment when children were four years or older. More information is needed on the long-term outcomes of scientifically valid, experimental studies of intensive and long-lasting early interventions (Farran 1990; Haskins 1989).

How much might the development of children from economically impoverished backgrounds be enhanced by an intensive program that begins early in the life span? An experimental examination of this question faces formidable barriers because ethical restrictions rightly limit the degree to which human lives are amenable to experimental manipulation. However, the increasing need for out-of-home care for infants permitted the investigators of the Abecedarian Project to design a prospective, longitudinal study to test the efficacy of early educational intervention that is delivered, beginning in early infancy, in an educational child-care setting. This study affords an experimental examination of outcomes from one of the most intensive (in degree of exposure to an educational milieu) early childhood educational programs ever provided for children of poor families.

Long-term cognitive and academic benefits of the Abecedarian Program across study participants' first ten years in school are the focus of this chapter. The results at the end of the preschool phase (Ramey and Campbell 1984; Ramey, Yeates, and Short 1984) and at time points during the elementary school years (Ramey and Campbell 1991; Campbell and Ramey 1994, 1995) have been reported in detail elsewhere and are summarized briefly here.

THE ABECEDARIAN PROJECT

Based on cross-sectional data, progressively lower intellectual test scores have been found as age increases among children being reared in poverty (Garber 1988). The intent of the Abecedarian Project was to test the degree to which continual, consistent enrichment of the early environment might alter this negative trend toward developmental retardation and also reduce subsequent academic failure in such children. The project's outcomes were evaluated within a multidisciplinary framework that included measures of cognitive functioning, social development, and health.

The target subjects were biologically healthy infants born to impoverished families living in a generally affluent southern college town of about fifty thousand people. The children were considered at high risk for suboptimal cognitive development based on thirteen family demographic characteristics and psychological risk indicators. Selection of participants was based on a High-Risk Index score derived from factors reported in the literature to be related to lower levels of intellectual functioning or academic failure (Ramey and Smith 1977). The thirteen factors included maternal and paternal educational levels, family income, absence of the father from the home, poor social or family support for the mother, indications that older siblings had academic problems, the receipt of welfare, parents working at unskilled jobs, indications of low parental IQ, family members seeking counseling, and other evidence of a need for support from community agencies. The greatest weight was given to parental educational levels and income. Families scoring above a predetermined cut point on this index were eligible to participate in the study.

Eligible children ($n = 111$) were identified typically during the last three months of pregnancy, using the Ramey and Smith High-Risk Index, and were assigned randomly shortly after birth to one of two experimental conditions. In the preschool control condition, children received developmental and pediatric surveillance, treatment, or referral, if necessary, and nutritional supplements; their families received family support services from social workers. These services were provided because the goal was to test the efficacy of the educational component of the intervention. The control participants received intervention services that were more intensive than those offered by many of today's early intervention programs, which makes the test of group differences a very conservative one.

In the preschool early intervention condition, these same services were provided *and* the children received a systematic early childhood educational program beginning at six weeks of age and lasting until they were enrolled in public kindergarten. Just before entering kindergarten, the early intervention and control groups each were divided randomly into two groups, and half of each original preschool group received a special Home-School Resource Program for the first three years of public school. Figure 6.1 presents the experimental design of the Abecedarian study showing the two phases of treatment and the two follow-up studies that have been completed to date. Overall, this study can be conceptualized as a 2 × 2 factorial design as indicated in figure 6.2. The 2 × 2 design contrasts outcomes in children with and without preschool as one factor and with or without home and school resource intervention as the second factor. The random assignment of children to the various treatment conditions is a very important feature of this study because it potentially permits robust causal inferences with respect to group differences as a function of treatment.

Table 6.1 gives family characteristics of the base sample. There were fifty-nine females and fifty-two males in the base sample, of whom fifty-seven (fifty-five families) were assigned to the early intervention treatment group and fifty-four (fifty-four families) were assigned to the early intervention control group. These children were admitted in four yearly cohorts of approximately twenty-eight children each year, with half of each group assigned to the educational intervention group and the other half assigned to the control group. As table 6.1 indicates, the families in the early intervention treatment and control groups were closely matched with respect to mean levels of maternal education, mean maternal IQ, maternal age, and percentage of single-parent households.

Over the years, subject attrition was low. Eighteen of the original 111 children were attrition cases, with fifteen lost during the preschool years and three thereafter. Thus ninety-three children could be properly placed in one of the four treatment cells and were eligible to enter the analysis of long-term benefits. The eighteen subjects lost to attrition did not differ significantly from the others on any entry-level demographic characteristics.

Figure 6.1 Design of Abecedarian Project

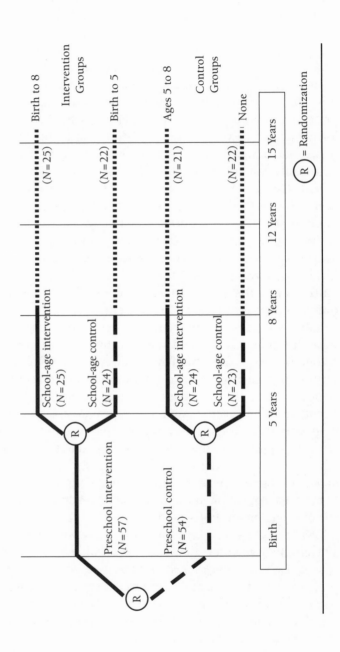

Figure 6.2 Experimental Conditions of the Abecedarian Project

Early Elementary School Intervention

		Yes	No
Preschool Intervention	Yes	Birth to Age 8	Birth to Age 5
	No	Age 5 to 8	No Educational Intervention

RESULTS

Figure 6.3 plots the mean IQ performance of intervention and control group participants at twelve, twenty-four, thirty-six, and forty-eight months of age.[1] The two groups did not differ at twelve months but did differ by an average of fifteen points at two, three, and four years of age. The function of the early intervention as evidenced in figure 6.3 was to prevent an IQ decline that occurred between one and two years of age in the control group.

Figure 6.4 shows the persistence of the preschool intervention's positive effect through fifteen years of age as well as the lack of impact of the school-age intervention on IQ performance. Thus, this

Table 6.1 Entry-Level Demographic Data for Preschool Experimental and Control Families

Variable	Experimental Group ($n = 55$)	Control Group ($n = 54$)	Total ($n = 109$)
Mean high-risk index	20.08 (5.72)	21.14 (5.88)	20.75 (5.81)
Mean maternal age	19.56 (3.88)	20.28 (5.77)	19.94 (4.89)
Mean maternal education	10.45 (1.75)	10.00 (1.89)	10.23 (1.83)
Mean maternal IQ	85.49 (12.43)	84.18 (10.78)	84.84 (11.61)
Female-headed family (%)	78	65	72
African American (%)	96	100	98

Note: Numbers in parentheses are standard deviations.

Figure 6.3 Bayley Mental Development Index (MDI) and Stanford Binet IQ at Twelve, Twenty-Four, Thirty-Six, and Forty-Eight Months of Age for Abecedarian Children

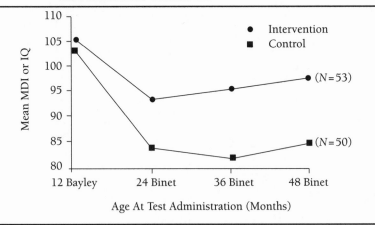

early intervention has been demonstrated to produce immediate and long-lasting positive effects on IQ performance.

ACADEMIC OUTCOMES

Figure 6.5 shows age-referenced standard scores for the Woodcock-Johnson Reading Cluster at three ages: eight, twelve, and fifteen years. At age eight the reading scores of the four groups were proportional

Figure 6.4 Full-Scale Wechsler IQ at Three Ages

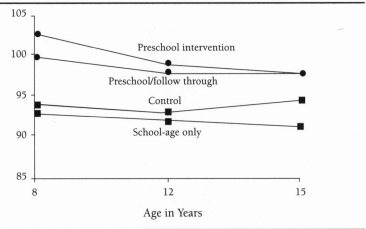

Figure 6.5 Woodcock-Johnson Reading Scores,
        Abecedarian Project

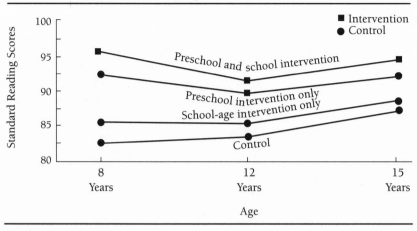

to the length of the intervention they received. Analyzed longitudinally, there was a main effect only for preschool intervention. The results for mathematics, graphed in figure 6.6, paralleled those for reading. Longitudinal analysis of mathematics standard scores also showed a significant main effect for preschool intervention relative to controls. There was no time x group interaction, implying that the

Figure 6.6 Woodcock-Johnson Mathematics Scores,
        Abecedarian Project

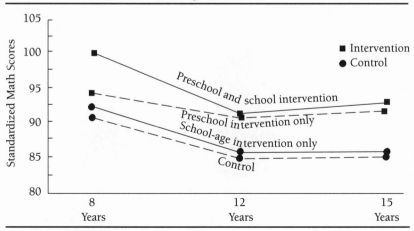

Preschool treatment $F (1,81) = 4.75, P < 0.04$

groups were parallel in their performance across time. In other words, the developmental advantage conferred by participation in the early intervention program persisted at a measurable level in both reading and mathematics.

SCHOOL PROGRESS

At age fifteen, there were differences in negative indexes of school progress (retention in grade or use of special education) as a function of early intervention. Through ten years in school, children who had the Abecedarian preschool treatment made better progress in school—fewer retentions in grade and fewer assignments to special education programs—than children in the preschool control group. Overall 31.2 percent of the early intervention group children were retained in grade by age fifteen compared with 54.5 percent of the preschool control group (figure 6.7).

Assignment to special education also showed a significant, positive difference related to preschool treatment. Overall, 24.5 percent of early intervention children were placed in special education compared with 47.7 percent of preschool control group children (figure 6.8).

DISCUSSION

The mid-adolescent cognitive and academic benefits associated with the Abecedarian preschool program represent the most durable positive effects of an early childhood educational program reported in the

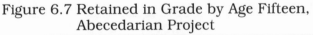
Figure 6.7 Retained in Grade by Age Fifteen, Abecedarian Project

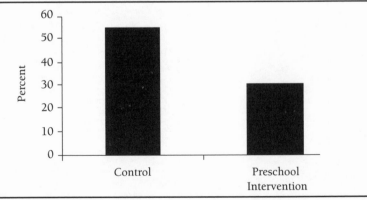

Figure 6.8 Placement in Special Education, Abecedarian Project, Age Fifteen

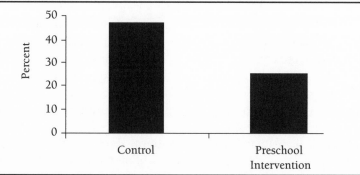

literature on early intervention. Because assignment to treatment and control conditions was random, it is plausible to conclude that the early educational treatment was responsible for the benefits found. The results generalize directly to African Americans because almost all the Abecedarian subjects were of that ethnic background. This heightens their importance because educational discouragement appears to be an especially serious problem for African American children (Alexander and Entwisle 1988). As this chapter shows, early failure among this population can be significantly reduced with an intensive preschool program.

Comparing academic test scores across the four Abecedarian treatment groups indicates that the preschool treatment was more strongly associated with improvement in academic achievement than was the later school-age intervention. Although inspection of the means suggests that, for reading test scores, a modest, long-lasting benefit was associated with having school-age treatment added to preschool experience, there was no evidence that the school-age program boosted mathematics performance above the level of gain associated with preschool treatment alone. For subjects not treated in preschool, the school-age program alone did not produce lasting improvement in reading or mathematics. The slight advantage in academic scores shown at age eight by the group who were preschool controls but who received the school-age intervention compared with the group who served as controls at both time points was not seen at age twelve or fifteen.

We cannot interpret with certainty all the reasons why five years of preschool education in a day-care setting produced larger and more enduring effects than did three years of school and family-mediated intervention during the primary grades because the design does not permit the effects of duration, timing, or modality of treatment to be disentangled definitively. The design unavoidably confounds duration (eight versus five versus three years), timing (infancy and early childhood versus the primary school years), and treatment delivery models (direct teaching of the child versus parent-mediated home activities) such that it is impossible to know for certain what factors were responsible for the stronger influence of preschool treatment on intellectual and academic outcomes. There are logical suppositions, however. If the primary factor were simply *duration of treatment*, then the group receiving both early and school-age intervention should outscore all others at all points from age eight onward. They did not do so, except in the case of reading. Neither IQ scores nor mathematics scores showed any advantage for students who received both school-age and preschool intervention. In contrast, there was always a strong academic advantage for students treated in the preschool years over those lacking such treatment and, to a lesser extent, also an advantage in IQ scores. Thus the data support the conclusion that five years of preschool are almost equally as effective at enhancing child IQ and academic achievement as five years of preschool with a three-year follow-through, and they are definitely more effective than intervention offered only from age five to eight. The Abecedarian outcomes may be interpreted as supporting the principle labeled by Kessen (1979) as the "primacy of early experience" because the results suggest that educational intervention early in the life span has a greater impact than experiences provided later.

COMPARISON WITH OTHER LONG-TERM STUDIES

It is of interest to compare the Abecedarian outcomes with those of similar early childhood programs. Two previous programs are of particular relevance: the Milwaukee Project (Garber 1988) and the High/Scope Perry Preschool Program (Schweinhart and Weikart 1980). All three programs were experiments in which children were assigned randomly to treatment and control conditions. All three programs treated children from economically disadvantaged families, primarily African American, but their selection criteria varied somewhat. The Milwaukee study sample was limited to children born to mothers with very low IQs (less than seventy-five); the Perry Preschool project enrolled children age three or four years, with three-year IQs between seventy and eighty-five points; the Abecedarian study used a weighted combination of scores reflecting family sociodemographic factors to determine eligibility. Also, the programs in which children were enrolled varied. The Perry Preschool provided a half-day center-based educational program for children ages three to five, with family visits in the afternoons. The Milwaukee and Abecedarian programs provided child-focused, full-day educational intervention within a day-care/preschool setting, from infancy through age five. The Milwaukee Project continued its educational program through the children's kindergarten year. In contrast, the two phases of the Abecedarian design involved staggered ages of entry (infancy or age five) and termination of treatment (age five or eight). Mid-adolescent intellectual and academic outcomes are available for all three programs, although the academic data from Milwaukee have not been published yet.

Table 6.2 contains means for mid-adolescent IQ scores reported by all three intervention studies. The Milwaukee and Abecedarian programs appear to have had a more enduring impact on the intellectual test performance of treated individuals than did the Perry Preschool project. Subjects treated in the Perry Preschool no longer showed a significant IQ advantage over controls by age seven. The groups differed by only one IQ point at age fourteen. In contrast, the children treated in the Milwaukee study consistently outscored controls through age fourteen. At that time, the last occasion for which scores are available, they maintained a ten-point IQ advantage over the Milwaukee controls. Abecedarian children treated in preschool also outscored controls through age fifteen, but not as dramatically. To provide a more comparable contrast between the Milwaukee and Abecedarian studies, the treatment/control difference in IQ was calculated for Abecedarian participants born to mothers with very low IQs. Thirteen of the Abecedarian mothers had IQ scores of seventy points or below. When mean IQ scores are compared for the twelve of these Abecedarian subjects (six in the preschool treatment group, six in the preschool control group) for whom age-fifteen child IQ data are available, the preschool treatment/control difference was 11.7 IQ points, very comparable to the age-fourteen Milwaukee treatment/control IQ difference.

Both the Abecedarian study and the Perry Preschool project obtained California Achievement Test (CAT) percentile scores for academic achievement in reading, mathematics, and language at eighth

Table 6.2 Adolescent Mean Intellectual Test Scores
for the Abecedarian, Milwaukee, and Perry
Preschool Early Educational Programs
and Academic Test Scores for the Abecedarian
and Perry Preschool Programs

Program	Treated Group	Control Group
Mean IQ score		
Abecedarian[a]	94.98	90.34
Perry Preschool[b]	81.02	80.71
Milwaukee[b]	101.06	91.13
California Achievement Test (range of percentile scores)		
Abecedarian	38–41	28–30
Perry Preschool	15–17	< 10

[a] Based on the Wechsler Intelligence Scale for Children-Revised (WISC-R).
[b] Based on the Wechsler Intelligence Scale for Children (WISC).

grade. Abecedarian children earned higher average scores than did the Perry Preschool project subjects: CAT percentile scores ranged between thirty-eight and forty-one for Abecedarian preschool experimental subjects, scores for the preschool controls were between the twenty-eighth and thirtieth percentile. In contrast, subjects treated in the Perry Preschool project earned academic achievement scores between the fifteenth and seventeenth percentiles, and their controls earned scores below the tenth percentile (L. J. Schweinhart, personal communication, May 1993). Thus for the Abecedarian and Perry Preschool studies, statistically significant academic benefits related to preschool programs were maintained into adolescence, long after treatment had ended. The Milwaukee study reportedly found no treatment/control differences in academic performance by seven years in school (H. Garber, personal communication, June 1992).

Even if one concedes that intervention in early childhood had a more powerful effect, it is still necessary to explain why mid-adolescent academic test scores and indexes of progress through school (or of failing to made satisfactory progress) still showed positive effects from an intervention that happened so many years earlier. The most parsimonious explanation appears to be that the early cognitive gains reflected in higher preschool IQ scores were associated with greater mastery of academics from the start, which led, in turn, to better performance thereafter. At least, through age fifteen, early mastery continued to be associated with higher scores on tests of reading and mathematics. There does appear to be support for the suggestion of Zigler and others (1982) that early academic success is associated with continued success. It does not appear to depend entirely on continued enhancement of IQ. In this study, IQ differences were less pronounced at age fifteen than were academic benefits, and the Perry Preschool study found mid-adolescent academic benefits in the absence of any demonstration of lasting IQ benefits.

Woodhead (1988) has speculated that, even in the absence of enduring differences in IQ or achievement tests, early intervention may change the psychosocial functioning of treated children, leading teachers to perceive the children in more positive ways and influencing the teachers' decisions to nominate a child for grade retention or assignment to special classes. In the Abecedarian study, there were both academic test score benefits and indexes of enhanced school progress (that is, fewer instances of retention or special education placement for students treated in preschool). The latter Abecedarian finding is consistent with the report by the Consortium for Longitudinal Studies of better school progress for students with preschool treatment (Lazar and others 1982). To what extent might teacher perceptions of the children or attitudes toward the Abecedarian program have played a role in enhancing the school progress of the Abecedarian students?

The attitudes of elementary schoolteachers toward the Abecedarian preschool program may have influenced their perceptions of its graduates, but there is little evidence on this point. The elementary school teachers did know which children had participated in the Abecedarian preschool study because they were asked to rate the children's classroom behavior and also to permit observations of target students in their classrooms. However, it is not clear that teachers could distinguish between children who had been treated in preschool and those who had not, because all of the study participants had the same sorts of data collected within the schools. Teachers whose pupils had the school-age phase of treatment were very much aware of it, because regular meetings between the classroom teacher and the home/school-resource teacher were essential to development of the supplemental curricula for the program.

The most pertinent data that exist relative to teacher perceptions of the students consist of teacher ratings of classroom adaptation made in the first three years of school. At that time, early elementary teachers showed a tendency to rate verbal intelligence higher for children with greater amounts of treatment (Ramey and Campbell 1991). However, there is also evidence that children treated in the preschool were not necessarily seen as better behaved (Haskins 1985). We therefore conclude that the elementary schoolteachers had no consistently positive bias toward these children, as a group.

Clearly, other factors in the homes, schools, and communities were involved in the lives of the Abecedarian students and students from the other pertinent studies, and these factors influenced outcomes in mid-adolescence. Speculatively, the twenty children treated in Milwaukee faced the worst odds in later life, given the intellectual limitations of their mothers and the urban ghetto communities in which they were reared. Despite better IQ test performance, they did not retain an academic advantage in their ghetto school environments and home environment in which parental support for learning was perhaps weak. Perhaps the Abecedarian and Perry Preschool students had somewhat more supportive educational settings across this time span, or their families were better able to facilitate their progress, or both. Of the three studies, the Abecedarian population was most heterogeneous with respect to initial ability levels of both parent and child, which could account for the higher academic test scores earned by its adolescent participants relative to those earned by participants in the Perry Preschool study.

POLICY IMPLICATIONS

The long-term results from the Abecedarian Project underscore the need for high-quality learning environments for impoverished infants, toddlers, and preschoolers. This study demonstrates that if such children are given high-quality educational experiences during the preschool years, their academic performance and school progress may be significantly enhanced through middle adolescence. The untreated control group of children, reared within their natural ecology, had high rates of academic failure, as reflected in more grade retentions and more assignments to special education. These outcomes are based on a sample of students almost entirely African American in ethnicity, but they may generalize more broadly. The program's essential elements were applied in the Infant Health and Development Program provided for almost one thousand low-birthweight children at eight sites nationwide. The large sample of infants was ethnically much more heterogeneous than the Abecedarian sample, having large numbers of whites and Hispanics as well as African Americans. Results through age three were comparable to those for Abecedarian subjects, for all but the lowest birthweight infants (Infant Health and Development Program 1990; Ramey and others 1992).

Some of the children in the Abecedarian control group were cared for at home by their mothers; others were cared for by relatives, some attended other early childhood programs. Within the preschool control group, exposure to preschool has been shown to facilitate cognitive development (Burchinal, Lee, and Ramey 1989).

Although the Abecedarian program involved parents in a number of ways, each child also received, in addition, consistent, individualized teaching over a period of years. Parents living in poverty face a number of problems that can interfere with their ability to optimize their children's development (McLoyd 1990). Although it certainly cannot replace parents, nor does it in any way minimize their importance, a high-quality preschool program can support and supplement parental efforts.

Based on the present results, the value of providing *only* a supplemental program in the primary grades of public school appears doubtful, being, by itself, not associated with enhanced academic outcomes. Even though it is easier to provide supplemental services for children once they are in school, those who plan interventions for poor children should be aware that elementary school programs may have less impact on the children's academic performance than would programs begun earlier in the life span. However, mean scores for reading were higher in students who had school-age treatment added to preschool treatment. Further research needs to be conducted on the interaction between school-age treatment and child and family factors to learn how they may potentiate one another.

Finally, a word must be said about the cost of the program. Based on a cost study conducted by the Early Childhood Research Institute of Utah State University, the average yearly cost of the Abecedarian preschool program was about six thousand dollars. Approximately 80 percent of those costs were attributable to personnel. Thus, although not inexpensive, the costs are reasonably consistent with current public school costs in a typical school system. Clearly, the Perry Preschool project has already demonstrated the cost-effectiveness of preschool intervention. We are currently planning a parallel cost analysis as soon as our follow-up at age twenty-one (which is under way) is completed.

CONCLUSIONS

The present study has shown, in a controlled, randomized trial, that substantially improved academic performance is possible for economically disadvantaged African American children. Extrapolating from long-term outcomes of the Perry Preschool project, it is our hope that the benefits found through mid-adolescence in our sample will eventually be reflected in better life circumstances in adulthood.

This research was supported by grants from the National Institute of Child Health and Human Development, the U. S. Department of Education, and the Administration for Children, Youth, and Families. We wish to express our thanks to the adolescents and their families who devoted so much time to this research effort. Without their cooperation, this study would not have been possible.

NOTE

1. All differences reported are significant at $p \le 0.05$ by appropriate statistical test. Details of the analyses can be found in Campbell and Ramey (1995).

REFERENCES

Alexander, K. L., and D. R. Entwisle. 1988. "Achievement in the First Two Years of School: Patterns and Processes." *Monographs of the Society for Research in Child Development* 53(2).

Berrueta-Clement, John R., Lawrence J. Schweinhart, W. S. Barnett, A. S. Epstein, and David P. Weikart. 1984. *Changed Lives: The Effects of the Perry Preschool Program on Youths through Age Nineteen.* Monograph 8 of the High/Scope Educational Research Foundation. Ypsilanti, Mich.: High/Scope Press.

Blair, Clancy, and Craig T. Ramey. 1997. "Early Intervention for Low Birthweight Infants and the Path to Second-Generation Research." In *The Effectiveness of Early Intervention: Directions for Second-Generation Research,* edited by M. J. Guralnick. Baltimore, Md.: Brookes.

Bloom, B. S. 1964. *Stability and Change in Human Characteristics.* New York: Wiley and Sons.

Burchinal, Margaret, Marvin Lee, and Craig T. Ramey. 1989. "Type of Day Care and Preschool Intellectual Development in Disadvantaged Children." *Child Development* 60(1): 128–37.

Campbell, Frances A., and Craig T. Ramey. 1994. "Effects of Early Intervention on Intellectual and Academic Achievement: A Follow-up Study of Children from Low-Income Families." *Child Development* 65(2): 684–98.

———. 1995. "Cognitive and School Outcomes for High-Risk African American Students at Middle Adolescence: Positive Effects of Early Intervention." *American Educational Research Journal* 32(4): 743–72.

Ceci, S. J. 1991. "How Much Does Schooling Influence General Intelligence and Its Cognitive Components? A Reassessment of the Evidence." *Developmental Psychology* 27(5): 703–22.

Cicirelli, V. G. 1969. *The Impact of Head Start: An Evaluation of the Effects of Head Start on Children's Cognitive and Affective Development.* Athens, Ohio: Westinghouse Learning Corporation.

Duncan, G. J. 1991. "The Economic Environment of Childhood." In *Children in Poverty: Child Development and Public Policy,* edited by Aletha C. Houston. New York: Cambridge University Press.

Farran, D. C. 1990. "Effects of Intervention with Disadvantaged and Disabled Children: A Decade Review." In *Handbook of Early Childhood Intervention,* edited by S. J. Meisels and J. P. Shonkoff. New York: Cambridge University Press.

Garber, H. L. 1988. *The Milwaukee Project: Preventing Mental Retardation in Children at Risk.* Washington, D.C.: American Association on Mental Retardation.

Garmezy, Norman. 1985. "Stress-Resistant Children: The Search for Protective Factors." In *Recent Research in Developmental Psychopathology,* edited by J. E. Stevenson. Oxford, England: Pergamon Press.

Gibbs, Jewell T. 1989. "Black American Adolescents." In *Children of Color: Psychological Interventions with Minority Youth,* edited by J. T. Gibbs, L. N. Huang, and Associates. San Francisco: Jossey-Bass.

Guralnick, M. J. 1997. *The Effectiveness of Early Intervention: Directions for Second Generation Research.* Baltimore, Md.: Brookes.

Haskins, Ron. 1985. "Public School Aggression among Children with Varying Day-Care Experience." *Child Development* 56(3): 689–703.

———. 1989. "Beyond Metaphor: The Efficacy of Early Childhood Education." *American Psychologist* 44(2): 274–82.

Hill, M. S., and G. J. Duncan. 1987. "Parental Family Income and the Socioeconomic Attainment of Children." *Social Science Research* 16(1): 39–73.

Horacek, H. J., Craig T. Ramey, Frances A. Campbell, K. P. Hoffmann, and R. H. Fletcher. 1987. "Predicting School Failure and Assessing Early Intervention with High-Risk Children." *American Academy of Child and Adolescent Psychiatry* 26(5): 758–63.

Hunt, J. McV. 1961. *Intelligence and Experience*. New York: Ronald Press Company.

Infant Health and Development Program. 1990. "Enhancing the Outcomes of Low-Birthweight, Premature Infants: A Multisite, Randomized Trial." *Journal of the American Medical Association* 263(22): 3035–42.

Kessen, William. 1979. "The American Child and Other Cultural Inventions." *American Psychologist* 34(10): 815–20.

Lazar, Irving, Richard Darlington, H. Murray, Jacqueline Royce, and Ann Snipper. 1982. "Lasting Effects of Early Education: A Report from the Consortium for Longitudinal Studies." *Monographs of the Society for Research in Child Development* 47(2–3, serial 195).

McKey, R. H., Larry Condelli, H. Ganson, B. J. Barrett, C. McConkey, and M. C. Plantz. 1985. *The Impact of Head Start on Children, Families, and Communities*. Department of Health and Human Services Publication OHDS 90-31193. Washington: U.S. Government Printing Office.

McLoyd, V. C. 1990. "The Impact of Economic Hardship on Black Families and Children: Psychological Distress, Parenting, and Socioemotional Development." *Child Development* 61(2): 311–46.

Ramey, Craig T., D. M. Bryant, Barbara H. Wasik, Joseph J. Sparling, K. H. Fendt, and L. M. LaVange. 1992. "Infant Health and Development Program for Low Birthweight, Premature Infants: Program Elements, Family Participation, and Child Intelligence." *Pediatrics* 89(3): 454–65.

Ramey, Craig T., and Frances A. Campbell. 1984. "Preventive Education for High-Risk Children: Cognitive Consequences of the Carolina Abecedarian Project." *American Journal of Mental Deficiency* 88(5): 515–23.

———. 1991. "Poverty, Early Childhood Education, and Academic Competence: The Abecedarian Experiment." In *Children Reared in Poverty*, edited by Aletha C. Huston. New York: Cambridge University Press.

Ramey, Craig T., K. O. Yeates, and E. J. Short. 1984. "The Plasticity of Intellectual Development: Insights from Preventive Intervention." *Child Development* 55(5): 1913–25.

Ramey, Craig T., and B. J. Smith. 1977. "Assessing the Intellectual Consequences of Early Intervention with High-Risk Infants." *American Journal of Mental Deficiency* 81(4): 319–24.

Scarr, Sandra. 1981. "Race, Social Class, and IQ." In *Race, Social Class, and Individual Differences in IQ*, edited by Sandra Scarr. Hillsdale, N.J.: Erlbaum.

Schweinhart, Lawrence J., H. V. Barnes, and David P. Weikart. 1993. "Significant Benefits: The High/Scope Perry Preschool Study through Age Twenty-seven." Monograph 10 of the High/Scope Educational Research Foundation. Ypsilanti, Mich.: High/Scope Press.

Schweinhart, Lawrence J., and David P. Weikart. 1980. "Young Children Grow up: The Effects of the Perry Preschool Program on Youths through Age Fifteen." Monograph 7 of the High/Scope Educational Research Foundation. Ypsilanti, Mich.: High/Scope Press.

Sullivan, M. L. 1993. "Culture and Class as Determinants of Out-of-Wedlock Childbearing and Poverty During Late Adolescence." *Journal of Research on Adolescence* 3(3): 295–316.

Woodhead, Martin. 1988. "When Psychology Informs Public Policy: The Case of Early Childhood Intervention." *American Psychologist* 43(6): 443–54.

Zigler, Edward, W. D. Abelson, P. K. Trickett, and Victoria Seitz. 1982. "Is an Intervention Program Necessary in Order to Improve Economically Disadvantaged Children's IQ Scores?" *Child Development* 53(2): 340–48.

CHAPTER 7

The Special Supplemental Nutrition Program for Women, Infants, and Children

Barbara Devaney

The Special Supplemental Nutrition Program for Women, Infants, and Children (WIC) provides supplemental foods, nutrition education, and health care and social service referrals to low-income pregnant, breast-feeding, and postpartum women, to infants, and to children up to age five who are at nutritional risk. The WIC program is based on the assumption that insufficient nutrition during the critical growth and development periods of pregnancy, infancy, and early childhood places many low-income individuals at risk of adverse nutrition and health outcomes. The WIC program is a supplemental food and nutrition program to help meet the special needs of low-income women, infants, and children during these periods.

The WIC program has been the focus of numerous and varied evaluations. In general, these studies have shown the effectiveness of participation in WIC, especially for pregnant women and infants (Batten, Hirschman, and Thomas 1990). This chapter presents detailed findings from one of these evaluations—the WIC-Medicaid Study (Devaney, Bilheimer, and Schore 1990, 1991)—and summarizes findings from other studies of the WIC program. The chapter describes the WIC program, presents findings from the WIC-Medicaid Study, and discusses the broader literature on the effectiveness of the WIC program.

THE WIC PROGRAM

The purpose of the WIC program is "to provide supplemental nutritious food as an adjunct to good health care during such critical times of growth and development in order to prevent the occurrence of health problems and improve the health status of these persons" (Public Law 95-627). WIC eligibility depends on three criteria: (a) categorical status as a pregnant, breast-feeding, or postpartum woman, an infant, or a child under age five; (b) income less than or equal to 185 percent of the poverty level (or adjunct eligibility through participation in the Medicaid program); and (c) evidence of nutrition risk. Categorical status is based on the importance of nutrition during the special periods of pregnancy, infancy, and early childhood. Income eligibility standards are based on evidence linking low income to poor nutrition and adverse health outcomes. The WIC program's nutrition-risk criteria are intended to target low-income individuals who either already have poor outcomes or are at the greatest risk of poor outcomes.

The WIC program is a comprehensive supplemental food and nutrition program providing three main benefits to participants: (a) supplemental foods, (b) nutrition education, and (c) referrals to health care and social service providers. Supplemental food is provided in the form of a "food instrument" (voucher or check) that can be exchanged for certain foods. The food instrument lists the quantities of specific foods, including brand names, that can be purchased with the instrument. WIC food packages consist of iron-fortified formula for infants, milk, cheese, eggs, iron-fortified adult and infant cereals, fruit and vegetable juices rich in vitamin C, dried peas or beans, and peanut butter. These foods target special nutrients lacking in the diets of low-income individuals—protein, vitamins A and C, calcium, and iron. By law, 80 percent of WIC funds must be spent on food. Supplemental foods are intended to improve the nutritional status of pregnant women, which, in turn, is expected to improve pregnancy outcomes and enhance the nutritional status of both mother and infant. Food supplements are also expected to reduce the prevalence of iron-deficiency anemia and to improve physical and mental growth and development of infants and children.

The WIC program also provides nutrition education that focuses on the relationship between nutrition and good health, assists individuals at nutritional risk to make positive changes in their food habits, and considers ethnic, cultural, and geographic preferences for food. Local WIC agencies must spend at least one-sixth of WIC administrative funds on nutrition education and counseling. At least two nutrition education sessions must be provided in each six-month certification period. However, participants cannot be denied food supplements if they do not attend the education sessions.

The WIC program also promotes good health care by referring participants to health care providers. WIC providers must advise clients about the types of health care available, the location of accessible facilities, the process of receiving health care, and the reasons why health care is useful; however, WIC funds cannot be used directly to provide health care to participants. For pregnant women, the health care referral system is expected to increase their use of prenatal and postpartum care; for breast-feeding and postpartum women, infants, and children, the WIC program promotes the use of routine preventive care as well as other health care services, such as immunization, family planning, smoking cessation, and substance abuse counseling and treatment.

The WIC program has become a major component of an ongoing effort to improve maternal and child health outcomes. Nationwide, the WIC program has grown from a 725 million dollar program serving 1.9 million women and children in fiscal year 1980 to a 3.5 billion dollar program serving an average of 6.9 million women and children per month in fiscal year 1995.

WIC-MEDICAID STUDY

The WIC-Medicaid Study was mandated by the WIC Amendments of 1987 and the Joint Resolution Continuing Appropriation for fiscal 1988. Its primary objective was to determine the savings in Medicaid costs during the first sixty days after birth for newborns and mothers due to participation in the WIC program during pregnancy. The secondary objective was to examine the effects of prenatal participation in the WIC program on two important birth outcomes—birthweight and gestational age.

The WIC-Medicaid Study entailed analyses of the relationship between Medicaid costs and prenatal WIC participation in five states: Florida, Minnesota, North Carolina, South Carolina, and Texas. The study period included all Medicaid births in 1987 for Florida, Minnesota, North Carolina, and South Carolina and all Medicaid births from January through June 1988 in Texas.

Table 7.1 provides background information on the five study states. Although only five states were included in the study, the selected states accounted for 18 percent of *all* U.S. births in 1987. Overall, the five states also provide striking contrasts in birth outcomes and peri-

Table 7.1 Birth Outcomes and Perinatal Risk Factors: United States and Study States, Various Years, 1980s

Indicator	United States	Florida	Minnesota	North Carolina	South Carolina	Texas
Total births, 1987	3,809,394	175,144	65,173	93,501	52,801	301,962
Infant mortality rate, 1987[a]	10.1	10.6	8.7	11.9	12.7	9.1
Percent low birthweight, 1987[b]	6.9	7.7	5.0	7.9	8.6	6.9
Percent of women ages fifteen through forty-four below poverty thresholds, 1984 to 1986						
<100 percent	15.2	15.4	11.4	14.0	17.3	15.2
<150 percent	24.3	26.8	19.4	24.2	29.4	25.5
<185 percent	31.0	34.4	25.0	32.3	37.6	33.1
Percent of births to teenagers, 1986	12.6	13.8	7.3	15.9	16.6	15.2
Percent of births to women receiving late or no prenatal care, 1986	6.0	8.6	3.8	4.6	8.1	11.5

Sources: National Center for Health Statistics 1988, 1989; Newacheck 1988; Hughes and others 1989.
[a] Number of infant deaths per 1,000 live births.
[b] Birthweight of less than 2,500 grams.

natal risk factors. Minnesota in 1987 had a lower proportion of low-income women and had birth outcomes that were more favorable than the other study states. The infant mortality rate, the percentage of low birthweight infants, the percentage of births to teenagers, and the percentage receiving late or no prenatal care in Minnesota were the lowest of the five states and were lower than the rates for the nation as a whole. At the other extreme, all of the three southeastern states had infant mortality rates and percentages of births to teenagers that were greater than the national average. In Texas the infant mortality rate was below the U.S. average, although the percentage of women receiving late or no prenatal care was considerably higher than the national average and was the highest of the five study states.

The WIC-Medicaid Study had three key components:

- Creating a database in each of the study states by combining information on Medicaid costs, prenatal WIC participation and costs, and birth outcomes

- Determining the savings in Medicaid costs due to prenatal WIC participation using statistical analysis

- Assessing the implications of the study findings for the states not included in the study and for recent changes in the WIC and Medicaid programs.

Each of these is discussed in turn.

DATABASE CONSTRUCTION

One of the key analytic challenges in this study was to construct a database with information on Medicaid costs from birth to sixty days after birth and on prenatal WIC participation. The database designed for this study had four major purposes: (a) to identify Medicaid newborns born in 1987 (the first six months of 1988 in Texas) and women with Medicaid claims for labor and delivery in 1987, (b) to provide information on Medicaid costs from birth to sixty days after birth, (c) to determine whether the mother participated in the WIC program while she was pregnant, and (d) to provide information on birth outcomes and descriptive data on the characteristics of WIC participants and nonparticipants.

The WIC-Medicaid database was constructed from Medicaid eligibility and claims files, Vital Records birth files, and WIC program files. To create the database, the information on Medicaid costs, birth outcomes, WIC participation and costs, and characteristics of Medicaid mothers and newborns was combined for each Medicaid birth in the study period. Four basic steps were used to link and combine the data files:

- *Internal Medicaid Linkage*   In this step, Medicaid newborns were linked to Medicaid mothers to create mother-newborn Medicaid birth records.

- *Medicaid to Vital Records*   Medicaid birth records were then linked to the Vital Records birth files to yield data on birth outcome and on both newborn and maternal characteristics (sex, race, age of mother, use of prenatal care).

- *Internal WIC Linkage*   WIC mothers and participating WIC newborns were linked mainly to obtain more information on WIC mothers (date of birth in particular).

- *Medicaid/Vital Records to WIC Linkage*   Medicaid births that were linked to Vital Records births were then linked to the WIC files to determine if the mother was a prenatal WIC participant.

The data linkage process for the WIC-Medicaid Study identified 111,958 Medicaid-covered births, ranging from just over 12,000 in Minnesota to just under 38,000 in Florida. Because the analysis relied heavily on data included in the birth files and because the U.S. birth registration system is very complete, only those Medicaid births that were linked to the Vital Records birth certificates were included in the final sample. With the exception of South Carolina, more than 93 percent of all Medicaid births identified in each state were linked with the Vital Records birth files. In South Carolina, 86 percent of Medicaid-covered births were linked with Vital Records.

The percentage in South Carolina was lower than in the other states for two reasons: (a) birth certificates for South Carolina residents giving birth in other states were not available; and (b) less identifying information from the Medicaid files was available in South Carolina than in the other four states. In all states, descriptive analyses of the cases deleted from the database indicated that deleted cases did not differ systematically from cases that were retained.

Table 7.2 shows the number of Medicaid births in each of the study states. Overall, the WIC Medicaid database included nearly 105,000

Table 7.2 Descriptive Data on Medicaid Births: Number of Births, Average Medicaid Costs, and Birthweight

Indicator	Florida	Minnesota	North Carolina	South Carolina	Texas
Medicaid births	35,558	11,592	20,441	11,641	25,472
To WIC participants	20,476	7,977	14,039	8,543	12,180
To nonparticipants	15,082	3,615	6,402	3,098	13,292
Percent WIC participants	57.6	68.8	68.7	73.4	47.8
Average Medicaid costs (U.S. dollars)[a]					
Newborns	—	—	1,733	—	1,867
Newborns and mothers	2,569	3,822	2,743	2,433[b]	3,248
Average birthweight (grams)	3,181	3,295	3,143	3,103	3,191
Percent low birthweight[c]	11.7	8.6	12.8	12.9	10.7

— Not available.

Source: WIC/Medicaid database for Florida, Minnesota, North Carolina, South Carolina, and Texas.

Notes: Medicaid births include all Medicaid mothers and newborns who were matched with a Vital Records birth certificate.

[a] Includes Medicaid costs from birth to sixty days after birth. Excludes births with costs less than or equal to $200.

[b] Includes hospital costs only.

[c] Birthweight of less than 2,500 grams (5.5 pounds).

Medicaid births. The proportion of these births to WIC participants varied across the study states, ranging from nearly half of the Medicaid births in Texas to almost three-quarters of the Medicaid births in South Carolina. Average Medicaid costs from birth to sixty days after birth for Medicaid newborns and mothers ranged from a low of $2,433 in South Carolina (hospital costs only) to $3,822 in Minnesota. The percentage of low-birthweight newborns was highest in North Carolina and South Carolina (12.8 and 12.9 percent) and lowest in Minnesota (8.6 percent).

It is important to realize that the study population consisted of a very low-income group of women and that the socioeconomic characteristics of the study populations in the five states were not comparable during the study period. At the two extremes, Minnesota was covering pregnant women whose incomes were up to 88 percent of the poverty level ($7,969 for a family of three), whereas Texas was covering only pregnant women whose incomes were up to 33 percent of the poverty level ($2,988 for a family of three). In Florida, North Carolina, and South Carolina, income eligibility changed from below 50 percent of the poverty level in the first quarters of the study year to 100 percent of the poverty level in the last quarter of the year. However, because expansions of eligibility typically require a considerable start-up period, the full impact of this change probably was not felt until 1988. Thus the Medicaid mothers and newborns in this study were very poor, with incomes well below the WIC income eligibility limit of 185 percent of poverty.

ANALYSIS FINDINGS

The basic analytic approach for measuring the differences in birth outcomes and savings in Medicaid costs attributable to the WIC program was to compare the birth outcomes and Medicaid costs of WIC participants with those of a comparison group. The comparison group used in this study consisted of a group of Medicaid mothers, who did not participate in the WIC program during pregnancy (nonparticipants), and their newborns. Such a comparison group is critical for providing information on what the birth outcomes and Medicaid costs for prenatal WIC participants would have been in the absence of WIC program. Multiple regression analysis provided estimates of the effects of prenatal WIC participation, after controlling for observed differences between WIC participants and nonparticipants that also may affect birth outcomes and Medicaid costs.

PRENATAL CARE

The differences between WIC participants and nonparticipants in the percentage of Medicaid mothers receiving inadequate levels of prenatal care are striking, as shown in table 7.3. In all five states, Medicaid mothers who did not participate in the WIC program were approximately two to three times more likely to have received inadequate prenatal care as WIC participants. Overall, 9.6 percent of the WIC participants in the five study states received inadequate levels of prenatal care, in contrast to 22.4 percent of nonparticipants. WIC participants were also much less likely than nonparticipants to have received no prenatal care at all.

MEDICAID COSTS

The principal finding from the analysis of Medicaid costs is that prenatal WIC participation is associated with substantial savings in Medicaid costs during the first sixty days after birth. In all five states, average predicted Medicaid costs from birth to sixty days after birth for women who did not participate in the WIC program exceeded predicted Medicaid costs for women who did participate. The difference between the predicted Medicaid costs with and without the WIC program is the estimated Medicaid cost savings, which are presented in table 7.4. Prenatal participation in the WIC program is associated with reductions in Medicaid costs for mothers and newborns combined that ranged from $277 in Minnesota to $598 in North Carolina, with intermediate values of $347, $493, and $565 in Florida, Texas, and South Carolina (hospital costs only), respectively.

In North Carolina and Texas, the only two states in which maternal and newborn Medicaid costs could be separated, the estimated savings in Medicaid costs for newborns due to prenatal WIC participation were even greater than the estimated savings in Medicaid costs for mothers and newborns combined. Specifically, estimated savings in newborn Medicaid costs from birth through sixty days were $744 in North Carolina and $573 in Texas. This finding reflects two phenomena: (a) high health care costs after birth are usually associated with high-cost newborns rather than mothers, and (b) some very

Table 7.3 Prenatal Care of Medicaid Mothers

Indicator	Florida WIC Participants	Florida Non-participants	Minnesota WIC Participants	Minnesota Non-participants	North Carolina WIC Participants	North Carolina Non-participants	South Carolina WIC Participants	South Carolina Non-participants	Texas WIC Participants	Texas Non-participants
Kessner Index										
Adequate	40.1	32.5	42.9	36.1	51.9	40.3	33.7	25.4	34.8	26.9
Intermediate	47.9	41.2	35.5	32.8	41.0	38.7	51.0	44.2	42.8	40.5
Inadequate	9.1	22.6	7.8	14.6	4.9	18.2	13.6	28.0	14.2	25.0
Unknown	3.0	3.7	13.8	16.6	2.1	2.8	1.6	2.4	8.1	7.7
Mean number of prenatal visits	10.3	8.3	9.8	8.7	11.2	9.2	8.9	7.1	9.1	7.7
Prenatal visits(%)										
0 visits	1.7	11.1	0.9	4.3	0.5	8.4	1.3	10.2	3.2	9.3
1–2 visits	2.5	5.4	1.9	4.2	1.4	5.6	4.0	8.4	4.2	7.1
3–6 visits	14.7	17.4	14.3	16.1	11.1	15.3	22.6	26.5	20.8	24.1
7–10 visits	39.7	36.3	33.1	30.0	27.6	24.9	37.7	30.5	35.5	30.8
11–12 visits	15.5	12.1	19.6	16.7	26.8	22.3	17.0	12.0	14.5	11.7
13 visits or more	24.9	16.6	17.2	13.1	32.4	23.1	16.3	10.9	18.0	13.3
Unknown	1.0	1.2	13.0	15.6	0.2	0.4	1.1	1.6	4.4	3.8
Number of Medicaid births	20,476	15,082	7,977	3,615	14,039	6,402	8,543	3,098	12,180	13,292
Percent of total	57.6	42.4	68.8	31.2	68.7	31.3	73.4	26.6	47.8	52.2

Source: WIC/Medicaid database for Florida, Minnesota, North Carolina, South Carolina, and Texas.

[a] The Kessner Index, as modified by the National Center for Health Statistics, combines information on the timing of entry into prenatal care with the number of visits recorded and the length of the pregnancy gestation. Thus, for example, for a full-term pregnancy, adequate prenatal care is defined as nine or more visits, with the first visit occurring during the first trimester of pregnancy, and inadequate care is defined as four or fewer visits. Intermediate care for a full-term pregnancy encompasses all levels of prenatal care between the two extremes. Adequate prenatal care for preterm births (births of less then thirty-seven weeks of gestational age) requires a decreasing number of visits as the length of gestation decreases.

Table 7.4 Savings in Medicaid Costs from Birth to Sixty
Days After Birth Associated with Prenatal
Participation in the WIC Program (U.S. Dollars)

| State and Group | Average Medicaid Costs | | Estimated Savings in Medicaid Costs[a] |
	With WIC Program	Without WIC Program	
Florida			
Newborns and mothers	2,341	2,688	347
Minnesota			
Newborns and mothers	3,733	4,010	277
North Carolina			
Newborns	1,425	2,169	744
Newborns and mothers	2,395	2,993	598
South Carolina[b]			
Newborns and mothers	2,288	2,853	565
Texas			
Newborns	1,567	2,140	573
Newborns and mothers	2,991	3,484	493

Source: WIC/Medicaid database for Florida, Minnesota, North Carolina, South Carolina, and Texas.
Notes: Medicaid costs are from birth to sixty days after birth. Births with costs less than or equal to two hundred dollars are excluded. Complete sets of regression estimates are available from the author.
[a] All estimated savings in Medicaid costs are statistically significant at the 0.01 level (two-tailed test), except in Minnesota where the estimate is statistically significant at the 0.07 level (two-tailed test) and at the 0.03 level (one-tailed test).
[b] Medicaid costs refer to hospital costs only.

high-cost newborns, whose mothers were not eligible for Medicaid during pregnancy, became eligible for Medicaid due to their high costs.

Table 7.5 presents ratios of the estimated savings in Medicaid costs per dollar of WIC program costs—the cost of the WIC supplemental food benefits plus an adjustment for administrative and nutrition education expenses. All ratios are greater than one, suggesting that the savings in Medicaid costs from birth to sixty days after birth exceed the costs of providing prenatal WIC benefits. For newborns and mothers, these estimates range from 1.77 in Florida to 3.13 in North Carolina, with values of 1.83 for Minnesota and 2.44 for both South Carolina and Texas. For newborns only, the benefit-cost estimates are 3.90 in North Carolina and 2.84 in Texas. Thus for every dollar spent on the prenatal WIC program, the associated savings in Medicaid costs during the first sixty days after birth

Table 7.5 Estimated Ratios of Savings in Medicaid Costs
to Prenatal WIC Costs (U.S. Dollars Unless
Otherwise Noted)

State and Group	Estimated Savings in Medicaid Costs[a]	Estimated Prenatal WIC Costs per Participant	Estimated Ratio of Savings to WIC Costs[b]
Florida			
Newborns and mothers	347	196	1.77
Minnesota			
Newborns and mothers	277	151	1.83
North Carolina			
Newborns	744	191	3.90
Newborns and mothers	598	191	3.13
South Carolina[c]			
Newborns and mothers	565	232	2.44
Texas			
Newborns	573	202	2.84
Newborns and mothers	493	202	2.44

Source: WIC/Medicaid database for Florida, Minnesota, North Carolina, South Carolina, and Texas.
[a] Medicaid costs are from birth to sixty days after birth. Births with costs less than or equal to two hundred dollars are excluded.
[b] All estimates are statistically significant at the 0.01 level (two-tailed test), except in Minnesota where the estimate is statistically significant at the 0.07 level (two-tailed test) and at the 0.03 level (one-tailed test).
[c] Medicaid costs refer to hospital costs only.

range from $1.77 to $3.13 for newborns and mothers and from $2.84 to $3.90 for newborns only.

An important caveat to these findings is that the estimated savings in Medicaid costs associated with prenatal WIC participation are *not* independent of any unmeasured or unobserved differences between WIC participants and nonparticipants that may also influence birth outcomes and Medicaid costs. WIC participants are a self-selected group of women who may choose to participate in the WIC program for underlying reasons that may lead independently to lower Medicaid costs. For example, some pregnant women may not participate in the WIC program because they lack access to public health programs, which may affect pregnancy outcomes. Thus the estimated savings in Medicaid costs related to WIC participation may overestimate the true savings because, relative to nonparticipants, WIC participants would have lower Medicaid costs even in the absence of the WIC program. Conversely, if the WIC program reaches high-risk, low-income pregnant women, WIC participants may be more likely to have higher-cost pregnancy outcomes than nonparticipants, and the estimated savings presented in this chapter would underestimate the true savings associated with prenatal WIC participation.

The problem introduced by self-selection may not be especially severe because (a) the adequacy of prenatal care is also likely to be related to any such underlying differences between WIC participants and nonparticipants, and (b) the analysis was able to adjust the estimated savings in Medicaid costs associated with prenatal participation for the adequacy of care. The potential implications of the self-selection issue, however, should be kept in mind when the study results are interpreted and generalized.

BIRTH OUTCOMES

Prenatal WIC participation by Medicaid recipients is also associated with increased birthweight and a lower incidence of low birthweight (births of infants who weigh less than 2,500 grams, or 5.5 pounds), as shown in table 7.6. The average increase in birthweight ranged from 51 grams in Minnesota to 73 and 77 grams in Florida and Texas, to 113 and 117 grams in South Carolina and North Carolina, respectively. Similarly, the reduction in the percentage of women who gave birth to low-birthweight newborns ranged from 2.2 percentage points in Minnesota to 5.1 percentage points in North Carolina and South Carolina. Prenatal WIC participation is also associated with increases in gestational age and reduced incidence of preterm births (births at less than thirty-seven weeks gestation).

In general, the pattern of the estimated effects of prenatal WIC participation on birthweight is consistent with the explanation that relatively heavier babies have relatively lower-cost births. The smallest effects on birthweight and Medicaid costs were observed in Minnesota, while the largest effects for birthweight and costs were observed in North Carolina and South Carolina.

GENERALIZATION OF STUDY RESULTS

The results of the WIC-Medicaid Study indicate that prenatal WIC participation improves birth outcomes and generates savings in Medicaid costs. What inferences can be drawn from these state-specific results about the nation as a whole? How stable are these conclusions over time?

Table 7.6 Estimated Effects of WIC Participation on Birthweight and Gestational Age

State and Indicator	Birthweight (Grams)[a]	Incidence of Low Birthweight (Percent)[b]	Gestational Age (Weeks)[a]	Incidence of Preterm Births (Percent)[b,c]
Florida				
With WIC program	3,225	9.5	39.6	11.8
Without WIC program	3,152	12.8	39.2	15.3
Estimated effect of WIC participation	73	−3.3	0.4	−3.5
Minnesota				
With WIC program	3,312	7.8	39.3	10.4
Without WIC program	3,261	10.0	39.1	12.7
Estimated effect of WIC participation	51	−2.2	0.2	−2.3
North Carolina				
With WIC program	3,179	11.1	39.6	13.2
Without WIC program	3,062	16.2	38.8	18.6
Estimated effect of WIC participation	117	−5.1	0.8	−5.4
South Carolina				
With WIC program	3,134	11.7	39.3	13.9
Without WIC program	3,021	16.8	38.7	20.2
Estimated effect of WIC participation	113	−5.1	0.6	−6.3
Texas				
With WIC program	3,231	8.8	39.5	11.5
Without WIC program	3,154	12.2	39.1	15.7
Estimated effect of WIC participation	77	−3.4	0.4	−4.2

Source: WIC/Medicaid database for Florida, Minnesota, North Carolina, South Carolina, and Texas.
Notes: Complete sets of regression estimates are available from the author. All estimated effects are statistically significant at the 0.01 level, except the effect on birth-weight for full-term births in Minnesota.
[a] Estimated with ordinary least squares regression.
[b] Estimated with probit analysis.
[c] Preterm births are those with a gestational age of less than thirty-seven weeks.

Important differences among the study states and changes in the program have occurred since the study period and are likely to influence the extent to which the findings can be generalized. In particular, Medicaid expansions for pregnant women and infants, in conjunction with increased coordination between the WIC and Medicaid programs, mean that a higher-income group of women is likely to participate in the WIC program. If prenatal WIC participation is more beneficial for lower-income women, then the benefits of prenatal WIC participation observed in 1987 may be greater than under the current Medicaid income-eligibility standards for pregnant women and infants, which range between 133 and 185 percent of poverty. However, the fact that the benefits of prenatal WIC participation by Medicaid beneficiaries were so clearly demonstrated in all five study states, with all their population and program differences, suggests that a nationwide study of the effects of prenatal WIC participation among Medicaid mothers would show improved birth outcomes for WIC participants.

STUDIES OF THE EFFECTS OF WIC ON INFANTS AND CHILDREN

In contrast to a large body of literature examining the effects of prenatal WIC participation, few studies focus on the effects of participation on infants and children. Nevertheless, some studies report positive effects of WIC participation, especially among infants. Data from the Pediatric Nutrition Surveillance System indicate that the prevalence of anemia among low-income children decreased during the 1980s, a finding attributed largely to improvements in iron nutrition status and to the effects of the WIC program (Yip and others 1987, 1992). In the National WIC Evaluation, Rush and others (1988) found significant effects of WIC participation on children's weight among children who had entered the WIC program in utero or within three months after birth. However, no change in weight was found in children who were more than three months of age when entering the program. Similar long-term benefits of WIC participation in utero on children's weight and height were found in an earlier evaluation by Hicks, Langham, and Takenaka (1982). Children's intake of iron, vitamin C, thiamin, niacin, and vitamin B6 was improved if they participated in the WIC program (Rush and others 1988). In addition, WIC participation is positively related to the proportion of infants and children with a regular source of health care and to the proportion of infants and children receiving some vaccinations (Paige 1983; Rush and others 1988).

SUMMARY

Overall, research evaluating the effectiveness of the WIC program shows positive effects for at-risk participants. The bulk of the literature has examined prenatal WIC participation and suggests that birth outcomes and reductions in Medicaid costs improve immediately after birth. Fewer studies have examined the effects of WIC participation by infants and children. These studies, however, have demonstrated some positive effects, especially reduced incidence of iron-deficiency anemia. Furthermore, results from several studies suggest that WIC participation may be associated with regular use of health care services and that children participating in WIC may be more likely than other low-income children to receive some form of immunization against disease.

REFERENCES

Batten, S., Jay Hirschman, and Denise Thomas. 1990. "Impact of the Special Supplemental Food Program on Infants." *Journal of Pediatrics* 117(2, pt. 2, August): S101–S109.

Devaney, Barbara, Linda Bilheimer, and Jennifer Schore. 1990. *The Savings in Medicaid Costs for Newborns and Their Mothers from Prenatal Participation in the WIC Program.* Vol. 1. Washington, D.C.: U.S. Department of Agriculture, Food and Nutrition Service, Office of Analysis and Evaluation. October.

———. 1991. *The Savings in Medicaid Costs for Newborns and Their Mothers from Prenatal Participation in the WIC Program.* Vol. 2. Washington, D.C.: U.S. Department of Agriculture, Food and Nutrition Service, Office of Analysis and Evaluation. April.

Hicks, Lou, Rose Langham, and Jean Takenaka. 1982. "Cognitive and Health Measures Following Early Nutritional Supplementation: A Sibling Study." *American Journal of Public Health* 72(10): 1110–18.

Hughes, Dana, Kay Johnson, Sara Rosenbaum, and Joseph Liu. 1989. *The Health of America's Children: Maternal and Child Data Book.* Washington, D.C.: Children's Defense Fund.

National Center for Health Statistics. 1988. "Advance Report of Final Mortality Statistics, 1986." *Monthly Vital Statistics Report (supplement)* 37(6, September), DHHS Publication PHS 88-1120, Hyattsville, Md.: Public Health Service.

————. 1989. "Advance Report of Final Natality Statistics, 1987." *Monthly Vital Statistics Report (supplement)* 38(3), Hyattsville, Md.: Public Health Service.

Newacheck, Paul. 1988. *Estimating Medicaid-Eligible Pregnant Women and Children Living below 185 Percent of Poverty.* Washington, D.C.: National Governor's Association.

Paige, David. 1983. *Evaluation of the WIC Program on the Eastern Shore of Maryland.* Baltimore, Md.: School of Hygiene and Public Health, Johns Hopkins University. May.

Rush, David, Jessica Leighton, Nancy Sloan, and others. 1988. "The National WIC Evaluation: Evaluation of the Special Supplemental Food Program for Women, Infants, and Children. Study of Infants and Children." *American Journal of Clinical Nutrition (supplement)* 48 (2, August): 484–511.

Yip, Ray, Nancy Binkin, Lee Fleshood, and Frederick Trowbridge. 1987. "Declining Prevalence of Anemia among Low-Income Children in the United States." *Journal of the American Medical Association* 258(12): 1619–23.

Yip, Ray, Ibrahim Parvanta, Kelley Scanlon, Ellen Borland, Carl Russell, and Frederick Trowbridge. 1992. "Pediatric Nutrition Surveillance System— United States, 1980–1991." *Morbidity and Mortality Weekly Report* 41(SS-7): 1–24.

CHAPTER 8

Preventing Adolescent Substance Abuse: Lessons from the Project ALERT Program

Phyllis L. Ellickson

During the late 1970s and early 1980s, illicit drug use rose so alarmingly that the Reagan Administration declared a "war on drugs." Many schools and communities instituted programs aimed at preventing teen drug use, and the late 1980s saw a significant decline, as efforts to delay or reduce drug use made impressive inroads. In the last six years, however, the gains began slipping away. The University of Michigan Survey Research Center recently released the results of its twenty-second national survey of American secondary-school students (Press release, University of Michigan, "The Rise in Drug Use among American Teens Continues in 1996," December 19, 1996). Those results indicate that both cigarette smoking and use of illicit drugs rose again in 1996, continuing a trend that began in 1991 among eighth graders and in 1992 among tenth and twelfth graders.

Although these results raise all the old and legitimate concerns about the immediate and long-term effects of teen substance abuse, one of the survey's directors saw cause for optimism: "While these levels of illicit drug use are certainly cause for concern . . . they are still well below the peak levels attained in the late 1970s. We are in a relapse period in the longer-term epidemic, if you will, but it is certainly not something over which society is powerless. Our great progress in the past at lowering rates of illicit drug use among our young people is proof of that" (Press release, University of Michigan, "The Rise in Drug Use among American Teens Continues in 1996," December 19, 1996).

One of the most rigorously designed and evaluated of the programs aimed at preventing drug use was the RAND's Project ALERT. Based on the "social influence" model, this program successfully prevented or reduced the use of cigarettes and marijuana among a diverse sample of seventh and eighth graders. The study followed this sample for six years, from the program's inception through the twelfth grade, with a low attrition rate. This chapter describes the lessons that Project ALERT has to teach about what kind of program can effectively curb substance abuse, for whom it is effective, and how long program benefits last with and without reinforcement.[1]

IMPETUS AND OBJECTIVES OF PROJECT ALERT

Project ALERT started with a question. In the early 1980s, the Hilton Foundation came to RAND and asked what a private foundation might do to help mitigate the problem of drug use among young people. RAND undertook a comprehensive eighteen-month assessment of the strategies employed in the United States to address the problem: law enforcement, treatment, and prevention. Our study team asked what was known about the patterns and antecedents of drug use, the kinds of strategies that had been used, and the effectiveness of these strategies (Polich and others 1984).

The major conclusion was that prevention held the greatest hope of making further inroads into the problem and that the most promising prevention approach was based on the social influence model. Several U.S. and Canadian universities had used that model in anti-smoking programs, which had achieved some success in delaying the initiation of smoking among teenagers (Evans and others 1979; Flay and others 1983; Murray and others 1984; Perry and others 1980). But no one knew if that approach would work with other substances. We suggested that investigating the possibilities might have a high payoff. Subsequently, the Hilton Foundation asked RAND to develop and test a prevention curriculum designed for the "gateway" drugs—alcohol, cigarettes, and marijuana.

The study aimed to answer several questions:

- Does a prevention program based on the social influence model curb the use of alcohol and marijuana as effectively as it curbs cigarette smoking?

- Is it equally effective in diverse school settings?

- Is it effective for both nonusers and adolescents who had experimented with the drugs before they were in the program?

- Is the program more effective if teen leaders assist teachers?

- Do booster sessions reinforce program effects and limit their erosion?

AIMS AND ASSUMPTIONS OF THE PROGRAM

Our primary aims for the Project ALERT program were (a) to keep those who were nonusers before the program from starting or using the drugs frequently and (b) to reduce or prevent frequent or regular use by those who were already experimenters and users. In developing the Project ALERT curriculum, we addressed several questions that are important for understanding the nature of the program.

First, what substances should receive the most attention? We focused on alcohol, cigarettes, and marijuana because these are the drugs of choice among adolescents and because each of them has serious health, safety, and developmental effects. Cigarettes and alcohol are responsible for more deaths in the United States than all other drugs combined (Rice 1993; U.S. Office on Smoking and Health 1990). Tobacco's highly addictive properties heighten the risk that early use will result in long-term exposure to its harmful effects, while drinking increases the likelihood that young people will engage in other high-risk activities such as unprotected sex, drinking and driving, or violent behavior. Chronic marijuana use has been linked with dropping out, delinquency, and difficulties in performing adult roles (Elliott, Huizinga, and Ageton 1985; Kandel and others 1986; Newcomb and Bentler 1988).

In addition, these three substances are "gateway" drugs: Research shows that young people are unlikely to try marijuana unless they have tried cigarettes and alcohol first and even less likely to try hard drugs unless they have used marijuana (Huba, Wingard, and Bentler 1981; Kandel and Faust 1975; Ellickson, Hays, and Bell 1992). Thus keeping them from starting to use these drugs may have a double payoff.

Second, why is the social influence model particularly promising? Early drug prevention programs focused largely on providing information about drugs or improving children's general skills in communication, decisionmaking, and the clarification of values. Both proved ineffective (Goodstadt 1978; Schaps and others 1986; Tobler 1986).

The first ignored research that documented the difficulty of changing behavior through knowledge alone; the second failed to link general skills with specific drug situations. Both approaches failed to counter the major reason for beginning drug use—the influence of others who use drugs or approve of drug use.

The anti-smoking programs, in contrast, viewed cigarette use as a social phenomenon—a response to the pro-smoking messages and examples presented by peers, adults, and the media. To counter these influences, the programs sought to help young people identify the pressures to use, counter arguments aimed at making them smoke, and learn to say "no" when directly offered cigarettes. They also tried to reinforce group norms against smoking and dispel beliefs that smoking is widespread, desirable, and harmless. Given adolescents' tendency to dismiss long-term health threats, the programs emphasized the negative effects that smoking has *now*, in their daily lives and social relationships.

Behavioral research supported the assumptions and the likely promise of the social influence model for more general drug prevention efforts. Adolescents typically start using cigarettes, alcohol, and marijuana in a group setting, among their friends or relatives (Orive and Gerard 1980; Friedman, Lichtenstein, and Biglan 1985). Before that, they have usually been around peers and family members who use these substances or approve of their use (Huba and Bentler 1984; Kandel, Kessler, and Margulies 1978). Because most teenagers want to look grown-up and independent, those who see drug use as an adult behavior are inclined to try it (Jessor, Chase, and Donovan 1980).

Third, when is the optimum time to offer drug prevention programs based on the social influence model? We assumed that the best time is before students start experimenting with or using drugs regularly, but when they are feeling the first heavy pressures to start. National data for the 1980s indicated that adolescents are particularly vulnerable to these pressures during the middle or junior high school years. Current use of cigarettes and marijuana was still quite low (2 percent or less) at ages twelve or thirteen. But both jumped sevenfold or more by the time students entered high school (ages fourteen to fifteen), and alcohol use nearly quadrupled (National Institute of Drug Abuse 1991. Moreover, grades eight and nine are peak years for antisocial behaviors like using drugs (Berndt 1979). This information argued for starting prevention by grade seven or earlier.[2]

Another consideration is the cognitive and developmental readiness of the student population. Most seventh graders have just made the transition that prepares them, socially and experientially, to learn resistance skills. They have left the more sheltered environment of the elementary school, are beginning to make decisions on their own, and are broadening their network of friends and acquaintances—and thus their exposure to peer pressure. They also have a stronger cognitive base for understanding difficult concepts like internal pressure (Ellickson and Robyn 1987). Based on all these considerations, we chose grade seven as the best time to offer Project ALERT.[3]

A RIGOROUS, EXPERIMENTAL DESIGN

Because we set out to design a rigorous, experimental test of a drug prevention program based on the social influence model, we needed to recruit schools from diverse community environments—not just the middle-class, homogeneous, largely white schools that had been the settings for most of the anti-smoking research. From a roster of all school districts in California and Oregon, we signed up thirty schools in eight districts from northern and southern California and northern, central, and southern Oregon. These eight districts encompassed urban, suburban, and rural communities. Nine of the thirty schools had a minority population of 50 percent or more, and eighteen drew from neighborhoods with a median income below the state median.

This diversity meant that Project ALERT would not be tested in wholly "favorable" or "unfavorable" settings. In the study schools, we could assess how well the curriculum worked with students from urban and rural communities, as well as suburban ones, and with students from homes with diverse racial and ethnic backgrounds and diverse income levels.

Another objective was to conduct an experimental test, to come as close to a clinical trial as is possible in a real-world environment. In practice, this meant randomly assigning schools to three experimental conditions: two treatment groups and one control. These procedures produced substantial pretreatment equivalence in student- and school-level characteristics potentially related to future drug use (Ellickson and Bell 1990).

In the twenty treatment schools, all students in the seventh grade received the same drug prevention program, but it varied in delivery. In ten of the schools, adults (teachers) taught the lessons. In the other ten, older teens from neighboring high schools assisted the teachers.

The ten control schools did not offer the Project ALERT curriculum but had the option of continuing to offer whatever traditional drug information or programs they might have (only four did so). The control schools served as the benchmark for measuring the curriculum's effect.

We varied the method of program delivery in order to find out whether including older teens would make the drug prevention program more effective. Older teens, who are close in age and experience to younger teenagers, are widely thought to outperform adults as credible communicators and attractive role models. Moreover, several of the early anti-smoking programs reported better results for students in peer-led versus teacher-led conditions (Botvin 1987; Murray and others 1989; Perry and Grant 1988). We chose older teens rather than same-age peers because the former have more experience in coping with social pressure. As role models for successful nonuse, their primary function was to provide personal examples of effective resistance and to help students believe that they, too, could successfully resist drugs.

CURRICULUM DESIGN AND COSTS

The original Project ALERT curriculum was comprised of eleven lessons. Eight were given in seventh grade, followed by three booster sessions in the eighth grade.[4]

Given the social influence approach, the curriculum was designed (a) to increase students' motivation to resist drugs and (b) to give them the skills they need to translate that motivation into effective resistance. To increase motivation, the curriculum focuses on helping students understand how drug use can affect their daily lives and social relationships. It also seeks to change norms about drug use— to help students recognize that most people are not drug users and that their peers might actually respect them for resisting pro-drug pressures.

To teach resistance skills, the curriculum has students role-play how to resist in different pressure situations, write down (and then discuss) how they could successfully respond to specific internal and external pressures, and watch videos of older teens coping with similar pressures. Because internal pressures are subtle and often difficult for young people to identify, the curriculum places particular emphasis on helping them recognize pressure that "comes from inside yourself"—as well as the more obvious external pressures from the media and from parents, peers, siblings, and others who use drugs.

Two theories heavily influenced curriculum design, the health be-lief model and the self-efficacy theory of behavioral change (Becker 1974; Bandura 1977). The former guided our emphasis on the per-sonal consequences of drug use (such as losing control, "ash-tray breath") and the adolescent's susceptibility to those consequences (many of these bad things can happen right away). It also influenced curriculum activities aimed at increasing the perceived benefits of nonuse and reducing the barriers to resisting drugs (for example, the inability to identify pro-drug pressures and beliefs that most people use or that resistance will not be successful).

Bandura's work on self-efficacy influenced our belief that "how you teach is as important as what you teach." The curriculum employs teaching strategies designed to enhance the belief that one can success-fully resist pro-drug pressures: *modeling* of the desired behavior by oth-ers (older teens in the classroom or on video); *active participation and performance accomplishment* through role playing, small group discus-sions, and question and answer exercises; and *reinforcement* for suc-cessful performance (verbal persuasion). Because they are so interactive, these methods allow teachers to adjust the program's content to diverse classrooms with different levels of information and exposure to drugs.

The expanded version of Project ALERT (eleven lessons plus three booster lessons) is made available through the BEST Foundation, which provides the curriculum and a one-day training for $85 per teacher.[5] If one teacher delivers the program to six classrooms of twenty-five stu-dents each, the cost per student for the two-year curriculum (including hiring a substitute for the training day) is about $1.50. If a different teacher delivers the program to each classroom, the cost per student is about $9.20 or $4.60 per year. These calculations assume that the teacher would be presenting some kind of drug prevention or health ed-ucation in the absence of Project ALERT; hence we do not include op-portunity costs for diverting resources from academic subjects.

RESEARCH DESIGN AND METHODS

The RAND team surveyed some sixty-five hundred seventh graders in 1984 to establish baseline conditions and measures before the pro-gram began. We conducted six follow-up surveys with nearly four thousand of these students over the next five years. The surveys com-pared students' drug use and related attitudes before, during, and after they participated in the lessons with similar data from the students in the control schools. The surveys were taken before and after the seventh-grade lessons, before and after the eighth-grade boosters, and once each during grades nine, ten, and twelve.

Figure 8.1 provides a drug use profile of the seventh graders before they entered the program. It indicates that the prospects for preventing *initiation* were limited from the beginning, particularly for alcohol. Although only 20 percent of the students had already tried marijuana, 75 percent had tried alcohol, and almost 50 percent had tried cigarettes. However, for the goal of curbing the transition to more regular use, the baseline prevention potential was more equal across the three target substances. The nonuser and experimenter groups accounted for 70 percent of the sample for alcohol, 80 percent for cigarettes, and 90 percent for marijuana.

As the figure suggests, teachers faced a great deal of diversity in their classrooms. They might be teaching some low-risk teens who had no experience with drugs and other teens whose risk of future use was considerably higher. Consistent with our research questions, this diversity reinforced the importance of assessing the program's effect on groups of students with different levels of risk for future use.

ANALYSIS GROUPS

We selected preprogram experience with the target drugs as the risk indicator because prior use is the single most important predictor of future use (Bachman, O'Malley, and Johnston 1984). For alcohol and cigarettes, the analysis identified nonusers (teens who had not used alcohol or cigarettes when they were surveyed at baseline), experimenters (those who had tried the substance once or twice, but not in the month before baseline), and users (those who had tried it three or more times or who currently drank or smoked). For marijuana, the risk groups differed slightly, because the pool of baseline nonusers was much larger. The analysis distinguished among (a) students who had not tried marijuana or cigarettes by seventh grade, (b) those who had tried cigarettes, but not marijuana, and (c) those who had already tried marijuana by that time.

RELIABILITY OF SELF-REPORTS

The assessments were based on student self-reports of drug use, collected through questionnaires administered in the classroom. As always with self-reports, this raised the question of reliability: would students tell the truth about socially undesirable behavior? We gave them a number of incentives to provide reliable, accurate data. Before admin-

Figure 8.1 Drug Use Among Seventh Graders, Project ALERT Baseline

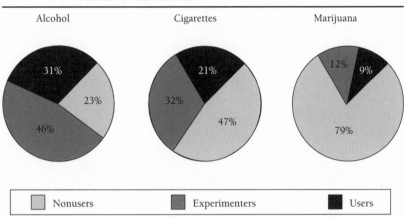

Alcohol	Cigarettes	Marijuana

☐ Nonusers   ◼ Experimenters   ■ Users

istering the questionnaire, the data collectors described the study's procedures for ensuring privacy (no names on questionnaires, no access by teachers or parents) and informed students of their right not to participate. Those who consented to participate were asked for saliva samples and told that these samples would be tested for drug use.

These procedures improved participation rates and accuracy of reports among adolescents in other research on drug use (Murray and others 1987) and seem to have worked in Project ALERT (Ellickson and Bell 1992). Fewer than 1 percent refused to fill out a questionnaire at baseline and in each wave of classroom data collection. Moreover, the saliva tests indicated that the great majority told the truth about tobacco use. Of students identified as recent tobacco users based on the laboratory tests, 95 percent also admitted to recent cigarette smoking or use of other tobacco products. Further, in checking consistency of answers across the first four waves of the survey, we found that the proportion who subsequently denied drug use that they had earlier admitted averaged only about 5 percent across substances. Only 1 percent of the students denied earlier admissions of frequent use (at least eleven times in the past year or six times in the past month).

METHODS OF ANALYSIS

Individuals were the unit of analysis for the self-reports, but the unit of assignment to the program was the school. In this situation, individual observations within a particular school are unlikely to be independent of one another, and statistical tests of significance for school-level variables like treatment curriculum will be overly liberal. Failure to correct for this "school effect" risks overstating the significance of treatment effects. To avoid this possibility, we estimated the within-school correlations, computed a corrections factor, and used that factor to adjust the tests of statistical significance (t-tests) downward. Hence, the analysis is more conservative than previous studies that failed to make this correction.

In order to rule out alternative explanations of program results, we controlled for a large number of baseline variables that might be related to subsequent drug use—gender, ethnicity, district, prior use, intentions to use, offers of drugs, and a composite variable that tapped numerous risk factors (such as early attitudes toward these drugs; use by peers, parents, and siblings; and parental and peer tolerance of use). The practical result of these controls was to decrease the preadjustment of program effects (Ellickson and Bell 1992).

SAMPLE ATTRITION

In this kind of research, attrition poses another challenge. Students are lost from the survey over time because they move, drop out of school, are absent on data-collection days, and so forth. By the end of the twelfth grade, we had retained 70 percent of the baseline sample, but the analysis sample for the assessment at grades ten and twelve was smaller, amounting to only 50 percent of the baseline respondents. Much of the loss was caused by variable absences, for example, students who filled out a tenth-grade survey but were absent on the twelfth-grade collection day (or vice versa). Nevertheless, this attrition did not threaten the internal validity of the experiment. Attrition rates or kinds of students lost did not differ across the three experimental groups (Ellickson, Bell, and McGuigan 1993).

Overall, however, the program did lose substantially more high-risk than low-risk students, such as those who were early smokers or marijuana users, came from disrupted families, or had poor grades. We also lost comparatively more African American or Hispanic students than white or Asian students. This loss limited our ability to generalize from our results about program effects on high-risk groups and some minorities. Nevertheless, we were able to assess the program's impact on the substantial number of high-risk students who had tried alcohol, cigarettes, or marijuana by the time they were in seventh grade.

SHORT-TERM BENEFITS, LONG-TERM NEEDS

Although several studies have reported short-term gains for drug use prevention programs, few have assessed the long-term effects. The Project ALERT study is one of those few. By following our seventh graders through twelfth grade, we established just how effective social influence programs can be and how long the effects can be expected to last in the absence of formal reinforcement during the high school years.

EFFECTS IN JUNIOR HIGH SCHOOL

For the junior high years (grades seven and eight), overall program results indicate that school programs based on the social influence model can make a real difference. They are not a panacea, but they do make an important contribution to drug prevention. Project ALERT curbed both marijuana and cigarette use; it held down both occasional and regular use; and it affected both low- and high-risk students.

Results for Marijuana and Cigarettes   The strongest and most consistent effects were for marijuana. For example, the program reduced initiation rates by about 30 percent among nonusers, that is, students who had no baseline experience with cigarettes or marijuana (see figure 8.2). For the lower-risk students who did begin using, Project ALERT reduced recent use (use in the past month) by 50 to 60 percent relative to use among the control group. In addition, the program had positive effects on marijuana use among higher-risk students. Among those who had already tried cigarettes, but not marijuana, by grade seven, it curbed frequent (monthly) marijuana use; for those who had already tried marijuana, it held down weekly use.

The results also revealed a pattern of positive effects for several different measures of cigarette use. The program's best results were among the experimenters (students who had tried smoking once or twice, but not in the month before the survey). These experimenters were about four times more likely than baseline nonsmokers to be regular smokers by the eighth grade and thus constituted a high-risk group. Project ALERT curbed both occasional and regular smoking among them and even made substantial inroads into heavy (daily) use (see figure 8.3). It had sharper effects on more serious levels of ciga-

Figure 8.2 Project ALERT's Impact on Marijuana Onset

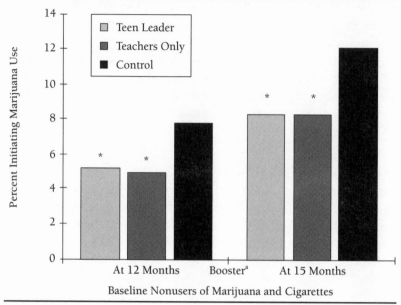

*Statistically significant at $p \leq 0.05$
[a]Eighth grade booster lessons delivered between twelve and fifteen month outcome measurements

rette use, cutting regular (weekly) smoking among these early experimenters by one-third to half compared to reductions of about 20 to 25 percent for use in the past month. In addition, the program induced some experimenters to quit.

Impact of Booster Lessons   These effects were achieved after only eleven lessons. That amounts to only eleven hours over a two-year period in the lives of these students—a fairly substantial benefit for such a limited investment of time. However, the eighth-grade booster lessons appeared critical for maintaining and extending program effects during junior high. Differences in smoking rates between treatment and control students did not become statistically significant until the former had received the full complement of lessons, eight during grade seven and three during grade eight. For marijuana, the booster lessons apparently maintained grade-seven results, and, in one case, they reversed the erosion of early effects: a 50 percent re-

Figure 8.3 Project ALERT's Impact on Heavy Smoking

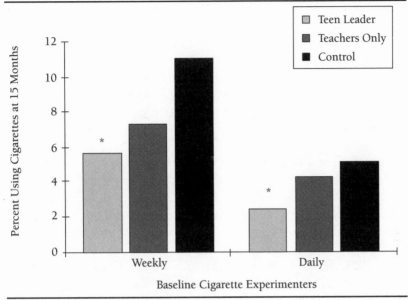

*Statistically significant at $p \leq 0.05$

duction in weekly use emerged right after exposure to the seventh-grade programs but disappeared following the summer break. After delivery of the three booster lessons, those early gains largely returned.

Effects in Minority Schools   The junior high analysis yielded several other results of interest to people involved in drug prevention policy or in program design, implementation, and evaluation. First, Project ALERT worked equally well in the high- and low-minority schools. We compared results in the thirteen schools with high-minority populations (at least 30 percent nonwhite in each school) with the seventeen schools with a 90 percent or more white enrollment. The treatment effects were similar for both groups. Moreover, where there were significant differences between the high- and low-minority schools, those differences tended to favor the high-minority schools. This outcome counters inferences from the results of some anti-smoking programs that prevention works only for white, middle-class teens.

Teen Leader Versus Teacher-Only Results   Second, and contrary to our expectations, the program that included teen leaders did not outperform the teachers-only program. Although the teen leaders were more effective with seventh graders who had experimented with cigarettes, they had a negative effect on the more committed users. And neither mode of delivery exhibited a clear pattern of dominance for marijuana and alcohol. Overall, both programs had positive effects, a finding that should be encouraging to adults, who too often hear that adolescents do not find them credible.

Impact on Alcohol Use   Some of the more instructive lessons involve prevention challenges. One is about alcohol. Immediately after the seventh-grade program, Project ALERT had modest, but significant, effects on the drinking behavior of adolescents at all three risk levels. Unfortunately, those early gains disappeared by eighth grade (see figure 8.4 for one example). Moreover, the booster lessons did not bring them back, despite the apparent importance of the eighth-grade boosters in maintaining the early gains for marijuana and in stimulating significant gains for cigarettes. In fact, nearly 90 percent of the students in both the treatment and the control schools had tried alcohol by the end of eighth grade. These results suggest that curbing alcohol use poses a more difficult and complex challenge than preventing or reducing the use of other gateway substances.

Impact on Committed Smokers   Another challenge is raised by the rebellious response of the early, more-committed smokers. Not only did Project ALERT not curb their smoking, it apparently made them smoke more. For these students, smoking was one element in a pattern of general deviance. They were much more likely than the experimenters or nonusers to have troubles at home, to be doing poorly in school, to have stolen something from a store, and to have a network of friends who smoked, drank, and used pot. Hence, a more general rebellion against society's norms may explain their negative response to Project ALERT.

Nevertheless, these multiple problems do not completely explain their response to the program, because the marijuana users, who had similar deviant profiles, did not respond negatively. One hypothesis is that adolescent smokers use smoking as a visible badge or marker of their deviant status. Faced with a prevention program that undermines the belief that smoking is "cool," adolescents who have adver-

Figure 8.4 Project ALERT's Impact on Alcohol Initiation

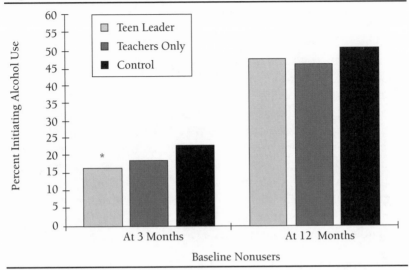

Baseline Nonusers

*Statistically significant at $p \leq 0.05$

tised their smoking may find themselves in a bind—either flaunt their choice or "betray" their image. Because marijuana use is likely to be much less public, students who have tried it are less likely to find themselves in that bind and thus less likely to rebel.

HIGH SCHOOL RESULTS

What happened after the students went to high school can be summarized very quickly. Once the lessons stopped, the program's effects on *behavior* stopped. Positive or negative, all the early behavioral effects washed away. For low- and moderate-risk students, the program's early effects on cigarette and marijuana use disappeared by ninth grade. In ninth, tenth, and twelfth grades, marijuana-initiation rates for baseline nonusers were not significantly different across the three experimental groups. The same was true for weekly cigarette smoking among the baseline experimenters.

In contrast, what the students learned in Project ALERT continued to have fairly significant effects on *cognitive* risk factors that we postulated as intervening variables—students' beliefs about the positive and negative consequences of use, about the likelihood of becoming dependent on drugs, about how many of their peers used drugs, and about whether their peers disapproved of drug use and would respect them for resisting (see table 8.1). Although these cognitive effects lasted longer—some of them throughout the high school years—they evidently were not sufficient to affect actual substance use.

The erosion of earlier program effects on two other intervening variables—personal expectations of use in the future and the belief that one can successfully resist pro-drug pressures—may partially explain the disappearance of behavioral effects. Expectations of future use have typically been stronger predictors of drug use behavior than other cognitive risk factors; hence the disappearance of program reductions in this key motivating variable may be critical. In addition, program-induced increases in resistance self-efficacy disappeared just after students entered high school, suggesting that their confidence in being able to resist new pressures needed strengthening.

LESSONS OF PROJECT ALERT?

The early results tell us much that is important for future social programs:

- First, school programs based on the social influence model can make a difference. With only eleven lessons, Project ALERT had significant effects on both marijuana and cigarette use for more than one risk group. Those results take on added importance because they occurred in schools with highly diverse student populations from urban, suburban, and rural areas. And they held up under rigorous experimental and statistical controls.

- Second, the program dispelled three myths that often discourage people about the prospects of drug prevention programs for adolescents—that they work only in middle-class, predominantly white, suburban environments; that they work only for low-risk teens; and that they prevent only trivial levels of use. The program worked in schools with large and small minority populations; in urban, rural, and suburban settings; and for high- and low-risk teens. It helped prevent students from trying marijuana, it helped students who had experimented with cigarettes from becoming regular users, and it even helped some of them to quit.

- Third, program outcomes alone do not justify the extra time and resources involved in using teen leaders in the classroom. Although the teen leader program produced longer-lasting effects on cognitive risk factors, neither mode of program delivery yielded clearly dominant effects on actual use. Coupled with findings from other studies (Fisher, Armstrong, and DeKlerk 1983), these results cast doubt on the belief that peer-led programs are superior to programs led by adults.

- Fourth, social influence programs are most effective when the prevailing social context reinforces their message. Project ALERT had only modest and short-lived effects on drinking, but it had much better results for cigarettes and marijuana. Other social influence programs have also had limited effects on alcohol use (Dwyer and others 1989; Hansen, Malotte, and Fielding 1988; Hansen and others 1988).

Why does alcohol present a problem seemingly different in kind from the challenge of other drug use? Probably because social attitudes and behavior differ for alcohol. In our society, most adults and older teens drink, and the prevailing norms foster use of alcohol in social situations. Consequently, prevention messages are repeatedly contradicted by messages from the media as well as from many parents and peers. Unless social attitudes toward drinking change substantially—as they have toward smoking and marijuana use—it seems unrealistic to expect prevention programs to stop teens from experimenting with alcohol.

There appears to be greater leverage for curbing drinking behaviors that society disapproves of—such as binge drinking and driving under the influence. However, it is a difficult challenge to develop programs that take advantage of the more favorable climate for preventing alcohol *misuse*, while also avoiding a message that promotes experimental drinking. Nevertheless, support for focusing on alcohol misuse has come from a program that successfully mitigated alcohol-related problems among young adolescents who had engaged in unsupervised drinking (Shope and others 1992).

Other studies indicate that the media and government officials can play an important role in creating societal norms and attitudes that support, rather than undermine, prevention messages. Media and government campaigns against smoking have been linked clearly with decreases in cigarette consumption (Warner 1981, 1989). Similarly, alcohol-related accident rates dropped after legislative action and publicity programs against drinking and driving increased (Decker, Graitcer, and Schaffner 1988). Recent increases in drug use

Table 8.1 Program Effects on Cognitive Risk Factors at Grades Ten and Twelve

Cognitive Risk Factor	Grade Ten (n = 3,685)			Grade Twelve (n = 3,640)		
	Teen Leader	Teachers Only	Control	Teen Leader	Teachers Only	Control
Consequences of use						
Risk of dependency	0.733	0.721*	0.797	0.702**	0.750	0.789
Social consequences	0.695***	0.755*	0.808	0.736*	0.770	0.781
Normative perceptions						
Prevalence of peer use	1.199***	1.288	1.300	1.389***	1.436	1.460
Friends approve of use	1.417**	1.513	1.487	1.531	1.565**	1.498
Friends do not respect refusal	0.942***	1.014*	1.095	0.898	0.946	0.931

Note: All outcomes range from zero (anti-drug) to three (pro-drug).
* p = 0.10, compared with control group.
** p = 0.05, compared with control group.
*** p = 0.01, compared with control group.

among adolescents of all ages have followed a precipitous decline in anti-drug messages from public officials, television and radio coverage, and advertising campaigns. Getting anti-drug messages back on the national media—and on the national agenda—may be critical to reversing the trend.

Our results also suggest that social influence programs are not a panacea. They do not work equally well for all substances nor do they help all children. Because classrooms and schools have diverse student populations, programs offered to an entire cohort do not necessarily meet the needs of all children within that cohort. Project ALERT, which focused on preventing initiation and the transition to regular use, triggered a rebellious reaction among more-confirmed smokers. Michigan's alcohol misuse curriculum, which emphasizes high-risk behavior, did not work for previous abstainers or for children whose previous drinking had been supervised. These variations in who benefits and who does not underscore the need for discovering how children who are not affected or are negatively affected can be helped.

The problems exhibited by Project ALERT's early smokers—delinquency, trouble at school, deviant friends, and poor relationships with parents—indicate that this group needs a much more intensive kind of intervention, one that also focuses on their environment and addresses their multiple problems. Such an intervention should come in the elementary school years and aim at mitigating familial, school, and other risk factors *before* they produce troubled teens.

Project ALERT's later results also offer clear lessons. The strongest is that we cannot expect program effects to last without continued reinforcement. The program had positive prevention effects in junior high, and some of the cognitive effects lasted into high school. But they no longer translated into behavioral effects. The students who received the lessons and boosters in junior high school were as likely as the control group to smoke and use marijuana in high school.

In retrospect, we probably should not have expected anything different. Maintaining behavioral changes is difficult. Many adults who try to quit smoking have three-to-four relapses before they succeed, and the same is true for losing weight and kicking drug habits. Why should adolescents be any different? Further, when they make the transition to high school, they do not enter a world that is free of pro-drug pressures. On the contrary, they face intensified pressures, quantitatively and qualitatively. High school students find themselves in new party or date situations that they have not encountered before and experience pressure from new and, often, older peers.

Given these pressures, maintaining behavioral gains in high school presents a real challenge for prevention programs. The National Institute of Drug Abuse recently funded RAND to address this challenge by developing an extended test of Project ALERT. The new program, ALERT Plus, will include a high school curriculum for grades nine, ten, and eleven; the evaluation will assess its effectiveness in maintaining and strengthening the middle-school program's effects on curbing drug use.

Support for high school boosters as a useful strategy for sustaining early prevention gains comes from research at Cornell Medical School (Botvin and others 1995). However, the best results for that program occurred when the high school boosters were implemented faithfully. Future prevention tests should give high priority to developing and evaluating methods for improving the fidelity of implementation.

Because we have little knowledge about effective programs for adolescents of high school age, we also need to develop and test a variety of program models for older teenagers. Older teenagers are more likely than younger adolescents to be users, to have a driver's license or ride in cars driven by other teenagers, and to use drugs as a coping mechanism. Hence they need programs that emphasize cessation strategies, drug-free driving, and alternative ways of handling stress. Project ALERT's middle-school results also suggest that high-risk adolescents need programs that are more intensive, and substantively different, from programs that work for lower-risk adolescents. The same is likely to be true for high-risk students in high school, many of whom may be attending alternative schools or no school at all. All of these differences highlight the need to evaluate different approaches for older teenagers.

Nevertheless, the best-designed and -implemented program will have only modest success if prevention messages are counteracted by societal norms that promote drug use. To realize their potential, school-based programs must be reinforced by the broader community. Truly effective drug prevention requires breadth of reinforcement as well as a sustained effort over time.

NOTES

1. Readers interested in the technical details of research design and evaluation and a fuller description of the Project ALERT curriculum can find that information in several articles and other publications that the study

has published. See, for example, Ellickson and Bell 1990, 1992; Ellickson, Bell, and McGuigan 1993; Ellickson, Bell, and Harrison 1993; Reinisch, Bell, and Ellickson 1991.

2. Current data show alarmingly high use rates for all three gateway drugs by grade eight: nearly one in ten adolescents is a current user of marijuana, one in five smokes cigarettes, and one in four drinks alcohol (Press release, University of Michigan, "Drug Use Rises Again in 1995 among American Teens," December 1, 1995). Although comparable information is not available for earlier grades, these figures reinforce the argument that prevention should start before the grade-eight upswing.

3. For children who attend middle school, sixth grade may be an option. These schools typically include sixth, seventh, and eighth grades; thus the sixth-grader going into middle school is making the transition that potentially makes him or her vulnerable to pro-drug pressures at an earlier age. Sixth grade may also be more advisable in neighborhoods with high use rates among older teenagers and adults. However, data contrasting program effects for a social influence program started at the fifth (versus the sixth) grade suggest that this approach is less appropriate for younger children (Dielman and others 1989).

4. The current version has three additional seventh-grade lessons: one on alcohol, one on smoking cessation, and one on inhalants. The first two are designed to address lessons learned during the evaluation; the third responds to evidence that use of inhalants is becoming increasingly prevalent among young adolescents.

5. The BEST Foundation is located in Los Angeles, California (1-800-ALERT-10).

REFERENCES

Bachman, J. G., P. M. O'Malley, and L. D. Johnston. 1984. "Drug Use Among Adults: The Impact of Role Status and Social Environment." *Journal of Personality and Social Psychology* 47(3): 629–45.

Bandura, Albert. 1977. "Self-Efficacy: Toward a Unifying Theory of Behavioral Change." *Psychology Review* 84(2): 191–215.

Becker, M. H., ed. 1974. "The Health Belief Model and Personal Health Behavior." *Health Education Monographs* 2(4): 324–508.

Berndt, T. J. 1979. "Developmental Changes in Conformity to Peers and Parents." *Developmental Psychology* 15(6): 608–16.

Botvin, Gilbert J. 1987. *Factors Inhibiting Drug Use: Teacher and Peer Effects.* Rockville, Md.: National Institute on Drug Abuse.

Botvin, Gilbert J., Eli Baker, Linda Dusendury, Elizabeth M. Botvin, and Tracy Diaz. 1995. "Long-Term Follow-up Results of a Randomized Drug Abuse Prevention Trial in a White Middle-Class Population." *Journal of the American Medical Association* 273(14):1106–12.

Decker, M. D., P. L. Graitcer, and William Schaffner. 1988. "Reduction in Motor Vehicle Fatalities Associated with an Increase in the Minimum Drinking Age." *Journal of the American Medical Association* 260(24): 3604–10.

Dielman, T. E., J. T. Shope, S. L. Leech, and A. T. Butchart. 1989. "Differential Effectiveness of an Elementary School-Based Alcohol Misuse Prevention Program." *Journal of School Health* 59(6): 255–63.

Dwyer, J. H., D. P. MacKinnon, M. A. Pentz, B. R. Flay, W. B. Hansen, E. Y. I. Wang, and C. A. Johnson. 1989. "Estimating Intervention Effects in Longitudinal Studies." *American Journal of Epidemiology* 130(4): 781–95.

Ellickson, P. L., and R. M. Bell. 1990. "Prevention in Junior High: A Multisite Longitudinal Test." *Science* 247(4948): 1299–1305.

———. 1992. "Challenges to Social Experiments: A Drug Prevention Example." *Journal of Research in Crime and Delinquency* 29(1): 79–101.

Ellickson, P. L., R. M. Bell, and E. R. Harrison. 1993. "Changing Adolescent Propensities to Use Drugs: Results from Project ALERT." *Health Education Quarterly* 20(2): 227–42.

Ellickson, P. L., R. M. Bell, and K. McGuigan. 1993. "Preventing Adolescent Drug Use: Long-Term Results of a Junior High Program." *American Journal of Public Health* 83(6): 856–61.

Ellickson, P. L., R. D. Hays, and R. M. Bell. 1992. "Stepping through the Drug Use Sequence: Longitudinal and Scalogram Analysis of Initiation and Regular Use." *Journal of Abnormal Psychology* 101(3): 441–51.

Ellickson, P. L., and A. E. Robyn. 1987. "Goal: Effective Drug Prevention Programs." *California School Board* 45(4): 24–27.

Elliott, D. S., Davis Huizinga, and S. S. Ageton. 1985. *Explaining Delinquency and Drug Use.* Beverly Hills, Calif.: Sage.

Evans, R. I., A. H. Henderson, P. C. Hill, and B. E. Raines. 1979. "Current Psychological, Social, and Educational Programs in Control and Prevention of Smoking: A Critical Methodological Review." In *Atherosclerosis Review.* Vol. 6, edited by A. Gotto and R. Paolettie. New York: Raven Press.

Fisher, D. A., B. K. Armstrong, and N. H. DeKlerk. 1983. "A Randomized Trial of Education for Prevention of Smoking in Twelve-Year-Old Children." Paper presented to the Fifth World Congress on Smoking and Health, Winnipeg, Canada.

Flay, B. R., J. R. d'Avernas, J. A. Best, M. W. Kersell, K. B. Ryan. 1983. "Cigarette Smoking: Why Young People Do It and Ways of Preventing It." In P. Firestone and P. McGrath, eds., *Pediatric and Adolescent Behavioral Medicine.* New York: Springer-Verlag.

Friedman, L. S., Edward Lichtenstein, and Anthony Biglan. 1985. "Smoking Onset Among Teens: An Empirical Analysis of Initial Situations." *Addictive Behavior* 10(1) 1–13.

Goodstadt, M. S. 1978. "Alcohol and Drug Education: Models and Outcomes." *Health Education Monographs* 6(3): 263–79.

Hansen, W. B., C. A. Johnson, B. R. Flay, J. W. Graham, and Judith Sobel. 1988. "Affective and Social Influences Approaches to the Prevention of Multiple Substance Abuse among Seventh-Grade Students: Results from Project SMART." *Preventive Medicine* 17(2): 135–52.

Hansen, W. B., C. K. Malotte, and J. E. Fielding. 1988. "Evaluation of a Tobacco and Alcohol Abuse Prevention Curriculum for Adolescents." *Health Education Quarterly* 15(1): 93–114.

Huba, G. J., and P. M. Bentler. 1984. "Causal Models of Personality, Peer Culture Characteristics, Drug Use, and Crucial Behavior over a Five-Year Span." In *Longitudinal Research in Alcoholism,* edited by D. W. Goodwin, K. T. Van Dusen, and S. A. Mednick. Boston, Mass.: Kluwer-Nijhof.

Huba, G. J., J. A. Wingard, and P. M. Bentler. 1981. "A Comparison of Two Latent Variable Causal Models for Adolescent Drug Use." *Journal of Personality and Social Psychology* 40(1): 180–93.

Jessor, R., J. A. Chase, and J. E. Donovan. 1980. "Psychosocial Correlates of Marijuana Use and Problem Drinking in a National Sample of Adolescents." *American Journal of Public Health* 70(6): 604–13.

Kandel, D. B., Mark Davies, Daniel Karus, and Kazuo Yamaguchi. 1986. "The Consequences in Young Adulthood of Adolescent Drug Involvement." *Archives of General Psychiatry* 43(8): 746–54.

Kandel, D. B., and Richard Faust. 1975. "Sequence and Stages in Patterns of Adolescent Drug Use." *Archives of General Psychiatry* 32: 923–32.

Kandel, D. B., R. C. Kessler, and R. Z. Margulies. 1978. "Antecedents of Adolescent Initiation into Stages of Drug Use: A Developmental Analysis." *Journal of Youth and Adolescence* 7(1): 13–40.

Murray, D. M., C. A. Johnson, R. V. Luepker, and M. B. Mittelmark. 1984. "The Prevention of Cigarette Smoking in Children: A Comparison of Four Strategies." *Journal of Applied Social Psychology* 14(3): 274–89.

National Institute of Drug Abuse. 1991. *National Household Survey of Drug Abuse: Main Findings, 1990.* Rockville, Md.: U.S. Department of Health and Human Services.

Newcomb, M. D., and P. M. Bentler. 1988. *Consequences of Adolescent Drug Use: Impact on Psychosocial Development and Young Adult Role Responsibility.* Beverly Hills, Calif.: Sage.

Orive, Ruben, and H. B. Gerard. 1980. "Personality, Attitudinal, and Social Correlates to Drug Use." *International Journal of the Addictions* 15(6): 869–81.

Perry, C. L., and Marcus Grant. 1988. "Comparing Peer-led to Teacher-led Youth Alcohol Education in Four Countries." *Alcohol Health and Research World* 12(4): 322–26.

Perry, C. L., Joel Killen, Michael Telch, L. A. Slinkard, B. G. Danaher. 1980. "Modifying Smoking Behavior of Teenagers: A School-Based Intervention." *American Journal of Public Health* 70(7): 722–25.

Polich, J. P., P. L. Ellickson, Peter Reuter, and J. P. Kahan. 1984. *Strategies for Controlling Adolescent Drug Use*. R-3076-CHF. Santa Monica, Calif.: RAND Corporation.

Reinisch, E. S., R. M. Bell, and P. L. Ellickson. 1991. *How Accurate Are Adolescent Reports of Drug Use?* N-3198-CHF. Santa Monica, Calif.: RAND Corporation.

Rice, D. P. 1993. "The Economic Cost of Alcohol Abuse and Alcohol Dependence." *Alcohol Health and Research World* 17(1): 10–11.

Schaps, Eric, J. M. Moskowitz, J. H. Malvin, and G. A. Schaeffer. 1986. "Evaluation of Seven School-Based Prevention Projects: A Final Report on the Napa Project." *International Journal of Addictions* 21(9–10): 1081–1112.

Shope, J. T., T. E. Dielman, A. T. Butchart, P. C. Campanelli, and D. D. Kloska. 1992. "An Elementary School-Based Alcohol Misuse Prevention program: A Follow-Up Evaluation." *Journal of Studies on Alcohol* 53(2): 106–21.

Tobler, N. S. 1986. "Meta-Analysis of 143 Adolescent Drug Prevention Programs: Quantitative Outcome Results of Program Participants Compared to Control of Comparison Group." *Journal of Drug Issues* 16(4): 537–67.

U.S. Office on Smoking and Health. 1990. *Executive Summary: Smoking and Health, a National Status Report. A Report to Congress*, 2d ed. DHHS Publication (CDC)87-8396. Washington, D.C.: U.S. Department of Health and Human Services, Public Health Service.

Warner, K. E. 1981. "Cigarette Smoking in the 1970s: The Impact of the Anti-Smoking Campaign on Consumption." *Science* 211(13): 729–31.

———. 1989. "Effects of the Anti-Smoking Campaign: An Update." *American Journal of Public Health* 79(2): 144–51.

CHAPTER 9

Preventing Adolescent Drug Abuse Through Life Skills Training: Theory, Methods, and Effectiveness

Gilbert J. Botvin

D rug use by American youth peaked in 1979 followed by a gradual decline that lasted until 1991. Since then, the prevalence of drug use by junior and senior high school students has increased steadily. According to national survey data, this upward trend in drug use is not isolated to a single group; rather it includes a broad range of youth from different regions of the country, racial and ethnic groups, and social classes. Since 1991, drug use has increased more than 30 percent, leading some experts to believe that we are on the verge of a new drug epidemic.

Efforts to combat the problem of drug abuse have involved a combination of strategies including education, treatment, and law enforcement. Billions of dollars have been spent by the federal government, much of this for efforts to interdict the flow of drugs both across and within our borders. These "supply reduction" efforts generally have been viewed as not only a dismal failure but also an extravagant waste of precious resources. Policy think tanks have been critical of the U.S. drug control policy in general and the proportion of federal drug control dollars spent on efforts to reduce supply and demand (treatment and prevention) in particular, arguing that the support for treatment and prevention should be substantially increased. There appear to be two major barriers to increasing the funding for treatment and prevention. The first reflects the government's (and perhaps the general public's) conceptualization of the drug problem as relating primarily to crime rather than health, thus warranting a solution based on law enforcement. However, with more than six hundred thousand deaths a year from drug abuse (more than four hundred thousand deaths from cigarette smoking alone), it is clear that drug abuse is not only the number one public health problem facing this nation, but also entirely preventable. Efforts to reduce demand using effective treatment and prevention approaches could produce dramatic reductions in the use and abuse of tobacco, alcohol, marijuana, and other illicit drugs.

The second major barrier to increasing the amount of funding available for demand reduction efforts is the widely held belief that such approaches are ineffective and therefore a waste of tax dollars. Despite advances in the development of more effective treatment and prevention approaches, the view that "nothing works" persists. This not only undermines any effort to increase the role played by treatment and prevention in our national drug control policy but also leads to the loss of hundred of millions of dollars in funding for treatment and prevention programs at federal agencies such as the Center for Substance Abuse Treatment, the Center for Substance Abuse Prevention, and the U.S. Department of Education, as lawmakers attempt to balance the federal budget.

Although no one would argue that *all* social programs work, it is clear that many do. As this volume indicates, there is considerable empirical evidence supporting the effectiveness of social and behavioral interventions designed to deal with our society's most pressing problems. This chapter describes an approach to drug abuse prevention called Life Skills Training and summarizes nearly two decades of evaluation research. This body of work demonstrates that school-based approaches to drug abuse prevention can reduce drug use up to 80 percent (relative to controls), that booster sessions can help maintain and even enhance prevention effects, that reductions in drug use for individuals exposed to a prevention program during junior high school can last until at least the end of high school, and that reductions in drug use during junior high school translate into reductions in more serious forms of drug involvement (heavy use, regular use of multiple substances, and use of illicit drugs other than marijuana). Finally, prevention effects have been demonstrated for a relatively broad range of students including white, suburban youth and inner-city minority (African American and Hispanic) youth.

THE PROBLEM OF ADOLESCENT DRUG ABUSE

Drug use among American youth is a problem of enormous proportions, and it is getting worse. According to the most recent national survey data (Johnston, O'Malley, and Bachman 1995), drug use in the

United States is at an unacceptably high level and, for most substances, there is a general developmental progression (see table 9.1). Drug use is at its lowest during the beginning of adolescence. Left unchecked, more and more individuals will begin using drugs each year as they progress through junior and senior high school. Because the onset of drug use typically begins during adolescence, prevention programs must target individuals either before or during junior high school.

The Sequence and Progression of Drug Use

The prevalence of drug use generally increases with age and progresses in a well-defined sequence (Millman and Botvin 1992). This sequence progresses in two ways. With the use of a single substance, the developmental progression occurs mainly with respect to the amount and frequency of use. Here the progression occurs with the transition from nonuse to initial use, to occasional (annual or monthly) use, and to more frequent (weekly and daily) use, along with an escalation of the amount used. With dependency-producing drugs, this escalation in both the frequency and amount of use typically eventuates in the development of tolerance (where larger or more frequent administrations of the drug are required to produce the same psychoactive effect) and in both physical and psychological dependence.

The other way the sequence of drug use progresses is related to the type of drug or drugs used. For most individuals, alcohol and tobacco are the first substances used, as are inhalants, because of their availability. Later, individuals progress to the use of marijuana. The use of these substances introduces adolescents to the world of drugs. For some individuals, their use may lead to the use of stimulants, opiates, hallucinogens, cocaine, and other illicit substances. The probability of using any substance in this developmental progression increases significantly with the use of one or more substances earlier in the progression. Thus the use of tobacco, alcohol, and inhalants significantly increases the risk of using marijuana, and the use of these "gateway" substances significantly increases the risk of using illicit drugs other than marijuana.

Moreover, any level of use (even trying a drug just once) significantly increases the risk of developing serious drug-related problems.

Table 9.1 Students' Use of Drugs in the United States, by Grade Level in 1994

Drug	Eighth Grade	Tenth Grade	Twelfth Grade
Ever used (%)			
Alcohol	56	71	80
Cigarettes	46	57	62
Illicit drugs	26	37	46
Used in past thirty days (%)			
Alcohol	26	39	50
Cigarettes	19	25	31
Illicit drugs	11	19	22

Source: Johnston, O'Malley, and Bachman 1995.

Thus experimentation with drugs or occasional use of drugs are risk factors for drug abuse and other drug-related problems. For this reason, drug abuse prevention programs targeting youth should focus on preventing the early stages of drug involvement as a method of reducing the risk of drug abuse. For middle or junior high school students, this might involve attempting to prevent "first use" or occasional (annual or monthly) use. For high school students, it might involve attempting to deter more serious levels of drug involvement (weekly or daily use of a single drug, use of multiple drugs, or "heavy" use) as well as preventing drug-related problems such as accidents or violence. Both because mortality and morbidity are associated with the use of tobacco and alcohol and because the use of marijuana dramatically increases the risk of using other illicit substances, drug abuse prevention programs should focus primarily on preventing the use of tobacco, alcohol, and marijuana. Because there is a direct relationship between the age of onset and the subsequent development of serious drug-related problems, prevention programs are likely to be valuable even if they merely delay the initiation of drug use or prevent the transition from occasional use to more serious levels of drug involvement.

Supporting Theory

It is now clear that there is no single factor or single pathway that serves as a necessary and sufficient condition leading to drug abuse. Drug abuse is the result of a multivariate mix of factors (Hawkins, Catalano, and Miller 1992; Newcomb and Bentler 1989). Some of these factors increase the risk of becoming involved with drugs, while other (protective) factors decrease the potential. Figure 9.1 presents a general domain model of the most important factors leading to drug-taking behavior. These factors can be grouped into broad categories or domains. The *sociocultural domain* consists of demographic factors (age, gender, social class), cultural factors (ethnic identity, acculturation), and drug availability. *Biological and genetic factors* include temperament and sensation-seeking. The *social and environmental* domain includes community factors (community resources and neighborhood organization), school factors (school bonding, school size, school climate), family factors (family management practices, communication, discipline, monitoring, parental drug use, and parental attitudes toward drug use), media influences promoting attitudes and norms conducive to drug use (television shows, movies, rock videos, and tobacco and alcohol advertising), and peer influences (friends' drug use and pro-drug attitudes). These factors both shape and interact with the adolescent's cognitive expectancies (attitudes, beliefs, normative expectations, drug-related health knowledge), general competencies (personal self-management skills, social skills), and a set of skills specific to resisting social influences from both the media and peers to use drugs. Vulnerability to factors that encourage drug use can be affected by psychological factors such as self-efficacy, self-esteem, personal control, psychological adjustment, and perceived life chances.

Figure 9.2 presents a general model of drug use initiation. This model incorporates key elements from the most prominent theories of drug use initiation including social learning theory (Bandura 1977), problem behavior theory (Jessor and Jessor 1977), self-derogation (Kaplan 1980), persuasive communications (McGuire 1968), peer cluster theory (Oetting and Beauvais 1987), and sensation-seeking (Zuckerman 1979). The variable domains presented in figure 9.1 are organized in the model contained in figure 9.2 into a causal framework in which these domains are conceptualized as superordinate constructs having specific relationships to one another. Although this model is designed to organize key factors associated with the onset of drug involvement into a coherent framework, it takes the perspective of how a preventive intervention may affect these factors and prevent drug use or abuse. For example, the model in figure 9.2 indicates that *psychological* factors mediate the impact of *general personal and social competence* on the risk of drug abuse. From a prevention perspective,

(*Text continues on p. 233.*)

Figure 9.1 Integrated Domain Model of Drug Use Behavior

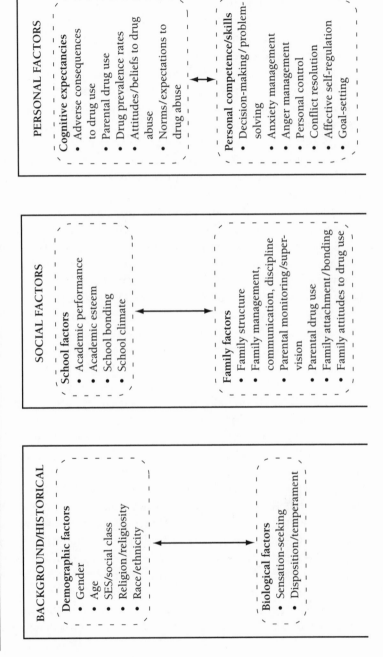

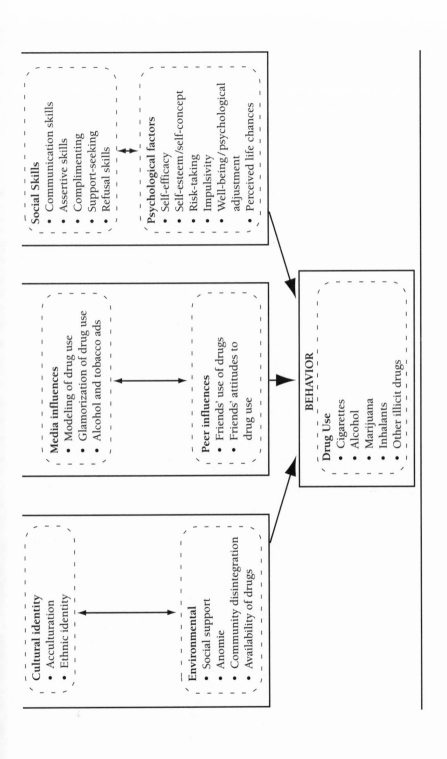

Social Skills
- Communication skills
- Assertive skills
- Complimenting
- Support-seeking
- Refusal skills

Psychological factors
- Self-efficacy
- Self-esteem/self-concept
- Risk-taking
- Impulsivity
- Well-being/psychological adjustment
- Perceived life chances

Media influences
- Modeling of drug use
- Glamorization of drug use
- Alcohol and tobacco ads

Peer influences
- Friends' use of drugs
- Friends' attitudes to drug use

Cultural identity
- Acculturation
- Ethnic identity

Environmental
- Social support
- Anomie
- Community disintegration
- Availability of drugs

BEHAVIOR

Drug Use
- Cigarettes
- Alcohol
- Marijuana
- Inhalants
- Other illicit drugs

Figure 9.2 Hypothetical Model of Drug Use Initiation

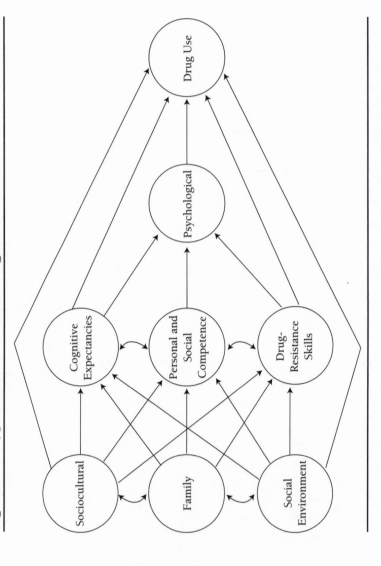

this suggests that a preventive intervention will have an impact on psychological factors associated with a reduced risk of drug abuse by improving personal and social competence. However, from the perspective of etiology, although psychological factors may certainly be associated with personal and social competence, they may not necessarily be consequences of personal and social competence. Instead, they may be antecedents of personal and social competence or occur simultaneously with it.

This type of model also has some inherent limitations. First, it suggests a temporal flow of causality that is static—little more than a snapshot of the underlying mechanisms in action. It does not capture the dynamic and recursive nature of these mechanisms. Second, although reasonably comprehensive, this model does not contain an exhaustive list of etiologic factors, nor does it posit all possible interrelationships. But it does provide a reasonably good method of organizing factors associated with drug use and understanding the etiology of drug use. It is also a useful means of formulating a prevention strategy.

Like other types of human behavior, drug abuse is conceptualized as being the result of a dynamic interaction of an individual and his or her environment. Social influences to use drugs (along with the availability of drugs) interact with individual vulnerability. Some individuals may be influenced to use drugs by the media (television shows and movies glamorizing drug use or suggesting that drug use is normal or socially acceptable as well as advertising efforts promoting the sale of alcohol and tobacco products). Others may be influenced to use drugs by family members, friends, and acquaintances who either use drugs or hold attitudes and beliefs supportive of drug use. Still others may succumb to peer pressure to use drugs because of intrapersonal factors such as low self-esteem, high anxiety, hopelessness, low personal control, or the need for excitement (sensation-seeking). The greater the number of risk factors that an individual has, the more likely it is that he or she will become a drug user and eventually a drug abuser, because the presence of multiple risk factors is associated with both initial drug use and the severity of later drug involvement (Newcomb and Felix-Ortiz 1992; Scheier and Newcomb 1991).

Inspection of the model contained in figure 9.2 suggests several potential points of intervention for either preventing or reducing the risk of drug abuse. Interventions can (and should) be developed to target individual, family, and community determinants of drug abuse.

However, most prevention research has focused on testing the effectiveness of school-based interventions targeting individual-level risk factors. A school-based intervention is likely to prevent drug abuse if it affects drug-related expectancies (knowledge, attitudes, and norms), drug-related resistance skills, and general competence (personal self-management skills and social skills). Increasing prevention-related drug knowledge and resistance skills can provide adolescents with the information and skills needed to develop anti-drug attitudes and norms as well as to resist peer and media pressure to use drugs. Teaching effective self-management skills and social skills (improving personal and social competence) offers the potential to affect a set of psychological factors associated with decreased risk of drug abuse (by reducing intrapersonal motivations to use drugs and the vulnerability to pro-drug social influences).

PROGRAM DESCRIPTION

The Life Skills Training (LST) Program is a drug abuse prevention program that targets individual adolescents, typically in school classrooms. It was designed to affect the individual-level variables contained in figure 9.1 under the heading of "personal factors." Although this is a logical point of intervention in view of what is known about the etiology of drug abuse, it clearly does not target *all* of the possible risk factors associated with either the initiation of drug use or the abuse of drugs. Recognizing the importance of other risk factors and the potential of other types of interventions, the LST Program was developed to determine the efficacy of this particular approach to prevention, knowing that the most effective prevention approach would need to target a broader array of risk factors through several different intervention modalities and delivery channels. From this perspective, the LST Program was viewed as merely a "first step" in the process of identifying and developing the set of preventive intervention components that will ultimately be necessary to attack the problem of drug abuse broadly and comprehensively for maximum effectiveness.

Accordingly, the research on the LST Program has sought not only to identify and refine an effective prevention program but also to discover underlying prevention principles. As research with the LST approach has proceeded over the past fifteen years, it has become clear that the program is suitable for implementation in other settings such as community centers and housing developments and with different populations. Moreover, the general prevention methods and underlying principles have been used to develop prevention programs for youth living in homeless shelters or participating in youth service organizations such as the Boys Club and even for parents. This chapter focuses on the school setting because most of the research on the LST Program has been conducted in schools.

Type of Prevention Approach

The LST Program is a *primary* prevention program. It is intended to target individuals who have not yet developed drug abuse problems—to prevent the early stages of drug abuse by decreasing the risk factors associated with drug abuse, particularly occasional or experimental use. Underlying this is the premise that preventing drug use with younger populations (junior high school students) will ultimately reduce the prevalence of drug abuse among these same individuals as they become older (seniors in high school). The LST approach is designed for all individuals in a given setting. As such, it is frequently referred to as a *universal* intervention as opposed to a selective or targeted intervention for individuals identified as being at "high risk."

Program Overview

Based on the model of drug abuse initiation specified in figure 9.1, the LST Program was developed to affect drug-related knowledge, attitudes, and norms; teach skills for resisting social influences that encourage drug use; and promote the development of personal self-management skills and social skills. Consistent with this, the LST prevention program can best be conceptualized as consisting of three major components. The first component teaches students a set of general self-management skills. The second component focuses on teaching general social skills. The third component includes information and skills related specifically to the problem of drug abuse. The first two components were designed to enhance overall personal competence and decrease both the motivation to use drugs and vulnerability to drug-use social influences. The problem-specific component was designed to provide students with material relating directly to drug abuse (drug resistance skills, anti-drug attitudes, and anti-drug norms).

Structure and Target Population

The LST Program consists of fifteen class periods (roughly forty-five minutes each) and is intended for middle or junior high school students. A booster intervention has also been developed that consists of ten class periods in the second year and five class periods in the third year. Except for our initial pilot research, all of the studies evaluating the LST Program have been conducted with seventh graders. When booster sessions were included, students received the LST Program in the seventh grade and the booster intervention in the eighth and ninth grades. Thus curriculum materials have now been developed and tested for all three years of junior high school. For school districts with a middle school, the LST Program can be implemented with students in grades sixth, seventh, and eighth. The following sections offer a brief description of the major components of the LST Program.

PERSONAL SELF-MANAGEMENT SKILLS COMPONENT

The personal skills component of the LST Program is designed to affect an array of self-management skills. To accomplish this, the personal skills component contains material to (a) foster the development of decision making and problem-solving (identifying problem situations, defining goals, generating alternative solutions, and considering consequences), (b) teach skills for identifying, analyzing, interpreting and resisting media influences, (c) provide students with self-control skills for coping with anxiety (relaxation training) and anger and frustration (inhibiting impulsive reactions, reframing [interpreting situations differently], using self-statements), and (d) provide students with the basic principles of personal behavior change and self-improvement (goal-setting, self-monitoring, self-reinforcement).

SOCIAL SKILLS COMPONENT

The social skills component is designed to affect several important social skills and enhance general social competence. This component contains material designed to help students overcome shyness and improve general interpersonal skills. This material emphasizes the teaching of (a) communication skills, (b) general social skills (initiation of social interactions, conversational skills, the giving of compliments), (c) skills related to boy and girl relationships, and (d) both verbal and nonverbal assertive skills.

DRUG-RELATED INFORMATION AND SKILLS COMPONENT

This component is designed to affect knowledge and attitudes concerning drug use, normative expectations, and skills for resisting drug-use influences from the media and peers. The material is similar to that contained in many psychosocial drug abuse prevention programs that primarily teach social resistance skills. Included is material concerning the (a) short- and long-term consequences of drug use, (b) knowledge about the actual levels of drug use among both adults and adolescents in order to correct normative expectations about drug use, (c) information about the declining social acceptability of smoking cigarettes and using other drugs, (d) information and class exercises demonstrating the immediate physiological effects of cigarette smoking, (e) material concerning media pressure to smoke, drink, or use drugs, (f) information concerning the techniques used by cigarette and alcoholic beverage advertisers to promote the use of these drugs and skills for resisting them, and (g) techniques for resisting direct peer pressure to smoke, drink, or use drugs.

BOOSTER INTERVENTION COMPONENT

In addition to the initial (primary) year of intervention, the LST approach contains a two-year booster intervention to be implemented in grades eight and nine. Designed to reinforce the material covered during the first year, the drug abuse booster curriculum consists of ten sessions in grade eight and five sessions in grade nine. This component focuses on the continued development of the general life skills that enable students to cope more effectively with the various pressures and problems confronting them as adolescents.

PROGRAM MATERIALS

Curriculum materials have been developed to standardize implementation of the LST Program and increase its exportability. These materials consist of a *Teacher's Manual* and *Student Guide* for each year of the program (published by Princeton Health Press). The *Teacher's Manual* contains detailed lesson plans consisting of the appropriate content and activities for each intervention session as well as the overall goal and objectives of each session. The *Student Guide* contains reference material for each session, class exercises, and homework assignments both to prepare students for specific sessions and to reinforce the skills and information already covered. The *Student Guide* also contains goal-setting principles, basic principles of self-directed behavioral change, and material for a semester-long "self-improvement" project.

PREVENTION TEACHING METHODS

Perhaps as important as the content of an effective prevention program are the methods used to teach that content. Prevention programs may fail because the material in the program does not adequately target the underlying risk and protective factors. They may, however, also fail because they rely on prevention methods that are ineffective in teaching the material contained in the prevention program. In developing effective interventions, attention must be given to both the content of the intervention and the method of delivery.

A variety of intervention methods have been used to teach the content of the LST Program, including the use of traditional didactic teaching methods, facilitation and group discussion, classroom demonstrations, and cognitive-behavioral skills training. Although lecturing and conventional didactic teaching methods are appropriate for some of the material taught in the LST Program, most of the material can be taught most effectively by facilitating group discussion and skills training, with *skills training* being the primary intervention method. Because a major emphasis of the LST Program is on the teaching of general personal self-management skills, social skills, and skills for resisting social influences to use drugs, the central role of intervention providers is that of skills trainer or coach. The cognitive-behavioral skills are taught using a combination of instruction, demonstration, behavioral rehearsal, feedback, social reinforcement (praise), and extended practice in the form of behavioral homework assignments.

INSTRUCTION AND DEMONSTRATION

The first step in the skills training process involves instruction and demonstration. Although they are generally used in combination, in some instances one may be used without the other. Instruction simply involves explaining a particular skill to students in a careful step-by-step fashion. Also important is a clear explanation of when to use the skill. Demonstration involves showing students how to perform a particular skill. This can be done by the program provider, by videotape, or even by a member of the class who has already learned the skill being taught. A good example of the use of instruction and demonstration can be seen anytime you fly on a commercial airline, when, prior to takeoff, a flight attendant explains and demonstrates how to use a seatbelt.

BEHAVIORAL REHEARSAL

The next step in the process of skills training involves behavioral rehearsal. Once the skill has been explained and demonstrated, students participating in the LST Program are given the opportunity to practice the skill being taught. This can be done in a number of ways. One common way is to have students take turns coming to the front of the room and participating in a brief role-play where they have the opportunity to practice the skill. Another is to divide the class up into small groups with the program provider circulating from group to group or with each group being led by a student. Role-play or behavioral rehearsal situations (scenarios) are clearly described by the provider or group leader and are as brief as possible (a minute or less each) so that as many students as possible have a chance to practice.

FEEDBACK

After students rehearse the skills being taught, they receive feedback concerning the strengths and weaknesses of their "performance." The provider conveys this information in a gentle and supportive manner so that students understand what aspects of the skill they performed well and what they need to improve, as well as how to improve. Emphasis is placed on constructive feedback designed to guide students as they strive to improve and "successively approximate" a mastery of the skills being taught.

SOCIAL REINFORCEMENT

Social reinforcement (praise) is closely related to the process of providing feedback and identifying aspects of the student's performance that approximate mastery of the skills being taught. The teacher or program provider reinforces each student for one or two positive elements of his or her performance of the skill. Although at times this may pose a challenge, the program provider simply identifies the *most* positive element of the student's performance. Because the primary objective of the LST Program is to reduce the risk of drug abuse, the goal of the training is to improve the target skills and self-efficacy of each student. Therefore, students are assessed individually with respect to improvement over their own baseline levels, however low.

EXTENDED PRACTICE

The final step is extended practice, which provides opportunities to practice the target skills in an effort to promote maximum development. This is accomplished through behavioral "homework" assignments. Examples are saying hello to one new person a day, practicing the technique for coping with anxiety once a day, giving assertive responses in three different situations (saying no, asking a favor, standing up for your rights). In addition to providing opportunities for practice in general, extended practice is intended to facilitate the use of these skills to situations outside the classroom, to promote generalizability to different situations, and to encourage students to use these skills in a natural way as part of their everyday lives. Program providers also provide feedback and reinforcement on an ongoing basis, as appropriate, outside the classroom.

INTERVENTION PROVIDERS, SELECTION, AND TRAINING

A critical element of any effective intervention is the intervention provider. The LST Program has been implemented successfully by several different types of intervention providers. These have included health professionals from outside the school (Botvin, Eng, and Williams 1980; Botvin and others 1994d), older peer leaders (Botvin and Eng 1982; Botvin and others 1984a), and regular classroom teachers (Botvin, Renick, and Baker 1983; Botvin and others 1984b; Botvin and others 1990). Because prevention effects can be produced with classroom teachers as well as other types of providers and because teachers are readily available, the most natural and logical provider for a school-based prevention program is a regular classroom teacher. In addition to availability, teachers are a logical choice because they generally have more teaching experience and better classroom management skills than other potential intervention providers. Peer leaders (same-age or older students) can assist teachers in implementing the curriculum and serve as positive role models for the kinds of skills and behavior being taught in the curriculum. Selection of program providers should be based on their interest, experience, enthusiasm, and commitment to drug abuse prevention; the extent to which they will be a positive role model; and their willingness to attend the training workshop, implement the intervention carefully and completely according to the provider's guide, and complete the necessary process evaluation forms. To enhance the potential for delivering the prevention program carefully and completely according to the intervention protocol, a spirit of collaboration should be engendered when recruiting providers.

Provider training consists of a one- or two-day training workshop. In one study (Botvin and others 1990), teachers were trained in one condition using a videotape. The purpose of the training workshop is to familiarize providers with the prevention program and its rationale and the results of prior studies and to provide them with an opportunity to learn and practice the skills needed to implement the prevention program (Tortu and Botvin 1989). Training for peer leaders has involved an initial half-day workshop that provides them with a general orientation to the prevention program and their responsibilities as well as with the information and skills needed to implement the program. Teachers meet with peer leaders prior to each session to prepare them for the upcoming session and debrief them regarding the last session.

EVIDENCE OF EFFECTIVENESS

The history of drug abuse prevention is full of countless theories and intervention strategies that have failed to withstand the scrutiny of evaluation research. Clearly the most serious challenge to the field of drug abuse prevention has been to prove that prevention works. Some approaches are easily shown to have an impact on knowledge and, in some cases, even on attitudes in a direction consistent with decreased risk of drug abuse. But this is weak proof that prevention works. The gold standard of whether or not a preventive intervention works is the extent to which it can affect drug use *behavior* (that is, reduce the incidence or prevalence of drug use). Using this as the standard, little credible evidence existed that drug abuse prevention worked until the end of 1970s and beginning of the 1980s. Since then, considerable research has been conducted, leading to several promising prevention approaches, including the Life Skills Training Program.

During the 1980s and up to the present, a series of evaluation studies have been conducted to test the effectiveness of drug abuse prevention approaches based on the LST model. These studies have been conducted in a logical sequence intended to facilitate the development of a prevention approach that is effective with different problem behaviors, when implemented by different types of providers, and with different populations. The focus of the early LST research was on cigarette smoking and involved predominantly white, middle-class populations. More recent research extended this work to other problem behaviors including the use of alcohol, marijuana, and, most recently, illicit drugs other than marijuana. In addition, this research has focused increasingly on the utility of the LST approach when used with inner-city minority populations. Finally, this research has assessed the long-term durability of the LST prevention model, its impact on hypothesized mediating variables, implementation fidelity, and methods of improving implementation fidelity. These studies are briefly described here, along with the key findings.

PREVENTING CIGARETTE SMOKING

The LST Program was developed as a smoking prevention program. Pilot research examined the short-term effectiveness of the LST approach for preventing cigarette smoking (Botvin, Eng, and Williams 1980). Participants were 281 students in the eighth, ninth, or tenth grades of two comparable suburban schools that were randomly assigned to either the experimental condition, in which students received the ten-session prevention program, or to a comparison control group. The prevention program was conducted by health professionals who were members of the project staff. This study found a 75 percent reduction in the number of new cigarette smokers after the initial post-test and a 67 percent reduction in new smoking at the three-month follow-up.

Effectiveness of Peer Leaders   A second study tested the effectiveness of this prevention approach when implemented by older peer leaders (eleventh and twelfth graders) with seventh graders ($n = 426$; Botvin and Eng 1982). In order to dramatize the immediate physical effects of cigarette smoking, an additional unit used biofeedback apparatus in class experiments. A methodological improvement to enhance the validity of smoking self-report data and to provide an objective measure of smoking status (saliva thiocyanate) involved the collection of saliva samples prior to the collection of self-report data in a variant of the procedure suggested initially by Evans and his colleagues (Evans and others 1979). Post-test results indicated that there were significantly fewer new smokers in the experimental group. These results were corroborated by the results of the saliva thiocyanate analysis, which showed a significant increase in smoking for students in the control group, but no increase for students in the experimental group. In addition, there was a 58 percent reduction in new smoking at the initial post-test and a 56 percent reduction in regular (weekly) smoking at the one-year follow-up. Significant treatment effects were also found on several hypothesized mediating variables, including smoking knowledge, psychosocial and advertising knowledge, social anxiety, and susceptibility to influence.

Teachers, Scheduling Format, and Boosters Effects A third study examined several important prevention issues (Botvin, Renick, and Baker 1983). This study was designed to test the efficacy of this prevention approach when implemented by regular teachers, to test two different implementation schedules, and to examine the efficacy of booster sessions for preserving initial prevention effects. Seventh-grade students ($n = 902$) from seven suburban New York schools were assigned randomly to three conditions: a treatment condition that involved conducting the prevention program once a week for fifteen weeks (E1), a treatment condition that involved conducting the program several times a week for about five weeks (E2), and a control condition. As in the previous study, saliva samples were collected to ensure high-quality self-reported data.

Significant treatment effects were found at the initial post-test using the monthly measure of cigarette smoking. A comparison of the relative effectiveness of the integrated weekly intervention format (E1) and the intensive minicourse format (E2) indicated that both conditions were equally effective in preventing the onset of new (monthly) smoking. Significant intervention effects for monthly, weekly, and daily smoking were found at the one-year follow-up. Students receiving additional booster sessions had half as many regular (weekly or daily) smokers as those not receiving booster sessions. Follow-up one and a half years after the conclusion of the prevention program showed lower rates of smoking onset for monthly, weekly, and daily smoking. These findings provided additional empirical support for the efficacy of the LST prevention program, this time when conducted by regular classroom teachers. These findings also indicated that the program is effective when implemented according to two different schedules (an integrated weekly schedule or a minicourse taught several times a week). Perhaps the most important finding of this study was its demonstration of the potential of booster sessions to maintain and even enhance the effects of the prevention program.

PREVENTING ALCOHOL USE

Several studies were conducted to determine the efficacy of this prevention approach with use of other types of substances. The first of these tested the impact of the LST prevention program on the frequency of alcohol use, episodes of drunkenness, and heavy drinking. The study was conducted with seventh graders from two comparable New York City public schools ($n = 239$) randomly assigned to experimental and control conditions (Botvin and others 1984b). The intervention was modified to include material concerning the potential consequences of alcohol use and, where appropriate, to teach skills in relation to situations that might promote alcohol use. Although no effects were evident at the initial post-test, program effects emerged at the six-month follow-up. Significantly fewer (54 percent) experimental students reported drinking in the past month, 73 percent fewer reported heavy drinking, and 79 percent fewer reported getting drunk at least once a month.

PREVENTING ALCOHOL AND MARIJUANA USE

Following the study testing the effectiveness of the LST Program with alcohol, a larger study was conducted to replicate the results for alcohol, test the generalizability of the LST approach to marijuana use, and test the relative effectiveness of this type of prevention strategy when implemented by older (tenth- and eleventh-grade) peer leaders or regular classroom teachers. The study included 1,311 seventh-grade students from ten suburban New York junior high schools who were randomly assigned to (a) teacher-led prevention curriculum, (b) peer-led prevention curriculum, (c) teacher-led prevention curriculum and booster sessions, (d) peer-led prevention curriculum and booster sessions, and (e) a control group.

Results at the end of the first year (Botvin and others 1984b) showed significant prevention effects for tobacco, alcohol, and marijuana use. Adolescents who participated in the LST Program drank significantly less alcohol per drinking occasion and were drunk less often, with students in the peer-led condition being superior to students in both the teacher-led and control conditions. With respect to marijuana, not only did fewer students report monthly and weekly marijuana use, but the magnitude of these effects was quite substantial. For students in the peer-led condition, the LST Program reduced experimental marijuana use by 71 percent and regular (weekly or daily) marijuana use by 83 percent. Effects were also evident on several cognitive, attitudinal, and personality variables in a direction consistent with decreased risk of drug use.

One-year follow-up results from this study (Botvin and others 1990) provide further support for the effectiveness of the LST prevention approach. Depending on the measure used, there were 79 to 82 percent fewer smokers in the peer-led booster group and 69 to 78 percent fewer marijuana users; 44 to 50 percent fewer smokers in the high-fidelity teacher-led group, 47 percent fewer experimenters with marijuana, and 51 percent fewer drinkers.

Evaluation Results from a Large-Scale Prevention Trial

One of the largest and most methodologically rigorous prevention studies ever conducted began in 1985. This randomized prevention trial involved 5,954 students from fifty-six schools in New York State. This study focused on the efficacy of the LST approach for preventing the use of all three gateway substances—tobacco, alcohol, and marijuana (Botvin and others 1990). The sample was approximately half male (52 percent) and predominantly white (91 percent). With spring 1985 smoking rates used as a blocking variable, schools within each of three geographic regions of New York State were randomly assigned to E1 (prevention program with training and support by project staff), E2 (prevention program with no involvement of project staff), and control conditions. Sample retention (based on all available students at the pre-test) was 93 percent at the initial post-test (mid-seventh grade), 81 percent at the sixteen-month follow-up (end of the eighth grade), 75 percent at the twenty-eight-month follow-up (end of the ninth grade), and 67 percent at the forty-month follow-up (end of the tenth grade). Retention rates were virtually identical across conditions.

Using both the *individual* and the *school* as the unit of analysis, prevention effects were found for drug use behavior as well as for several hypothesized mediating variables at the twenty-eight-month follow-up and the forty-month follow-up for students who received at least 60 percent of the intervention program. The results of the individual-level analysis at the twenty-eight-month follow-up found significantly less smoking and marijuana use among the E1 and E2 groups and less problem drinking in the E2 group than among controls. Results of the school-level analysis at the twenty-eight-month follow-up revealed that both the E1 and E2 groups had significantly less cigarette smoking than controls. At the forty-month follow-up, there was significantly less marijuana use in the E1 group and less excessive drinking in both the E1 and E2 groups than among controls.

Evidence of Long-Term Effectiveness

Although a growing number of evaluation studies have demonstrated prevention effects, these studies typically focus on short-term effectiveness. In order to determine the durability of drug abuse prevention in general and the LST approach in particular, a long-term follow-up study was conducted (Botvin and others 1995a). Students ($n = 3,597$) from fifty-six schools in New York State who participated in the drug abuse prevention trial that began in 1985 (when they were in the seventh grade) were located. Data were collected at the end of the twelfth grade by surveys in school, on the telephone, or through the mail. The average length of follow-up was six years after the initial baseline assessment. Follow-up results indicated that there were significantly fewer smokers, "heavy" drinkers, or marijuana users among students who received the LST prevention program during the seventh grade and had booster sessions during the eighth and ninth grades.

In order to assess the impact of the prevention program on more serious levels of drug involvement, treatment and control students were also compared in terms of polydrug use (defined in this study as the monthly or weekly use of multiple gateway substances). At the end of the twelfth grade, there were 44 percent fewer LST students than controls who used all three gateway drugs (tobacco, alcohol, and marijuana) one or more times a month and 66 percent fewer LST students who used all three substances one or more times a week. Prevention effects were also found for twelve hypothesized mediating variables in the direction of decreased risk of drug abuse. The strongest prevention effects were produced for the students who received the most complete implementation of the prevention program.

Finally, although prevention effects were produced regardless of whether providers were trained at a formal training workshop with periodic feedback and consultation from project staff or merely viewed a provider training videotape without feedback or support, the strongest effects were produced by teachers who attended annual training workshops and received ongoing support. Prevention effects were found using both the individual and school as the unit of analysis. A potential weakness of long-term follow-up studies concerns differential attrition, which can either undermine the initial (pretest) equivalence of the treatment and control groups and make it impossible to determine whether any observed follow-up effects are the result of the intervention or the result of differential attrition. In this study, attrition rates were equivalent for treatment and control conditions, as were pretest levels of drug use for the final analysis sample. This supports the conclusion that prevention effects were the result of the intervention and not the result of differential attrition or pretest lack of equivalence.

PREVENTING ILLICIT DRUG USE

Long-term follow-up results from the large-scale prevention trial also provided evidence that the LST prevention program can reduce the use of illicit drugs. An underlying assumption is that if primary prevention efforts prevent or reduce the use of tobacco, alcohol, or marijuana, they will have a corresponding impact on the use of other substances further along the developmental progression. In other words, preventing the use of gateway drugs will reduce the use of illicit drugs such as cocaine or heroin in the future. Although this rationale is commonly used to justify targeting gateway drug use, it has never been tested.

The impact of the LST Program on illicit drug use was addressed by analyzing data collected from an anonymous subsample of students involved in the long-term follow-up study. Data were collected by mail from 454 individuals (mean age = 18.86 years) who were contacted after the end of the twelfth grade. The length of follow-up was six and a half years from the initial baseline. The survey assessed the use of thirteen categories of illicit drugs following those used by the University of Michigan *Monitoring the Future* study (Johnston, O'Malley, and Bachman 1994). Significantly lower levels of drug involvement (relative to controls) were found for the LST students on two composite measures of illicit drug use as well as for specific categories of illicit drugs. There were lower levels of illicit drug use for the composite measure that assessed use of any illicit drug and for the measure that assessed use of illicit drugs other than marijuana. By individual drug category, significantly lower levels of use were found in the E1 group for LSD (lysergic acid diethylamide) and other psychedelics as well as for PCP (phenyl cycl-piperidine). Significantly lower levels of heroin use were found for both the E1 and E2 condition. Finally, significant prevention effects were found for the use of inhalants for both LST groups.

TESTING THE GENERALIZABILITY OF THE LST APPROACH TO MINORITY YOUTH

Several studies have been conducted to determine the impact of the LST approach on the drug use of racial- and ethnic-minority youth. This work is important not only because it examines the effectiveness of the LST approach for preventing drug use with minority youth but also because it addresses a gap in the drug abuse prevention field concerning a general lack of high-quality research with minority populations. In developing preventive interventions for minority populations, two strategies have been followed. One strategy, based on the assumption that the etiology of drug abuse is different for different populations, involves the development of interventions designed to be population-specific. The other strategy, based on the assumption that the etiology of drug abuse is more similar than different across populations, involves the development of interventions designed to be generalizable to a broad range of individuals from different populations.

Research with the LST Program has followed the second course, making modifications where warranted to maximize generalizability, cultural sensitivity, relevance, and acceptability to varied populations. Although there are only limited data concerning the etiology of drug abuse among minority populations, existing evidence suggests that there is substantial overlap in the factors promoting and maintaining drug use and abuse among different racial and ethnic groups (Bettes and others 1990; Botvin and others 1993a, 1993b, 1994c; Dusenbury and others 1992; Epstein and others 1995). A second reason for pursuing this course is that most urban schools contain individuals from multiple racial and ethnic groups. Therefore, even if differences across populations warranted different interventions, it would be extremely difficult to implement separate interventions for different racial and ethnic groups for both logistical and political reasons. Given the choice of two or more effective interventions, it is important to consider feasibility as well as effectiveness.

Although some Asians have been included in the studies conducted with the LST Program, the major racial and ethnic groups involved in the most recent research studies with minority populations have been African American and Hispanic youth. As was the case with previous research with white, middle-class youth, the initial focus of this research was on cigarette smoking, followed by a focus on other gateway substances. Research testing the generalizability of the LST prevention approach to inner-city, minority youth has progressed through the following sequence: (a) exploratory and qualitative research consisting of focus-group testing and key informant interviews, (b) expert review of intervention methods and materials, (c) consumer-based review of intervention materials and methods, (d) small-scale pilot studies, and (e) large-scale randomized field trials. Intervention materials and methods were modified, as necessary, throughout the process of development and testing. None of the modifications deriving from the etiologic literature concerning minority youth or the review process changed the underlying prevention strategy. Rather, these changes related to the reading level of intervention materials, the inclusion of appropriate graphics (illustrations or pictures of minority youth), language, role-play scenarios, and examples appropriate to the target population.

Prevention Research with Hispanic Youth   The first study testing the effectiveness of the LST approach with a minority population involved predominantly Hispanic youth (Botvin and others 1989b). The study included 471 seventh graders (46 percent male) attending eight public schools in the New York metropolitan area. The sample consisted of predominantly lower-income Hispanic students (74 percent) as well as a small percentage of African American (11 percent) and white (4 percent) students. Schools were assigned randomly to conditions. Significant post-test differences between the experimental and the control group were found, controlling for pretest smoking status, gender, social risk for becoming a smoker, and acculturation. Intervention effects were also found for knowledge concerning the immediate consequences of smoking, prevalence of smoking, social acceptability of smoking, decision making, normative expectations concerning adult smoking, and normative expectations concerning peer smoking.

Data from a large-scale randomized trial also demonstrated significant program effects when implemented with predominately Hispanic urban minority students (Botvin and others 1992). This study involved 3,501 students from forty-seven public and parochial schools in the greater New York City area. Intervention materials were modified (based on the results of our pilot study and input from consultants, teachers, and students) to increase their relevance to Hispanic youth as well as to ensure a high degree of cultural sensitivity. Schools were assigned randomly to experimental and control conditions. Using *school means* as the unit of analysis, significant reductions in cigarette smoking were found for the adolescents who received the LST Program when compared with controls at the end of the seventh grade. Adolescents who received the LST Program had monthly prevalence and onset rates that were nearly 30 percent lower than for controls. Follow-up data demonstrated the continued presence of prevention effects through to the end of the tenth grade (Botvin 1994).

Prevention Research with African American Youth   Before testing the LST approach on African American youth, the intervention materials and methods were once again subjected to an extensive review to determine their cultural appropriateness for this population. Following this, a small-scale study was conducted with nine urban junior high schools in northern New Jersey (Botvin and others 1989a). The pretest involved 608 seventh-grade students. Of these, 221 were in the treatment group, and 387 were in the control group. The sample was 87 percent African American, 10 percent Hispanic, 1 percent white, and 2 percent other. Schools were assigned randomly to treatment and control conditions within each of the three participating communities. Students in the treatment schools received the LST Program; students in the control schools received the smoking education curriculum normally provided by their school. Throughout the prevention program, classroom observation data and teacher feedback were collected.

A series of multivariate statistical analyses were computed to assess the impact of this intervention approach on cigarette smoking. Pretest scores, age, grades, and social risk for smoking (the smoking status of friends) were used as covariates. Results indicated that there were 57 percent fewer post-test smokers in the treatment group (3 percent) than in the control group (7 percent) based on smoking status in the past month. Significant treatment effects were also found for knowledge of the consequences of smoking, normative expectations regarding the prevalence of smoking among adults, and normative expectations regarding the prevalence of smoking among peers.

A large-scale prevention trial involving predominantly African American youth from forty-six inner-city schools in northern New Jersey provided additional empirical support for the effectiveness of this prevention approach with this population (Botvin and Cardwell 1992). Schools were assigned randomly to treatment ($n = 21$) and control ($n = 25$) conditions after first controlling for schoolwide smoking rates. Students ($n = 2,512$) were pretested in the spring of 1990 while they were in the seventh grade, post-tested in the early winter of 1991, and post-tested again in the spring of 1991 at the end of the eighth grade. In the treatment condition, all eligible classes in participating schools received the LST intervention; in the control group all classes received the health (smoking) education normally provided to students. The final sample was 97 percent minority and 3 percent white; of the total sample, 78 percent were African American, 13 percent were Hispanic, 1 percent were Native American, 1 percent were Asian, and 3 percent classified themselves as "other." Initial post-test results showed significantly less smoking for students in the treatment group who received the intervention in the seventh grade and booster sessions in the fall of the eighth grade when compared with both the nonbooster treatment group and the controls. At the final follow-up, students who received booster sessions and the original intervention had a 92 percent lower rate of smoking during the past month than the controls (1 and 13 percent, respectively).

TAILORING LST TO MINORITY YOUTH

Although research has demonstrated the generalizability of the LST approach to minority youth, it is often argued that the strongest prevention effects are likely to come from an intervention approach tailored to the specific population targeted. A recently completed study tested the relative effectiveness of the LST approach and a prevention approach specifically tailored to African American and Hispanic youth (Botvin and others 1994d). Both prevention approaches were similar in that they taught students a combination of generic "life skills" and skills specific to resisting offers to use drugs. However, the tailored or culturally focused approach was designed to embed the skills training material in myths and legends derived from the African American and Hispanic cultures. Six junior high schools containing predominantly minority students (95 percent) were assigned to receive either (a) the LST Program, or (b) the culturally focused prevention approach, or to serve as (c) an information-only control group. The sample was 48 percent African American, 37 percent Hispanic, 5 percent white, 3 percent Asian, and 8 percent other. Students were pretested and post-tested during the seventh grade.

Results indicated that students in both skills training prevention conditions had lower intentions to drink beer or wine relative to the information-only controls and that students in the LST condition had lower intentions to drink hard liquor and use illicit drugs. Both skills training conditions also affected several mediating variables in a direction consistent with nonuse of drugs. According to these results, both prevention approaches were equally effective, significantly reducing behavioral intentions to drink and use illicit drugs and suggesting that a generic approach to drug abuse prevention with high generalizability may be as effective as one tailored to individual ethnic populations. These data, therefore, support the hypothesis that a single strategy of drug abuse prevention can be used effectively with multiethnic populations.

Follow-up data ($n = 456$) collected two years later, at the end of the ninth grade, found significant prevention effects for both approaches (Botvin and others 1995b). Students in both prevention conditions drank alcohol less often, became drunk less often, drank less alcohol per drinking occasion, and had lower intentions to use alcohol in the future relative to the controls. The magnitude of these effects was reasonably large. For example, there were 50 percent fewer adolescents drinking alcohol during the past month than in the control group (6 and 12 percent, respectively). However, these data also showed that the culturally focused intervention produced significantly stronger effects on these variables than the generic LST approach. The findings of the follow-up study are particularly interesting because, while they suggest that it may be possible to develop a preventive intervention that is effective for a relatively broad range of students, they also indicate that tailoring interventions to specific populations can increase effectiveness with inner-city minority populations.

FROM RESEARCH TO ACTION

For many years, the challenge to prevention researchers and public health professionals has been to identify promising approaches, carefully test them, and provide evidence that they work. That challenge has largely been met. A considerable amount of information is known at this point about the causes of drug abuse and how to prevent it. Although more work is needed to further refine existing approaches and develop even more effective ones, the current challenge concerns bridging the gap between research and practice. Recognizing this, efforts are under way to disseminate information concerning effective approaches to drug abuse prevention in order to move from research to action. National conferences during the past year by the National Institute on Drug Abuse, the U.S. Department of Education, and the Justice Department's Office of Juvenile Justice and Delinquency Prevention have all focused on communicating the results of research showing that a small group of prevention approaches, such as the Life Skills Training Program, have been demonstrated to work. Speakers at these conferences have exhorted practitioners to use research-based approaches.

One issue that will have to be addressed is cost. Although most prevention programs are inexpensive, schools and communities will have to allocate some of their resources to cover the cost of prevention materials and training. The Life Skills Training Program costs approximately five dollars to ten dollars per student per year including the cost of materials and training. To the extent that several schools in a state or region can coordinate training and the purchase of curriculum materials, the costs can be closer to five dollars per student due to cost-efficiencies and volume discounts. Although a formal economic analysis of cost-benefit or cost-effectiveness is planned for the Life Skills Training Program, none has been conducted to date. However, compared to the expense of treatment or imprisonment, which can exceed thirty thousand dollars a year, a prevention program like Life Skills Training is extremely inexpensive.

SUMMARY, CONCLUSIONS, AND FUTURE DIRECTIONS

Despite a general downward trend in the use of drugs by high school seniors over the past ten years, recent data indicate that drug use is once again on the rise. The etiology of drug abuse is complex, involving multiple determinants and numerous developmental pathways. Prevention approaches, to be effective, need to target these determinants as comprehensively as possible. Approaches that focus on drug-related health knowledge or attitudes have not been effective. Similarly, the use of scare tactics or affective education has also failed to produce an impact on drug use behavior. The most effective prevention approaches have focused on teaching social resistance skills either alone or in combination with general life skills.

The Life Skills Training Program is the most extensively evaluated school-based prevention approach available today. More than a decade and a half of research has demonstrated prevention effects with respect to tobacco, alcohol, and marijuana use, gateway poly-drug use, and illicit drug use as well as hypothesized mediating variables. The reported effects of these approaches typically have been relatively large in magnitude, with most studies demonstrating initial reductions (relative to controls) of 50 percent or more. These studies have generally produced reductions in both occasional (experimental) drug use as well as more serious levels of drug involvement. Research with the Life Skills Training approach includes studies testing its short-term effectiveness as well as its long-term durability, studies testing different delivery methods and the effectiveness of booster sessions, studies testing its effectiveness when conducted by different program providers, and studies testing its effectiveness with different populations. These studies have ranged from small-scale pilot studies involving two schools and a few hundred adolescents to large-scale, multiple-site, randomized field trials involving more than fifty schools and several thousand adolescents.

Although progress has been made in the past decade, further research is clearly needed. Additional research is under way to improve our understanding of the mechanism(s) through which this approach prevents drug use, to understand its effectiveness with different populations (particularly minority youth), and to determine its generalizability to other empirically and theoretically related behaviors such as violence.

REFERENCES

Bandura, Albert. 1977. *Social Learning Theory*. Englewood Cliffs, N.J.: Prentice Hall.

Bettes, Barbara A., Linda Dusenbury, J. F. Kerner, Susan James-Ortiz, and Gilbert J. Botvin. 1990. "Ethnicity and Psychosocial Factors in Alcohol and Tobacco Use in Adolescence." *Child Development* 61(2): 557–65.

Botvin, Gilbert J. 1994. "Smoking Prevention among New York Hispanic Youth: Results of a Four-Year Evaluation Study." Unpublished manuscript.

Botvin, Gilbert J., Eli Baker, E. M. Botvin, Linda Dusenbury, John Cardwell, and Tracy Diaz. 1993a. "Factors Promoting Cigarette Smoking among Black Youth: A Causal Modeling Approach." *Addictive Behaviors* 18(4): 397–405.

Botvin, Gilbert J., Eli Baker, E. M. Botvin, A. D. Filazzola, and R. B. Millman. 1984a. "Alcohol Abuse Prevention through the Development of Personal and Social Competence: A Pilot Study." *Journal of Studies on Alcohol* 45(6): 550–52.

Botvin, Gilbert J., Eli Baker, Linda Dusenbury, E. M. Botvin, and Tracy Diaz. 1995a. "Long-Term Follow-up Results of a Randomized Drug Abuse Prevention Trial." *Journal of American Medical Association* 273(14):1106–12.

Botvin, Gilbert J., Eli Baker, Linda Dusenbury, Stephanie Tortu, and E. M. Botvin. 1990. "Preventing Adolescent Drug Abuse through a Multimodal Cognitive-Behavioral Approach: Results of a Three-Year Study." *Journal of Consulting and Clinical Psychology* 58(4): 437–46.

Botvin, Gilbert J., Eli Baker, N. L. Renick, A. D. Filazzola, and E. M. Botvin. 1984b. "A Cognitive-Behavioral Approach to Substance Abuse Prevention." *Addictive Behaviors* 9(2): 137–47.

Botvin, Gilbert J., H. W. Batson, S. Witts-Vitale, V. Bess, Eli Baker, and Linda Dusenbury. 1989a. "A Psychosocial Approach to Smoking Prevention for Urban Black Youth." *Public Health Reports* 104(6): 573–82.

Botvin, Gilbert J., and John Cardwell. 1992. "Primary Prevention (Smoking) of Cancer in Black Populations." Grant contract N01-CN-6508. Final Report to National Cancer Institute. Cornell University Medical College, Ithaca, N.Y.

Botvin, Gilbert J., Linda Dusenbury, Eli Baker, Susan James-Ortiz, E. M. Botvin, and J. F. Kerner. 1992. "Smoking Prevention among Urban Minority Youth: Assessing Effects on Outcome and Mediating Variables." *Health Psychology* 11(5): 290–99.

———. 1989b. "A Skills Training Approach to Smoking Prevention among Hispanic Youth." *Journal of Behavioral Medicine* 12(3): 279–96.

Botvin, Gilbert J., and Anna Eng. 1982. "The Efficacy of a Multicomponent Approach to the Prevention of Cigarette Smoking." *Preventive Medicine* 11(2): 199–211.

Botvin, Gilbert J., Anna Eng, and C. L. Williams. 1980. "Preventing the Onset of Cigarette Smoking through Life Skills Training." *Preventive Medicine* 9(1): 135–43.

Botvin, Gilbert J., J. A. Epstein, S. P. Schinke, and Tracy Diaz. 1994c. "Predictors of Smoking among Inner-City Youth." *Developmental and Behavioral Pediatrics* 15(2): 67–73.

Botvin, Gilbert J., C. J. Goldberg, E. M. Botvin, and Linda Dusenbury. 1993b. "Smoking Behavior of Adolescents Exposed to Cigarette Advertising." *Public Health Reports* 108(2): 217–24.

Botvin, Gilbert J., Nancy Renick, and Eli Baker. 1983. "The Effects of Scheduling Format and Booster Sessions on a Broad-Spectrum Psychosocial Approach to Smoking Prevention." *Journal of Behavioral Medicine* 6(4): 359–79.

Botvin, Gilbert J., S. P. Schinke, J. A. Epstein, and Tracy Diaz. 1994d. "The Effectiveness of Culturally Focused and Generic Skills Training Approaches to Alcohol and Drug Abuse Prevention among Minority Youth." *Psychology of Addictive Behaviors* 8(2): 116–27.

Botvin, Gilbert J., S. P. Schinke, J. A. Epstein, Tracy Diaz, and E. M. Botvin. 1995b. "Effectiveness of Culturally Focused and Generic Skills Training Approaches to Alcohol and Drug Abuse Prevention among Minority Adolescents: Two-Year Follow-up Results." *Psychology of Addictive Behaviors* 9(3): 183–94.

Dusenbury, L., J. F. Kerner, Eli Baker, Gilbert J. Botvin, Susan James-Ortiz, and A. Zauber. 1992. "Predictors of Smoking Prevalence Among New York Latino Youth." *American Journal of Public Health* 82(1): 55–58.

Epstein, J. A., Gilbert J. Botvin, Tracy Diaz, and S. P. Schinke. 1995. "The Role of Social Factors and Individual Characteristics in Promoting Alcohol among Inner-City Minority Youth." *Journal of Studies on Alcohol* 56(1): 39–46.

Evans, R. I., A. H. Henderson, P. C. Hill, and B. E. Raines. 1979. "Smoking in Children and Adolescents: Psychosocial Determinants and Prevention Strategies." In *Smoking and Health: A Report of the Surgeon General,* edited by U.S. Public Health Service. Washington, D.C.: U.S. Department of Health, Education, and Welfare.

Hawkins, J. D., R. F. Catalano, and J. Y. Miller. 1992. "Risk and Protective Factors for Alcohol and Other Drug Problems in Adolescence and Early Adulthood: Implications for Substance Abuse Prevention." *Psychological Bulletin* 112(1): 64–105.

Jessor, Richard, and S. L. Jessor. 1977. *Problem Behavior and Psychosocial Development: A Longitudinal Study of Youth.* New York: Academic Press.

Johnston, L. D., P. M. O'Malley, and J. G. Bachman. 1994. *National Survey Results on Drug Use from the Monitoring the Future Study, 1975–1993.* Vol. 1: *Secondary School Students.* Rockville, Md.: U.S. Department of Health and Human Services.

———. 1995. *National Survey Results on Drug Use from the Monitoring the Future Study, 1975–1994.* Vol. 1: *Secondary School Students.* Washington, D.C.: U.S. Department of Health and Human Services.

Kaplan, H. B. 1980. *Deviant Behavior in Defense of Self.* New York: Academic Press.

McGuire, W. J. 1968. "The Nature of Attitudes and Attitude Change." In *Handbook of Social Psychology,* edited by G. Lindzey and Elliot Aronson. Reading, Mass.: Addison-Wesley.

Millman, R. B., and Gilbert J. Botvin. 1992. "Substance Use, Abuse, and Dependence." In *Developmental-Behavioral Pediatrics,* 2d ed., edited by Melvin Levine, N. B. Carey, A. C. Crocker, and R. T. Gross. New York: W. B. Saunders Co.

Newcomb, M. D., and P. M. Bentler. 1989. "Substance Use and Abuse among Children and Teenagers." *American Psychologist* 44(2): 242–48.

Newcomb, M. D., and Maria Felix-Ortiz. 1992. "Multiple Protective and Risk Factors for Drug Use and Abuse: Cross-Sectional and Prospective Findings." *Journal of Consulting and Clinical Psychology* 63(2): 280–96.

Oetting, E. R., and Fred Beauvais. 1987. "Peer Cluster Theory, Socialization Characteristics, and Adolescent Drug Use: A Path Analysis." *Journal of Consulting and Clinical Psychology* 34(2): 205–13.

Scheier, L. M., and M. D. Newcomb. 1991. "Psychosocial Predictors of Drug Use Initiation and Escalation: An Expansion of the Multiple Risk Factors

Hypothesis Using Longitudinal Data." *Contemporary Drug Problems* 18(3): 31–73.

Tortu, Stephanie, and Gilbert J. Botvin. 1989. "School-Based Smoking Prevention: The Teacher Training Process." *Preventive Medicine* 18(2): 280–89.

Zuckerman, Mort. 1979. *Sensation-Seeking: Beyond the Optimal Level of Arousal.* Hillsdale, N.J.: Lawrence Erlbaum Associates.

CHAPTER 10

Models of Community Treatment for Serious Juvenile Offenders

Patricia Chamberlain and Kevin Moore

Violent juvenile crime is growing at an alarming rate. Citizens are reaching for solutions, and getting youths who commit crimes off the streets to prevent them from causing more harm has become a high priority in most communities. This is especially true for violent and sexual offenders. Increased capacity for incarceration is an option that many states have taken. However, long-term incarceration has disadvantages. Given the young age of juvenile offenders, incarceration is a costly solution. Yet results on the effectiveness of community-based rehabilitation programs have been disappointing. Rehabilitation efforts for serious and violent juvenile offenders have fallen short and have led policymakers to conclude that, when it comes to changing "hard-core delinquents," nothing works. This chapter identifies potential flaws in the structure of many delinquency treatment programs, discusses features of the programs' designs that virtually ensure that the treatment provided to high-risk juvenile offenders will fail, and presents an alternative model.

Many policymakers and treatment providers accept the notion that adolescents are beyond adult influence. From the literature on adolescents and from our own personal experience in growing up, we "know" that the influence of peers takes on enormous proportions during the teenage years, especially in relation to the influence of parents. Therefore, it seems logical that treatment approaches must abandon or at least not rely on parental efforts to supervise and discipline youngsters in the face of the emerging power of the peer group. Yet, in the scholarly literature on the development and maintenance of delinquency, there has been consistent empirical support for the powerful role of negative (or deviant) peer relations (Elliott, Huizinga, and Ageton 1985).

Association with deviant peers has been shown to be a strong predictor of involvement in and escalation of aggressive and delinquent behavior. For example, peer support for aggressive behavior in the classroom increases aggression (Guerra and others 1995). Interaction with negative peers predicts substance use (Dishion and Andrews 1995; O'Donnell, Hawkins, and Abbott 1995). Research in sociology and developmental psychology over the past twenty-five years has shown that youngsters who have strong bonds with delinquent peers are at far greater risk for becoming delinquent in the first place and for escalating delinquency over time than those who associate with nondelinquent peers.

It is ironic, then, that most delinquency treatment programs put youngsters with criminal histories together in groups that can potentially facilitate further bonding and development of common social identities among group members. These treatments run the risk of maintaining and enhancing friendship cliques among delinquents (Elliott, Huizinga, and Ageton 1985).

Most widely used treatments for delinquency, such as Positive Peer Culture (Vorrath and Brendtro 1985), attempt to use the "group process" to gain a therapeutic effect. The assumption is that the peer group can best motivate and influence youths to change their behaviors and attitudes. However, it seems unreasonable to expect youngsters with histories of serious delinquent behaviors to function as a group and somehow become good influences on one another or establish positive social norms or values. These approaches may vastly underestimate the influence that adult-initiated norms and rules of conduct can have in the face of day-to-day involvement in a peer-dominated culture. A more sensible intervention would involve minimizing the influence of peers and immersing the youngster in a nondelinquent culture.

In 1991 we designed a study to test the effectiveness of two treatment models for male adolescents with histories of chronic delinquency. The two models used very different approaches to handling exposure to delinquent peers; one attempted to use peer-group interactions therapeutically, and the other attempted to isolate boys from their delinquent peers and to maximize the influence of mentoring adults and prosocial peers. Eighty boys who were mandated into residential treatment by the juvenile court were assigned randomly to placement in group care (GC) or Treatment Foster Care

(TFC). In group care, boys lived with six to fifteen other boys who had similar histories of delinquency. In Treatment Foster Care only one boy was placed in a home with a family that had been recruited from the community. TFC parents were trained in the use of behavior management skills and were closely supervised throughout the boy's placement. In both conditions, treatment lasted for an average of seven months. Boys who participated were from twelve to seventeen years old (average age, 14.3 years) and had an average of thirteen previous arrests; half had committed at least one crime against a person.

The Treatment Foster Care model had been pilot tested in two previous studies where we explored the feasibility of using this model for adolescents referred for delinquency and for youngsters leaving the state mental hospital (Chamberlain 1990; Chamberlain and Reid 1991). Results showed that TFC was not only feasible but also cost-effective, compared with alternative residential treatment models, and that the outcomes for children and families were better. For example, during a two-year follow-up period, the number of days that delinquent youngsters were incarcerated in the state training school was lower for participants in TFC than for a comparison group of youngsters placed in group care programs. The savings in incarceration costs alone were $122,000.

Shortcomings of the study were that we examined incarceration records only and that we were not able to obtain data on arrest rates. Also the study design used a matched comparison group rather than assign cases randomly to conditions, which is a preferable strategy for ensuring that groups are equivalent. In another study comparing TFC to "treatment as usual" in the community, we followed children and adolescents leaving the state mental hospital for one year after their discharge. This time we were able to use a random assignment design, and we looked at children's daily adjustment as well as their rehospitalization rates. Again, participants in TFC fared better than those in community-based group care settings. These findings encouraged us to apply for federal funding to conduct a full-scale clinical trial on the efficacy of TFC for adolescents with serious and chronic delinquency. When designing the study, in addition to looking at the relative effectiveness of the treatment models, we were interested in the broader issue of understanding what factors or key treatment components led to success or failure for individual participants.

Researchers and policymakers agree that development of effective interventions for youngsters with severe conduct problems should take advantage of the substantial body of basic research that addresses the life course development of aggression and antisocial behaviors. Further, to be most useful, expensive intervention trials need to provide experimental tests of their underlying theoretical model of change (Mrazek and Haggerty 1994). Thus an efficient intervention study must serve two purposes: evaluate the effectiveness of the intervention and provide specific information that can guide the development of better interventions in the future. Therefore, the goals of our study were (a) to evaluate systematically the immediate and longer-term outcomes of the interventions and (b) to evaluate the contribution of the interventions' key variables to changes in outcomes.

Measurement of study outcomes was fairly straightforward. We collected data on official arrests, including each boy's history of arrests prior to entering the study. In addition, we collected confidential self-reports of criminal activity from each boy. The number of days each boy was incarcerated or "on the run" was tracked, as was information on school attendance and academic advancement. Mental health outcomes were also assessed. Boys were assessed at baseline and then every six months throughout a two-year follow-up period. To assess the contribution of key treatment components, we first identified variables that were likely to influence a boy's success or failure in treatment. To do this, we turned to the scholarly literature on the development of aggression and delinquency. Problems with adult supervision, disciplinary practices, as well as attachment and involvement with the child have been shown to be powerful predictors of a child's conduct problems. In addition, the influence of negative peers appears to play a key role, especially in the escalation of delinquency, once problems already exist. To examine the relative contribution of these variables to individual outcomes, we conducted an assessment with the boy and his caretaker (line staff in group care, TFC parent in Treatment Foster Care) in the placement setting after he had been there for three months. We then examined the relationship between scores on these in-program variables and case outcomes.

IMMEDIATE AND LONGER-TERM OUTCOMES OF TREATMENT FOSTER CARE

From April 1991 to April 1996, eighty boys referred to substitute (out-of-home) care due to chronic delinquency were randomly assigned to Treatment Foster Care (one boy per home; $n = 40$) or to one of eleven group care placements (six to fifteen boys per placement; $n = 40$). Boys were assessed at baseline, at three months after placement, and at six-month intervals thereafter. At the time of this writing, all boys had completed their treatments, and their rates of criminal behavior had been examined for the twelve-month period following discharge from their programs.

Frequency of Arrests, Incarcerations, and Runaways

When they entered the study, boys in group care had been arrested an average of 6.7 times during the prior year, and TFC boys had been arrested an average of 8.5 times. This difference was not statistically significant. At one year after being discharged from treatment, the average arrest rate for boys in group care was more than twice that for boys in TFC (GC mean = 5.4; TFC mean = 2.6), producing a statistically significant difference ($p = 0.003$) between the two groups, favoring those in TFC. In figure 10.1, data are shown for the arrest rates for boys from the year before entering the study (baseline) through one year after leaving the treatment program. We examined the percentage of boys in each group who had no arrests after enrollment in the study. In the GC group, 7 percent ($n = 3$) had no further arrests from baseline to twelve months post-discharge. In the TFC group, 41 percent ($n = 15$) had no arrests during that same period. These data include all boys who were originally enrolled in the study, whether they completed or dropped out of treatment.

Timing of Arrest

Another way to look at differences in arrest rates is through the use of survival analysis. In survival analysis, the relationship between a predictor (treatment group membership) and the time until something important happens (an arrest) can be investigated. Figure 10.2 illustrates the survival function for the first seventy subjects (TFC, $n = 35$; GC, $n = 35$) in the two groups for time to first arrest after enrollment in the study. At each point in time, the value of the function on the y-axis is the percentage of subjects who had not been arrested again. A log rank test revealed that the survival functions for the two groups were significantly different, ($X^2[1] = 9.69, p < = 0.01$). The median survival times were 237 days for subjects in Treatment Foster Care and 55 days for subjects in group care.

Figure 10.1 Annual Arrest Rates of Two Groups, from
Preplacement to Two Years After Placement,
Mediator's Study

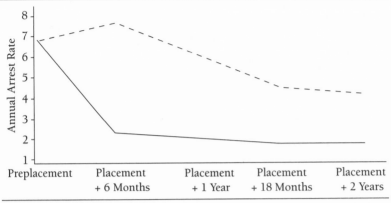

F(1,34) for interaction = 3.0, p < 0.10
– – –   GC n = 19
———   TFC n = 17

INCARCERATION AND RUNAWAY RATES

During the one-year follow-up period, GC subjects had been incarcerated for significantly more days than subjects in the TFC group. This included fewer days in local detention facilities (TFC mean = thirty-two days; GC mean = seventy days) and fewer days in the state training schools (mean = twenty-one and fifty-nine days, respectively). Further, GC boys ran away from their placements at a significantly greater rate than TFC boys (58 percent of GC boys ran away at least once compared with 31 percent of TFC boys). A greater proportion of TFC boys ultimately completed their programs (73 and 36 percent, respectively). By the one-year follow-up, boys in TFC had spent nearly twice as much time living with parents or relatives as had boys in GC.

IN-PROGRAM PEER AND ADULT ASSOCIATION PATTERNS AND SUPERVISION AND DISCIPLINE PRACTICES

At the three-month assessment, the boy's primary caretaker and the boy were interviewed during a face-to-face visit to the program and during five telephone interviews conducted over two weeks. Tele-

Figure 10.2 Survival Time to First Arrest of Boys in Treatment Foster Care and Group Care

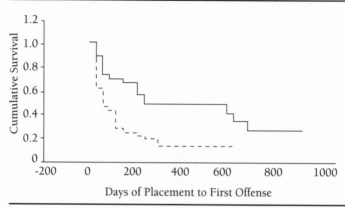

Days of Placement to First Offense

—— TFC *n* = 35; median = 237 days
– – – GC *n* = 35; median = 55 days
GC versus TFC $p < 0.001$

phone interviews were conducted to assess boy and caretaker reports of the boy's behavioral problems, involvement in disciplinary situations, and patterns of association with adults and delinquent peers during the past twenty-four hours. Telephone interviews were arranged so that the boy and caretaker could not hear one another.

On average, caretakers in both GC and TFC programs reported that boys engaged in about the same number of problem behaviors during the previous day (3.7 and 3.6, respectively). However, boys in the two groups differed considerably in their own reports of how many problem behaviors they engaged in per day: GC boys reported an average of 6.6, while TFC boys reported 3.0. On discipline given and received, caretakers in TFC said they gave disciplinary consequences more frequently than those in GC (62 and 34 percent of the times the boy misbehaved, respectively). Boys in TFC said they were disciplined 37 percent of the times they misbehaved, and boys in GC reported being disciplined 15 percent of the times.

On the peer and adult contact variables, as could be expected given the fundamental differences in the program structures, boys in GC spent significantly more time with delinquent peers than did those in TFC. In addition, we measured how much time boys spent with delinquent peers living outside their program and how much they felt they were negatively influenced by delinquent peers. Boys in GC reported spending significantly more time with delinquent peers than their caretakers reported. In TFC the findings were in the opposite direction: boys reported spending less time with delinquent peers than their caretakers reported. Boys in GC reported that they were influenced more negatively by delinquent peers than did boys in TFC ($p < 0.02$). Boys in TFC spent more time with adults than boys in GC (five and three hours a day, respectively). Group care boys reported that they spent an average of seventy-nine minutes a day unsupervised, and TFC boys reported an average of twelve minutes a day unsupervised.

IMPLICATIONS OF THE FINDINGS

In terms of the design of future treatment strategies for highly delinquent youngsters, a most interesting finding was that key variables measured while boys were in placement predicted their rates of arrest one year after leaving their treatment programs. The amount and quality of supervision and discipline they received during placement—and their patterns of association and relationships with adults and peers—predicted both the total number and the seriousness of arrests at the one-year follow-up, regardless of treatment condition. In other words, no matter whether they were placed in GC or TFC settings, boys with poor supervision, less consistent discipline, less positive contact with mentoring adults, and more association with delinquent peers had more arrests during follow-up than their well-supervised and disciplined counterparts who associated more with positive adults and less with delinquent peers. During placement, association with delinquent peers also predicted a reliable increase in the seriousness of offenses committed at follow-up (see table 10.1).

These findings suggest that it is easier to supervise and discipline a boy who has severe problems with delinquency when he is not part of a group of peers who have the same type of problems. Boys themselves reported that the more they associated with delinquent peers the more those peers negatively influenced them. In group care, there were greater discrepancies between what boys and their caretakers

Table 10.1 Correlations Between Discipline, Delinquency, and Arrests (Baseline to One Year)

Indicator	Total Arrests	Seriousness of Arrests	Change in Seriousness
Discipline	−0.160	−0.330*	−0.270*
Association with delinquent peers	0.430*	0.370***	0.380**

* $p < 0.06$.
** $p < 0.03$.
*** $p < 0.005$.

reported was going on than in family care. The differences between these two program models are important only if they relate in a lawful way to case outcomes. In our study, scores on these four key variables predicted later criminal offenses, as well as the seriousness of that offense. These findings imply that regardless of the program structure or model, to the extent that treatment programs provide youngsters with consistent consequences for daily rule-breaking, provide children with positive adult contact, and help youngsters avoid contact with peers who are engaging in delinquency, they will be successful in preventing or lessening the probability of future criminality.

In TFC we have developed methods and strategies for providing participants with high levels of adult supervision and contact and with consistent and fair discipline. We attempt to isolate youths from contact with delinquent peers, and after they have been stabilized and are doing well at home and in school, we encourage contact with pro-social peers. An overview of TFC follows.

THE COMPONENTS OF TREATMENT FOSTER CARE

Implementation of a Treatment Foster Care model is based on intervention work conducted at the Oregon Social Learning Center since the 1960s (Patterson and Brodsky 1966) and is continuing today (Dishion and Andrews 1995; Reid 1991). Development of the Oregon Social Learning Center's TFC model was also influenced by the early work of Bryant (1983), Hawkins (1989), Hawkins and others (1985), and Meadowcroft (1989), who were the first to use and advocate for TFC in community-based settings. The Oregon Social Learning Center's TFC model was designed to provide an alternative to group residential care for adolescents removed from their homes by the courts.

In TFC, community families are recruited, screened, trained, and supervised to provide treatment to the adolescent placed with them in conjunction with case management and therapy provided by clinical staff of the Oregon Social Learning Center (Chamberlain 1994; Moore and Chamberlain 1994). A detailed description of the model is available in Chamberlain (1994). A brief overview of key components is given here.

RECRUITMENT AND TRAINING OF TREATMENT FOSTER CARE PARENTS

Both two- and one-parent families from diverse social, ethnic, and economic backgrounds have served as successful TFC parents. We attempt to select strong and nurturing families who are willing to work actively, consistently, and cooperatively toward specific behavioral goals with the teenager placed in their care. Recruitment is done through word-of-mouth and newspaper advertising. Existing TFC parents are paid a $100 "finders fee" for referring families that we eventually train. During training, in addition to teaching basic behavior management skills (close supervision, fair and consistent discipline), there is emphasis on both preventing contact with antisocial peers and engaging youngsters in prosocial activities. Training includes an emphasis on exposing teenagers to enriching activities and materials (movies, sports, books). The aim is to increase the "vocabulary" or repertoire of positive skills and experiences they have with which to talk to prosocial peers. In addition, TFC parents are taught methods for turning problem situations into teaching opportunities and for responding to aggressive behavior in nonreactive ways. TFC parents are taught to use the point/level system adapted from the Achievement Place Program (Phillips and others 1972) and from our own work using similar systems in parent training treatments. Reinforcement is emphasized with points given for participation in routine daily activities. Points are taken away for low-level behavioral problems that are likely to alienate prosocial peers, such as swearing and telling "war stories."

CASE MANAGEMENT

A case manager supervises the TFC parent's implementation of the point system and, prior to the youth's involvement in the program, meets with the teenager and explains how the daily system works. The case manager, who has a maximum caseload of ten, conducts a weekly foster parent meeting and coordinates treatment in the TFC home with the youngster's individual and family therapist. The case manager is on call twenty-four hours, delivers crisis intervention, and arranges for psychiatric services, as needed. The case manager also schedules home visits and coordinates the assignments given to the biological parents or relatives in the family therapy sessions.

DAILY STRUCTURE AND SUPPORT

Supervision and monitoring are systematized through use of a point program. School attendance, homework completion, and classroom behavior are tracked using a daily school card, and TFC parents follow through with daily rewards and sanctions. Clear rules for unsupervised time are provided. Discipline for serious violations of the rules or persistent or intense problems include repetitive activities such as writing sentences and performing work chores. In extreme cases, short stays in detention are used. TFC parents are telephoned daily (Monday through Friday) to obtain information on the youth's behavior and points earned and lost within the past twenty-four hours and to troubleshoot current or anticipated clinical problems. In weekly foster parent meetings, each case is reviewed, and the point program is adjusted. For example, individualized behavioral targets are identified, refined, and then included in treatment plans; plans for behavioral development or improvement are then implemented through the point program.

Family therapy is aimed at working with parents (or relatives or other after-care resource) to implement the same or similar support, supervision, and disciplinary procedures as those used in the TFC home. As parents progress in their skills, longer home visits are scheduled. During visits, case managers are on call to offer the parents advice and crisis intervention. In instances where the youth's return home or placement with relatives is not possible, long-term placement in the foster home can be negotiated with Child Welfare. This has occurred for about 15 percent of cases. After-care parent groups are offered weekly for twelve months following the youth's return home.

Individual therapy occurs weekly and emphasizes skill-building in the areas of (a) negotiation and problem-solving, (b) skills required for living successfully in a family setting, (c) modulation of the expression of anger, including techniques for expressing dissatisfaction and distress directly as opposed to through retaliation, (d) development of an educational and occupational plan that incorporates the youngster's interests and any academic strengths that have been identified, and (e) identifying the problems associated with being in a delinquent peer group and development of prosocial skills needed for relating to "normal" peers. In the individual sessions, the playing of roles and practicing of skills are emphasized, and youngsters are assigned homework to do during the week between sessions. The therapist provides small rewards for completing these tasks. The therapist works with the case manager to identify potential future job opportunities and to explore what education or training is required. Whenever feasible, the youngster is matched with a community mentor who can discuss the occupation or profession and possibly arrange visits or volunteer opportunities at the mentor's workplace.

Program Costs

The TFC program described here was funded by the Oregon Youth Authority at $76 per boy per day or $2,356 per month. In addition, the local mental health division was billed for family therapy at the rate of $76 per week, making the total case cost $18,620 for seven months of treatment. This funding level, with annual 3 percent cost-of-living adjustments, has been in effect since 1983 when the program started. Group care programs varied in cost from $120 to $160 per day for a total cost of $26,040 to $34,720 for seven months of treatment.

CASE EXAMPLE: EDDIE S.

Because the TFC model is designed to serve "one child at a time," the treatment plans are completely individualized, depending on the specific needs and potential of the participant. This section presents a brief case example describing treatment for a boy with complex mental health problems in addition to delinquency.

Eddie, a fourteen-year-old boy, was referred to TFC from juvenile corrections where he had been living in detention for eight months. Eddie had been in group care since age seven when he was removed from his home. From early infancy until age six, Eddie had received both physical and sexual abuse from his father, who later left the state to avoid prosecution. One day, after his mother fled from his father, Eddie attempted to pull down the pants of his three-year-old brother and then later in the day, while his mother was driving the car, he attempted to choke his brother. His mother, overwhelmed with her circumstances and Eddie's behavior, called Child Welfare asking for help. Both children were immediately removed from her care, and she was investigated for child abuse. Once she was cleared of abuse, her youngest child was returned to her care, but Eddie was placed in foster care.

By the time he was referred to TFC, it appeared that Eddie's problems stemmed not only from the initial abuse but also from the trauma of being removed from his home and placed in the custody of the state. He had multiple foster home placements that failed (five in six months). Finally, he was placed in long-term residential care. His mother was advised (by professionals and her own family members) to terminate her parental rights so that Eddie could be adopted. She ended up consenting to relinquish her parental rights, and an adoptive family was found for Eddie. That adoption failed and was followed by two long-term placements in residential care, where he was extremely aggressive, and his emotional and conduct problems worsened.

After the state Child Welfare agency decided that no further adoption attempts would be made, Eddie's mother wanted to reopen her relationship with him. For more than three years, staff at the residential facility where Eddie lived told her he was potentially homicidal and sexually aggressive, and because of this they would not allow home visits. In addition, Eddie's mother reported that she was advised to "beg off" visits with her son at the residence. Residential staff reported that Eddie would act up before and after visits with his mother. Finally, he was placed in the county detention facility. At the time of referral to our TFC program, he had been in detention for eight months. He had been referred to and rejected from several residential care programs throughout the state.

At the time of referral, Eddie's symptoms were many. He was paranoid, felt isolated from his peers, had erratic mood swings, exhibited impulsive behavior, was obsessed with violent material, had outbursts of anger that included physical attacks on others, was nervous, had difficulty sleeping, and demonstrated an array of conduct problems that reportedly included making inappropriate sexual comments. He had been charged with three counts of assault that were later pled to one lesser count. He was diagnosed as having a post-traumatic stress disorder and conduct disorder. In school, Eddie had been designated as being seriously emotionally disturbed and had an Individualized Educational Plan. However, prior to placement in our Treatment Foster Care program, Eddie had not attended public school since the first grade. Intellectual testing at ages eight and thirteen found him to be in the normal range of ability. Eddie scored well above average on measures of depression, anxiety, and antisocial tendencies.

His mother reported that this history of failure and mutual rejection contributed to an extreme sense of shame, defensiveness, and depression for her. She also reported that Eddie told her that he thought she hated him and was choosing his brother over him. The negative fallout from these numerous changes was exacerbated by Eddie's transition into adolescence, when identity issues became more important. His isolation from his mother and other family members was very painful for him. He despaired not because the attempted adoption had failed but because his mother had "put him up" while his brother stayed with her.

TREATMENT FOSTER CARE TREATMENT PLAN

The treatment plan devised for Eddie focused on his adjustment in multiple settings (the TFC home, his relationship with his mother, and school and community activities). Years of individual therapy focused on insight had not worked for Eddie, and he was on a negative trajectory with a backlog of behavior and emotional problems.

To prepare for Eddie's placement we (a) provided specialized training for a TFC parent, including how and when to use crisis on-call services from our staff, (b) explained the point/level contingency management system to Eddie, (c) introduced Eddie to his individual therapist and had two sessions with him prior to placement, (d) obtained psychiatric consultation to review management of his medication, (e) set up school planning and consultation, including a plan for crisis intervention, and (f) initiated family involvement with Eddie's mother prior to placement. Eddie's mother reported that she wanted to be involved, but that she was quite nervous about whether she could handle him. She hoped that he would eventually be able to return home.

These treatment components were coordinated by a case manager who also provided support and close supervision, including daily contact with the TFC parents. After implementing a structured behavior management plan in the TFC home for two weeks, other services were added, including (a) family therapy, first with Eddie's mother alone and later with both families, (b) regular home visits, (c) psychiatric evaluation and management of medication, (d) ongoing planning and consultation with the school, including supportive services for the teacher, and (e) recreational activities conducted by junior program staff that focused on teaching Eddie social skills targeted at improving his peer relationships.

There were several crises during the first three months in which Eddie became extremely angry and verbally abusive. He also ran away for two to three hours at a time, usually hanging around the neighborhood and refusing to come inside. We used consequences such as point and privilege loss, short work chores, and sentence writing in these and other more minor instances of rule-breaking behavior. These consequences were short and given in a neutral manner with little or no talk about "why" he did what he did. On several occasions, program staff were dispatched to "help" him do or finish his consequence. In addition, TFC staff, program staff, school personnel, and later his mother worked together to follow through with cross-setting consistency. In instances of extreme anger on his part, we used brief (twenty-four-hour) stays in detention as a consequence. Eddie responded positively to the high degree of structure provided in the foster home and to the large amount of positive reinforcement provided. His individual therapist helped him understand that his outbursts were triggered by his feelings of failure and thoughts that others were viewing him negatively. He had an almost zero tolerance for failure, which he saw everywhere. Over a six-month period, Eddie began to like and feel supported by his TFC family and program staff. He wanted to please them and over time began to believe that they valued and cared about him.

FAMILY THERAPY

Special care was taken when involving Eddie's mother in his treatment. During the first several sessions, she described both the history of what had happened in the family and her accompanying emotional experience. The family therapist was very careful to frame her decisions as courageous and to acknowledge her feelings of being overwhelmed and alone during the early years of this family crisis. Eddie's mother felt a tremendous sense of shame and guilt for not protecting Eddie better or leaving her husband sooner. She had never received treatment for herself, and this was the first time the she had been asked to tell her side of the story without punishment or blame. She said that she had married as a teenager and moved away from her family to a rural and isolated area. Her husband had not allowed her to work, and she had no money. She was from a family with three generations of fundamentalist preachers, so the decision to leave her marriage had not been made lightly.

Eddie's mother was encouraged to discuss her specific fears about being involved in Eddie's life and having him return to her care. These fears included not having the skills to cope with his behavior, wanting to protect his younger brother who was reportedly doing very well, and being afraid of disrupting her relationship with her new spouse. We supported Eddie's mother by acknowledging that these were important and legitimate concerns, and we asked her to help us develop Eddie's treatment plan.

Numerous professionals had diagnosed Eddie as being seriously emotionally disturbed. We attempted to move away from this explanation because we thought it left a fearful and hopeless feeling about what could be done to remedy this complex situation. Instead, we focused on a "developmental disability" theory to conceptualize his treatment. The idea was that Eddie had several learning deficits in areas such as knowing how to respond calmly and appropriately to frustration and stress. We would work with him to improve these skills. We noted that Eddie would probably need long-term support for learning and maintaining these skills and that he might be vulnerable throughout his life to overreacting to stress.

School

Initially, school was very difficult and not very successful. Eddie was placed first in our program and then in public school in April, where he attended a middle school with a self-contained classroom of students classified as seriously emotionally disturbed. He started with one period a day and gradually moved up to a full day of school. Eddie was not used to public school: he was nervous and anxious, lacked many academic skills, and was unable to cope with any frustration. He was especially vulnerable to provocations from his peers. He would swear and threaten teachers and students, run in and out of the classroom, and refuse to move or be quiet. As part of our prespecified crisis plan, we would respond to calls from the school and remove him in these instances. School administrative staff were very frustrated with Eddie, became increasingly intolerant of any transgression, and would quickly call us to remove him from campus.

During the summer months, we targeted several problems that had emerged during the school year, including Eddie's preference for hanging out with highly delinquent peers at school. The plan involved one-on-one tutoring for Eddie. We contracted with a local agency and requested their most experienced tutor (who was paid by the school district). We jointly designed a treatment plan in which they would work on improving his reading and math skills and at the same time work on his compliance and ability to take criticism and feedback from the teacher. He earned daily rewards for participating. At the same time, two staff members took turns involving him in community-based activities that were fun. Intensive social skills training was embedded in these activities.

Toward the end of summer, we paid for Eddie to attend a soccer camp (run by one of our former therapists). The coach, who ran one of the best high school programs in the state, took Eddie under his wing and provided a high level of positive reinforcement. We had to retrieve Eddie on two occasions when he was too disruptive (cussing and trying to fight), but overall he did well and was learning to get along with nondelinquent peers.

Eddie had a successful summer, he liked his tutor and his community experiences, and he really liked his soccer uniform. His tolerance for frustration increased, and his swearing and bizarre talk and behavior declined dramatically. Before school began, we had him meet his new teacher, who was experienced working with youngsters with behavioral and emotional problems. There were only a few days during the first part of the year when we had to get Eddie from school, and his negative verbal and physical behaviors were nearly zero by January. He also did not like hanging out with delinquent peers because they might "get me in trouble."

THE TRANSITION HOME

We scheduled home visits beginning with a one-hour visit, building up to overnight visits, and then becoming extended visits during school holidays. His mother received twenty-four-hour backup from program staff, who on several occasions had to get Eddie from home when he became agitated and noncompliant. She was taught to use the point and level contingency management system and to apply consequences. She was encouraged and assisted to change the system to make it fit with her home and family. We then worked to eliminate the need to remove Eddie when he became agitated at home. This was done by teaching his mother not to react emotionally to his outbursts, to use consequences, and, if these failed, to call us. Once Eddie learned that he could settle matters between his mother and himself without intervention, he worked hard to control himself at home and was successful. In November, Eddie was successfully reunited with his mother. He had been in TFC for seventeen months.

AFTER CARE

Eddie's after-care program included (a) continuing social skills training, (b) individual and joint family sessions, (c) participation of Eddie's mother in an after-care group designed to support parents caring for delinquent or behaviorally and emotionally troubled adolescents (in fact, she was invited to become a paid parent advocate for a local parent support network), and (d) ongoing psychiatric management of medications. Eddie was initially prescribed a combination of lithium and halidol; once home with his mother, he was gradually taken off these medications.

CONCLUSIONS

Treatment Foster Care is a model that is effective for working with children and adolescents who have serious problems. It is less costly than group residential care and allows individual treatment plans that fit the unique needs of each participant.

Support for this project was provided by grant R01 MH47458 from the Center for Studies of Violent Behavior and Traumatic Stress and grant P50 MH46690 from the Prevention Research Branch, both of the National Institute of Mental Health, U.S. Public Health Service.

REFERENCES

Bryant, Brad. 1983. *Special Foster Care: A History and Rationale*. Verone, Va.: People Places, Inc.

Chamberlain, Patricia. 1990. "Comparative Evaluation of Specialized Foster Care for Seriously Delinquent Youths: A First Step." *Community Alternatives: International Journal of Family Care* 2(2): 21–36.

———. 1994. *Family Connections: Treatment Foster Care for Adolescents with Delinquency*. Eugene, Ore.: Castalia Press.

Chamberlain, Patricia, and J. B. Reid. 1991. "Using a Specialized Foster Care Treatment Model for Children and Adolescents Leaving the State Mental Hospital." *Journal of Community Psychology* 19(2): 266–76.

Dishion, T. J., and D. W. Andrews. 1995. "Preventing Escalation in Problem Behaviors with High-Risk Young Adolescents: Immediate and One-Year Outcomes." *Journal of Consulting and Clinical Psychology* 63(4): 538–48.

Elliott, D. S., David Huizinga, and S. S. Ageton. 1985. *Explaining Delinquency and Drug Use*. Newbury Park, Calif.: Sage Publications.

Guerra, N. G., L. R. Huesmann, P. H. Tolan, R. VanAcker, and L. D. Eron. 1995. "Stressful Events and Individual Beliefs as Correlates of Economic Disadvantage and Aggression among Urban Children." *Journal of Consulting and Clinical Psychology* 63(4): 513–28.

Hawkins, R. P. 1989. "The Nature and Potential of Therapeutic Foster Family Care Programs." In *Therapeutic Foster Care: Critical Issues*, edited by R. P. Hawkins and James Breiling. Washington, D.C.: Child Welfare League of America.

Hawkins, R. P., Pamela Meadowcroft, B. A. Trout, and W. C. Luster. 1985. "Foster Family–based Treatment." *Journal of Clinical Child Psychology* 14(3): 220–28.

Meadowcroft, Pamela. 1989. "Treating Emotionally Disturbed Children and Adolescents in Foster Homes." In *Specialist Foster Family Care: A Normalizing Experience*, edited by Jay Hudson and Burt Galaway. New York: Haworth Press.

Moore, Kevin J., and Patricia Chamberlain. 1994. "Treatment Foster Care: Toward Development of Community-based Models for Adolescents with Severe Emotional and Behavioral Disorders." *Journal of Emotional and Behavioral Disorders* 2(1): 22–30.

Mrazek, P. J., and R. J. Haggerty, eds. 1994. *Reducing Risks for Mental Disorders: Frontiers for Prevention Intervention Research*. Washington, D.C.: National Academy Press.

O'Donnell, Julie, D. J. Hawkins, and R. D. Abbott. 1995. "Predicting Serious Delinquency and Substance Use among Aggressive Boys." *Journal of Consulting and Clinical Psychology* 63(4): 529–37.

Patterson, G. R., and Gerald Brodsky. 1966. "A Behaviour Modification Programme for a Child with Multiple Problem Behaviours." *Journal of Child Psychology and Psychiatry* 7: 277–95.

Phillips, E. L., E. A. Phillips, D. L. Fixsen, and M. M. Wolf. 1972. *The Teaching-Family Handbook*. Lawrence, Kans.: Bureau of Child Research, University of Kansas.

Reid, J. B. 1991. "Mediational Screening as a Model for Prevention Research." *American Journal of Community Psychology* 19(6): 867–72.

Vorrath, H., and L. K. Brendtro. 1985. *Positive Peer Culture*. Chicago: Aldene.

CHAPTER 11

Are Welfare Employment Programs Effective?

Lawrence M. Mead

The employment programs that states have implemented for welfare recipients since the 1980s constitute a promising development in social policy, but how promising is disputed. Some experts say that the programs are effective, others that they are not. Much of the debate turns on what one means by "effective." "Welfare" here largely means Temporary Assistance for Needy Families (TANF), the new name for Aid to Families with Dependent Children (AFDC)—the controversial family assistance program—after Congress restructured it in the Personal Responsibility and Work Opportunity Reconciliation Act (PRWORA) of 1996.[1]

Congress first established work requirements for AFDC adults in 1967, when it enacted the Work Incentive Program (WIN). WIN was supposed to place employable welfare adults in work or training, but it never seriously affected more than a small part of the caseload, due to weak funding and implementation. After allowing states to experiment for much of the 1980s, Congress in 1988 replaced WIN with the Jobs Opportunities and Basic Skills Training Program (JOBS). JOBS was implemented from 1989 to 1995, and some states obtained waivers of normal federal rules to continue to run experimental work programs differing in some details (for the politics and policy developments surrounding WIN and JOBS, see Mead 1986, 1992). In 1996, PRWORA ended specific authorization for JOBS by folding its funding into the new block grant supporting TANF. But it raised work requirements still higher than before, and this will require states to keep running welfare employment programs of some kind. Thus the issue of what these programs achieve lives on.

The following sections describe various meanings of program effectiveness and argue that welfare employment programs are more successful than the evaluation literature suggests. Impacts tend to be understated for technical reasons, and they vary with how fully programs are implemented. Evaluations also neglect effects on client activity and miss diversion effects on welfare caseloads. Work requirements have substantial potential to deter entry to welfare and thus reduce dependency. Wisconsin provides a dramatic illustration. Well-crafted work programs also save money for government, and again the effects are understated due to diversion; whether the recipients gain is less clear. Reforming welfare through work is really an administrative challenge. TANF assumes that work programs can drive the rolls down substantially. Today, it is no longer disputable that work requirements have effects. Rather, the question is the nature of these effects, and whether the poor population is better or worse off as a result.

MEANINGS OF EFFECTIVENESS

When we say that a social program is "effective," we mean, at the least, that it achieves something.[2] Evaluators have taught the policy world that it is not enough to spend money on doing good. The criterion of success should not be mere *inputs* to a program. Nor should it be mere *outputs* in the sense of services delivered to clients. Nor should it even be *outcomes,* meaning the changes in the clients' condition or status, such as income or employability, that occur during or after a program treatment. Rather, it should be *impact,* meaning the *change* in outcomes that is actually *due to* the program and not something else.

OUTCOME VERSUS IMPACT

A positive change in outcomes is not itself evidence of impact. Improved results such as job entries may have occurred for reasons unrelated to the program. Suppose a work program has managed to place its clients in jobs. Perhaps it succeeded only because it chose motivated clients or because the economy was favorable. The jobs would have been obtained, that is, even without the program, and thus it should receive no credit for them. Impact must be measured against the counterfactual, against what would have occurred otherwise. That need is especially great in the case of welfare. People usually go on aid because they have lost jobs or spouses. Many rebound into employment or remarriage and thus leave aid, whether or not anything is done to help them. A welfare employment program should not receive credit for this turnover. It achieves impact only if it causes *more* recipients to take jobs and leave aid than would have done so *without* the program.

The rationale for experimental evaluations is that they separate the true from the apparent effects of a program. A random sample of clients is drawn from the population to be served, and then this sample is allocated randomly to two groups, one of which receives the experimental treatment, while the other—the control group—does not. Due to random assignment, the program cannot choose the most motivated people to serve. The experimental clients will probably not differ systematically in any attribute, either measured or unmeasured, from the controls. If they realize better outcomes, therefore, that gain can truly be attributed to the program. The difference is an unbiased measure of impact.[3] The Manpower Demonstration Research Corporation (MDRC), the main evaluator of welfare employment programs, has built its reputation on this sort of study.

Is the Impact Test Demanding?

From one point of view, the impact criterion is demanding. It means that programs must "really" have effects, not only appear to. A program does not succeed because it generates appealing success stories, let alone because it has good intentions. The social programs of the 1930s, such as the Works Progress Administration, are fondly remembered as having helped overcome the Great Depression. But they did not undergo serious evaluations, so we do not really know if they achieved an impact or not.

The designers of the War on Poverty in the 1960s were liberals who believed that government could help the poor, but many were also economists who insisted on evaluating the new programs rigorously. Unfortunately, measured against the impact test, many popular education and training programs, such as Head Start, proved disappointing. The effect of this sort of social science was ultimately conservatizing, bringing ambitious social programming into question (Aaron 1978). The experience gave rise to Rossi's Law: "The expected value of any net impact assessment of any large-scale social program is zero" (Rossi 1987, 4).

From another viewpoint, however, the impact criterion is lenient, for it requires only impact. That is, it asks that a program show effects on a social problem, but not that it fully overcome that problem. Commonly, experimental evaluations find that a program has some impact on skills, earnings, or other outcomes, even if not a large one. Yet a small impact can be enough to justify the program's expense in cost-benefit terms, especially if consideration is given to far-in-the-future reductions in crime or welfare by the clients. The program is then judged to be a rational investment, and its designers advocate that society spend more on it.[4] But the effects on the problem in question—for example, school failure by disadvantaged students—may still be too small or long-term for anyone but the evaluators to notice. Thus conventional evaluation can declare programs successful without their having any effects on social problems that the public can see. This disjuncture grows greater the better-designed an evaluation is. Studies with large samples can detect quite small differences in outcome between experimentals and controls.

These conflicting notions of effectiveness underlie much of the debate over the value of anti-poverty programs. The public clearly wants government to solve social problems, not only to affect them. Government's apparent inability to reduce crime or welfarism or elevate school performance contributed to the image of incompetence in domestic policy that dogged the federal government in the 1970s and 1980s. This, in turn, fomented the rightward political trend of those years (Mead 1992). Republicans took power—in the White House with Ronald Reagan in 1981 and in Congress with Newt Gingrich in 1995—promising to cut back anti-poverty programs. As their rationale, they had only to cite the long series of disappointing evaluations—mostly done by liberal evaluators—in education, training, criminal justice, and other areas. That record gave credence to the further charge that social programs, particularly welfare, had actually exacerbated poverty by rewarding the poor for failing to marry and work (Murray 1984).

But, on the other side, liberals retorted that the effect of tested programs is seldom actually zero and rarely negative. Most do show some impacts, even if they are smaller than we would wish. Some programs, notably the Perry Preschool project in Ypsilanti, Michigan, have demonstrated long-term benefits that make them look more successful after years than they did at first (Berrueta-Clement and others 1984). The view that government always fails is, thus, ignorant and unfair. Good programs can make some headway against poverty, provided government is prepared to "invest" in them for the long term (Schorr 1988; Susan Mayer and Christopher Jencks, "War on Poverty:

No Apologies, Please," *New York Times*, November 9, 1995, A29). But again, effectiveness in this sense does not satisfy the public's desire to solve social problems visibly in the present.

EFFECTIVENESS IN WELFARE EMPLOYMENT

A persuasive definition of effectiveness ought to include both impact and what I will call sufficiency. That is, the effective program is one that has clear effects on the problem it addresses *and* which substantially or visibly overcomes that problem in the present, or could do so if it were implemented fully. In welfare-to-work policy, the chief goals are to raise the earnings and employment of welfare adults and to reduce the dependency of their families. These aims are rarely in conflict, because for the adults to go to work usually raises incomes and often takes the families off welfare, if not out of poverty.[5] To achieve impact and sufficiency, therefore, welfare work programs should clearly improve employment and reduce dependency, and they should be able to do this for the bulk of welfare adults.

This would imply achieving and sustaining employment at least for the recipients who are judged to be employable. Experts judge that the employable include perhaps four-fifths of the women who ever go on welfare and about two-thirds of those on the rolls at a given time, who tend to be the more disadvantaged (Maynard 1995; Gueron 1996, 555; Mead 1992, 124–27). Alternatively, effectiveness might mean driving the employable off welfare so that the rolls were radically reduced, even if the remaining cases could not work enough to escape dependency.

UNDERSTATED IMPACTS

Are welfare employment programs effective in these terms? There is at least hope. If anything has repealed Rossi's Law, it is the welfare work programs evaluated by MDRC since the early 1980s. These projects showed more consistent impacts in experimental evaluations than any previous class of social program serving large populations. The first of the projects, in San Diego, showed as early as 1984 that it could raise the employment of welfare applicants and reduce their dependence on aid (Goldman and others 1984). From that point, the whole debate in Washington about welfare and poverty took a more hopeful turn. The perception grew that these programs worked, and for this reason the Family Support Act (FSA) of 1988 was devoted mainly to the creation of JOBS, the most ambitious welfare work structure up till then (Wiseman 1991a).

Small Differences   Analysts at the political extremes, both right and left, tend to dismiss welfare employment impacts as inconsequential. This serves their political agenda, which is to argue that reformism must fall and that radical change—either to the right or left—is unavoidable. Libertarians say that dependency is the product of the welfare state (Murray 1994), while leftists blame it on the capitalist economy (Piven and Cloward 1993). Once work programs are seen as feeble palliatives, the first group hopes to abolish national antipoverty programs, while the second wants government to intervene forcefully in the economy to guarantee employment.

From a certain point of view, the effects are indeed small. Table 11.1 describes the average impacts from the nine primary evaluations of welfare employment programs that MDRC has completed from 1985 to the present. The middle column shows the effects expressed as absolute differences between the experimental and control groups. It is difficult to believe that a rise in earnings of $329 or in employment of three percentage points could transform the welfare system. For several reasons, however, impacts expressed this way are understated.

Percentages of Baseline   It is reasonable to ask not only how large impacts are in absolute terms, but how large they are relative to where recipients began. If impacts are expressed as percentages of the control-group mean, as in the right-hand column of table 11.1, they appear more substantial. Perhaps the average program raises employment or reduces welfare by only three points, but as a percentage of the baseline, the typical improvement is two to four times as great. Admittedly, the percentage gain is inflated by the smallness of the base.

In the most notable programs evaluated by MDRC, however, the effects were sizable by any measure. The Saturation Work Initiative Model (SWIM) in San Diego and California's Greater Avenues for Independence (GAIN) in Riverside County recorded earnings impacts of $658 and $1,010 a year, respectively, representing 29 and 40 percent of the control-group mean. The programs also reduced annual welfare payments by $553 and $584, or 14 and 17 percent of the base, respectively. Over three years, Riverside raised the share of its clients who worked by a quarter and their earnings by close to half, compared to controls (Riccio, Friedlander, and Freedman 1994, 7, 120; for details about SWIM and GAIN, see table 11A.1). Impacts on this

Table 11.1 Average Results from Nine Main MDRC Welfare Employment Evaluations

Impact	Control Mean	Experimental-Control Difference	Percentage Change
Average earnings (dollars)	1,992	329	16
Percent employed at end of final year	28.4	3.0	11
Average AFDC payments (dollars)	2,409	−175	−7
Percent on welfare at end of final year	55.2	−3.1	−6

Note: For details of individual studies and sources, see table 11A.1.

scale approach sufficiency because they are visible to people other than evaluators.

Late Randomization Impacts are understated, furthermore, because the baseline against which effects are measured is higher than many people realize. The idea of an experimental evaluation suggests that the treatment group gets a new program and the control group gets nothing at all. But in practice, the control clients often receive treatment much like that given to the experimentals. For one thing, it is not always possible to keep the controls entirely out of an experiment. In MDRC's Florida study, 20 percent of the control group were inadvertently exposed to various aspects of the experimental program, a mistake that reduced the measured impacts of the program by as much as 20 percent (Kemple, Friedlander, and Fellerath 1995, 55, 57, 101–104).

More subtly, in several of the MDRC projects, the controls received some elements of the welfare employment treatment by design. An evaluation that tests all dimensions of a work test would separate the experimental and control clients at the point when they first applied for welfare or were found to be mandatory for the work requirement.[6] But of those required to enter welfare work programs, only two-thirds or less actually do so, in part because they never complete their applications or they leave welfare quickly (in seven MDRC studies, the percentage of clients referred to work programs who ever participated in them ranged from 38 to 64 percent; see Gueron and Pauly 1991, 128–34). One reason may be that they hear a message about the need to work and avoid dependency. Not facing the same requirements, the controls hear such a message less and are more likely to go on aid and stay there. The difference is a diversion effect that represents part of a work program's impact. If randomization occurs at the time of application, the experiment will get credit for it, just as it will for any success in moving clients into jobs after they enter the program. In MDRC's studies in Baltimore, Florida, San Diego, and Virginia, this was the research design.

However, in the five other MDRC projects (Arkansas, California GAIN, Cook County, San Diego SWIM, and West Virginia), randomization was done only among recipients who had been assigned to work *and* who had reported to the work program for registration and orientation. Only then were some admitted to the program and some consigned to a control group. This meant that the program could get credit only for impacts produced after entering the program, typically by moving its clients toward work. It could not get credit for diversion occurring between application and registration. Also, by attending registration and orientation, the controls got some of the message about the need to work intended for the experimentals. For both reasons, all else being equal, the achievements of the programs should appear smaller than if randomization were at the time of application.[7]

Controls Served by Other Programs   Further, clients in the control groups may well be exposed to suasions unrelated to the tested program. By the time MDRC began its projects in the early 1980s, welfare mothers whose youngest children were at least six years old were already supposed to enroll in the WIN program, as were other welfare adults without family or school responsibilities. Clients relegated to control groups in the MDRC studies escaped the experimental work program but were still subject to WIN. The top panel of table 11.2 shows activity levels in studies where MDRC compared participation by the experimentals in the tested program to participation by the controls in WIN. This comparison is only rough, because studies differed in many respects, including the point of randomization.[8] Activity was much lower in WIN than in the newer programs, chiefly because WIN had less funding and was more leniently administered. The WIN levels, though, are not zero. Although WIN generally was ineffective, any effect it did have reduced the measured impact in these experiments.

Controls were also able to obtain education and training services entirely outside welfare employment. In several projects where MDRC had information from community colleges, nonwelfare training programs, or surveys of clients, it was able to show participation

Table 11.2 Activity Levels of Experimentals and Controls in MDRC Evaluations (Percent)

Study	Experimentals	Controls
Using WIN data		
In any employment and training activity	40	5
In job search or job club	35	1
Using other data		
In any employment and training activity	56	29
In job search or job club	40	6
In education or training	30	23

Notes: Intervals covered vary. For details of individual studies and sources, see table 11A.2.

in these activities as well. The lower panel of table 11.2 shows average activity levels for experimentals and controls in these studies. Again, the comparison is only rough. However, participation by controls is much higher than when only WIN was considered: 29 percent of the controls had some involvement in employment-related activities, mostly in education or training. Again, if these services were of any benefit, the effect was to reduce the measured impact of the welfare work experiment.

The problem of the nonzero baseline would be slight if the experiment being tested were the only program of its kind. Welfare work programs, however, were instituted in the 1970s and 1980s, at a time when the ground was already encumbered with many other federal and local training and education programs. Recipients consigned to the control group for an MDRC experiment could obtain similar training from local programs operating under the Job Training Partnership Act (JTPA), vocational education, or local community colleges, and many did. Often in a locality, all these programs compete for clients, and not enough eligibles remain outside the system to construct a truly unserved control group to evaluate any of them.

IMPACTS AND IMPLEMENTATION

Likewise, one may presume for several reasons that the evaluated impacts of welfare employment programs vary with the degree of implementation. As work requirements are implemented more fully, their effects will probably rise. That gives hope that work programs could show a sufficient impact on the welfare problem, not only a detectable one.

The Averaging Problem

Just as the control group can include people who receive services, so the experimental group can include people who do not, and again measured impact is reduced. In the experimental method, the impact is estimated by the difference in *average* outcomes between experimentals and controls, with the means for both groups computed over all their members, whatever happened to them.[9] But, as noted, not all experimental clients enter the tested program. This means that the experimental average includes many people who did not actually receive the treatment.

Nonparticipation is minor in voluntary programs, where it is assumed that clients apply for benefits and receive them if they are admitted. It is substantial, however, in mandatory programs, which serve a population many of whom do not come forward on their own.[10] In both WIN and JOBS, the vast majority of clients enrolled only because they were required to as a condition of welfare eligibility.[11] Inevitably, many will drop out and not be served, depressing recorded impact.

It makes sense to test a program's effects on the whole experimental group if it is meant in principle to serve an entire clientele, as is true for mandatory work programs. It is also necessary methodologically. The estimate of impact is valid only if the experimental and control groups are truly equivalent. They will be equivalent reliably only if the estimate considers all individuals in both groups—whether or not they actually participated actively. One cannot single out the clients who were active and calculate an impact just for them. They might differ, in measured or unmeasured ways, from the control group, and the estimate would no longer be untainted by selection bias.

A consequence, however, is to understate considerably how much welfare adults may gain from participation or employment. Impacts can look small, in part, because the group averages merge the improvements in earnings, or reductions in dependency, realized by clients who go to work, with a lot of zeros for the nonworkers. In SWIM, for example, the average experimental earned $2,903 during the program's second year, but since only 49 percent of this group worked during that year, the average *employed* experimental earned about twice that much (Gueron and Pauly 1991, 145). If one focuses on the gains of the working recipients and not on the average impacts, the potential of work programs to solve the welfare problem looks greater.

The point here is not that the impacts of the programs are really twice what they seem. We cannot assume that the recipients who work and realize large gains do so because of the program. Nor is it reasonable to compare the results for working experimentals with the averages for controls. Averaging also occurs among the controls, and there too people with earnings will do considerably better than the average. The difference in average impact is still a fair test of the program.

Rather, the point is that impact is likely to vary positively with participation rates. If work programs have any good effect, they have it by causing more recipients to work and thus realize the gains typical of the workers. The more clients actually partake of the program, the greater will be the number who are likely to have earnings and other favorable outcomes. Then a higher proportion of experimentals will contribute something to the averages, and measured impact will rise (Greenberg and Wiseman 1992, 39–40, 45–46). This will happen even if the gains per employed experimental do not improve at all, and perhaps even if they drop. A demanding work program might cause more reluctant clients to work than a lenient one would. Their jobs would pay less on average than those of the more advantaged clients placed by the lenient program.[12] Average wages and earnings would fall *among employed experimentals*. However, they would also rise *among all experimentals,* and thus measured impacts would rise.[13]

Conversely, if programs fail to show effect, a major reason is simply that so many recipients referred for work never participate. The difference between typical gains and working gains was enormous even for SWIM, which achieved one of the highest participation rates ever realized in welfare employment. The gap would be even greater in a typical program with lower participation. Thus the evaluations of welfare employment programs are tests of the level of participation more than the efficacy of services. An evaluation of a program with low participation is not a good indicator of what that program, if fully implemented, might achieve.

REACHING BELOW THE CREAM

Impacts will rise for another reason as well. As a higher proportion of the eligibles participate in a work program, the additional clients tend to be those for whom impact will be higher. When a work program first serves a welfare caseload, the clients who most readily participate are typically the most employable. They tend to be motivated, and they often have a high school diploma and a work history. They enter the program as volunteers or with little suasion, and they quickly get jobs, often at good wages, and leave welfare.[14] However, clients like this would typically succeed even without the program. Their fortunes will be little different from those of equivalent controls who find work on their own, so the program generates little impact by serving them. These easy-to-serve cases comprise about a third of the adults on welfare, and it was this third that welfare employment chiefly served prior to the experiments evaluated by MDRC. That largely explains why WIN had little palpable effect on the caseload (Mead 1992, 167–68, 171–72).[15]

To maximize impact, a program must reach deeper down in the employability barrel. A close study of the MDRC projects revealed that most of their effects on employment and welfare did not come from fresh applicants to welfare, who tend to be the most employable. They came rather from applicants returning to welfare after a break and, in some instances, from recipients already on the rolls—groups that are less employable (Friedlander 1988). This implies that, to maximize impact, welfare employment programs must expand their participation so that they reach at least the top two-thirds of the caseload.[16] Because programs cannot achieve these levels voluntarily, they must be mandatory and must enforce participation stringently.[17]

It is quite possible that impacts would eventually fall as the bottom of the barrel was reached. This is because the most disadvantaged clients have too many problems to benefit much from conventional employment and training treatments. They might be given assignments short of actual work, such as participation in community activities (Herr, Halpern, and Conrad 1991), but these would not much increase employment or lower dependency. However, in most places participation rates in work programs are still well short of this point.

THE GROWTH OF IMPACTS

One can argue that the impacts recorded by work programs serving the disadvantaged have already grown as those programs have become more demanding. Most would say that the welfare employment programs evaluated, as a group, show stronger effects on employment and earnings than voluntary government training programs run under the auspices of the Comprehensive Employment and Training Act (CETA) of 1973 to 1982 or the Job Training Partnership Act (JTPA) since 1982. While most of the welfare work programs at least show effects, JTPA's impacts in a national evaluation were mostly nonsignificant and, for some groups, negative (Bloom and others 1992). A reason why the welfare employment programs perform better probably is that they reach more of the ambivalent clients where there is greater potential to produce change.

Impacts among the welfare employment projects studied by MDRC have improved as it has become clearer how to run effective programs. Considering all the MDRC studies, there is no general trend for impacts to grow over time, but there is for projects within California, the state that has had the largest influence on national developments.[18] There, the record of each program has shaped it successor. The initial San Diego effort of the early 1980s started the vogue for welfare employment. Its successor, SWIM, improved on those impacts primarily by enforcing participation more stiffly. By emphasizing job search as well as participation, Riverside GAIN then improved on SWIM. The GAIN evaluation obtained impacts in six counties comparable to the initial San Diego results, even though, of the six programs tested, only those in San Diego and Riverside were conspicuously well run. Recently, counties throughout California have come under pressure to run JOBS more as Riverside does. In 1995 the state legislature amended GAIN to weaken the strong presumptions of remediation contained in the original legislation and to require more recipients to look for work up-front. Los Angeles is now shifting its vast program toward the Riverside model (Weissman 1997).

Recently, MDRC released preliminary results from a nationwide evaluation of JOBS that look even more encouraging. The data come from three local sites (Atlanta, Georgia; Grand Rapids, Michigan; and Riverside, California) that are testing two different versions of JOBS. One is a labor force attachment model stressing job search and immediate work; the other is a human capital development approach that encourages clients to enter education or training in preference to work in hopes of getting better jobs later. Table 11.3 shows the impacts for both models after two years. The labor force attachment results are much the stronger. Admittedly, this may be partly because impacts from remediation may take more than two years to appear. The labor force attachment results are also considerably better than the averages in table 11.1. They are comparable to Riverside's, and they are now produced through a common program philosophy in three different localities.[19] That again suggests that as work programs are better implemented, they will show higher impacts around the country.

Table 11.3 Preliminary Impacts from MDRC National JOBS Evaluation

Model and Outcome	Control Mean	Absolute Impact	Percentage Change
Labor force attachment model			
Average earning (dollars)	2,712	696	25.8
Percent with earnings	34.4	8.1	23.5
Average AFDC payments (dollars)	3,312	−732	−21.9
Percent on AFDC	68.3	−11.1	−16.2
Human capital development model			
Average earnings (dollars)	2,508	−24	−0.8
Percent with earnings	32.4	2.6	8.1
Average AFDC payments (dollars)	3,420	−456	−13.5
Percent on AFDC	68.8	−4.2	−6.1

Source: Freedman and Friedlander 1995.
Note: Dollar figures are annualized from data for months.

In light of these and other evaluation results, it has become reasonably clear that the best work programs are those that (a) maximize participation and (b) require that participants actually work or look for work in preference to entering education or training. An effect on national policy is apparent. Where WIN was largely voluntary, JOBS was considerably more demanding about participation, although it favored education and training over actual work as the activity within work programs. PRWORA both raises the participation threshold far above that of JOBS and shifts the nature of participation sharply toward work.

IMPACTS ON LIFESTYLE

If we look beyond orthodox evaluation studies such as MDRC's, there is additional reason to call welfare employment programs effective. Economic effects capture vital dimensions of program performance, but not the noneconomic dimensions that are politically most important.

One would imagine from the MDRC studies that the goals of the programs were simply to raise recipients' earnings so that more of them can leave welfare and money is saved. But it is clear that the main controversies in welfare politics are not economic. The public and politicians are not exercised about welfare primarily because it costs money. Welfare budgets are well below those of larger social insurance programs such as Social Security or Medicare (for summaries of studies of public opinion about welfare and poverty, see Mead 1986, 1992).[20]

Rather, the chief controversy in welfare is about the lifestyle of adult recipients. While about half of welfare families go on the rolls for two years or less, the other half stays on longer, and the rolls at a point in time are dominated by these chronic cases (Bane and Ellwood 1994, chap. 2). The long-term recipients remain dependent largely because they do not work regularly and often have children out of wedlock. Who is responsible for these behaviors? Could the adults work more than they do? Are they to be seen as "deserving" of aid, or as "undeserving"? These are the issues that dominate controversy about welfare, not the costs of the programs.

Public opinion studies show that the public wants to enforce good behavior on welfare adults but also to help families in need. That combination makes voters uneasy at proposals simply to spend more or less on welfare. Spending more does not change behavior, and spending less might put the needy at risk. Most people would prefer to turn AFDC into a work program, in which families receive an income in return for work, just as taxpayers do. Then good behavior is enforced while families are assured of income. If a work-oriented welfare program costs more money, in order to guarantee jobs or child care for the recipients, voters accept that, provided that the work demand is serious. Politically, putting adults to work is much more important than getting them off welfare, although the former will often accomplish the latter. From the public's perspective, the key aim of welfare employment is to change lifestyle—simply to have welfare adults do more to help themselves. Actually working or leaving aid may be the final goal, but to show effort in that direction is also an end in itself.

RAISING ACTIVITY LEVELS

The Family Support Act was crafted only in part to maximize economic impacts. States were required to spend 55 percent of their federal JOBS money on disadvantaged groups of clients likely to generate economic gains, and federal officials were told to draft performance measures for the program that would promote impacts.[21] These provisions generated little debate.

Rather, the main controversy surrounding FSA was about whether participation levels in JOBS would be high enough to satisfy the public thirst to see work effort on the rolls. Congressional Republicans and the Reagan White House demanded that activity standards be much higher than in WIN, which was required to serve only 15 percent of its eligibles annually. FSA required states to involve 20 percent of their employable recipients in JOBS on a monthly basis by 1995, a much stiffer standard. Regulations written by the Bush Administration defined participation to require assigned activities of at least twenty hours a week, a level many localities protested as excessive (Mead 1992, chap. 9). Nevertheless, in the debates leading to PRWORA, Democrats and Republicans competed to set still tougher requirements, leading to very severe new work and participation standards.

Thus the activity levels indicated in table 11.2 have great importance in themselves, quite aside from the influence that activity may have on impacts. Although controls are active enough to understate the measured effects of experimental programs, there is still an enormous difference in level between them and the experimentals. To take the more conservative numbers from the lower panel, *almost twice as many* recipients do something to help themselves when they are subject to a work program than when they are not. And while experimentals participate in education and training only slightly more often than controls, they enter job search *more than six times* more often. Looking for work is the activity the public most wants to see from dependent adults.

A related idea is "coverage." The broadest goal of a work program is to make the caseload accountable for lifestyle in various ways. This it may do by causing more recipients to go to work or look for work, but also by ensuring that those who do not comply absorb a sanction (a reduced grant) or leave welfare. A caseload that must do one of these things is "covered" in a sense meaningful to the public, even if only part of it goes to work. In seven studies, MDRC estimated that programs achieved coverage of 75 to 97 percent of their eligibles over nine to twelve months (Gueron and Pauly 1991, 133–34). In SWIM, the most stringent example, only 3 percent of clients managed to remain on welfare and in SWIM without participating in the program, undertaking education or training on their own, working, or incurring a sanction (Hamilton 1988, 140–42).

These effects on activity dwarf any of the economic impacts. Politically, they are probably at least as important, and more should be made of them as a justification for welfare employment programs. Effects on lifestyle, not on earnings or dependency, are where the programs approach closest to sufficiency.

IMPACTS ON DEPENDENCY

It would be difficult to argue for sufficiency, however, unless work programs show more effect on the welfare rolls than they have thus far. As table 11.1 suggests, measured impacts on dependency or on welfare payments have generally been smaller than effects on employment or earnings, both absolutely and relative to the baseline.

Earnings gains in welfare work programs apparently translate poorly into welfare reductions. The main reason is probably that gains are concentrated among the more advantaged recipients who leave welfare quickly even without a program. These clients generate little welfare savings when compared to similar controls. The discrepancy appears greatest in training-oriented programs. Work-oriented programs are more able to shorten welfare stays (Friedlander and Burtless 1995, 78–87, 194–95).

It is understandable, in part, that employment impacts should exceed welfare impacts. Not all welfare adults who go to work earn enough money to leave the rolls, although their grants should be reduced. Welfare rules allow recipients who work to keep some of their earnings rather than reduce their grants by the full amount, a "work incentive" meant to promote employment. The more generous such incentives, the more possible it is to work without leaving welfare.[22] Meanwhile, many controls leave the rolls for a variety of reasons (work, remarriage, ineligibility). Against a baseline with such turnover, it is harder for work programs to show an impact on dependency than on employment (Gueron and Pauly 1991, 149, 152).

UNDERSTATED IMPACTS

Again, however, welfare impacts are understated, for reasons beyond those mentioned. One of these is that not all the jobs that recipients enter are reported to welfare. Some clients work off-the-books, so they can receive their earnings without any reduction in their welfare grant. When surveyed by the government, only 8 percent of AFDC mothers reported that they were working, even part-time (U.S. Congress 1996, 474). But according to analyses of the Panel Study of Income Dynamics, an academic database, the real level is probably a quarter, and 51 percent of welfare mothers work at some time while on welfare (Moffitt 1983, 1029; Harris 1993, 329–30). According to an interview study of 214 welfare mothers, 15 percent of their income came from various forms of employment, legal or illegal, most of it unreported (Edin 1995, 2–3).

Failure to detect such jobs reduces the anti-dependency impact of a work program. This assumes that the program should receive some credit for the jobs and that the skills and motivation it gives to its clients will make them more likely to obtain jobs secretly than clients in a control group. At the same time, the program also makes it more likely that unreported jobs will be detected. One of the purposes is to "smoke out" recipients who are working off-the-books by assigning them to activities that they cannot discharge consistent with their jobs. Presumably, smoke-outs will occur more among participants in a work program than among controls not subject to these pressures. If the recipients who are flushed out give up the jobs in order to join the program, impacts might be depressed, whereas if they give up welfare and keep the jobs, impacts would rise.[23]

Even when welfare caseworkers know about jobs, they may not adjust grants or close cases because of the paperwork involved. According to some accounts, caseworkers may discourage recipients from working or reporting earnings for fear that the case will become "error-prone" and trigger quality-control sanctions (Bane and Ellwood 1994, 6–7, 126–27). Failure to reduce grants for earnings is no doubt one reason why recipients who work do not have their benefits "taxed" away at the rate legislators intend. Between 1967 and 1981, AFDC adults who took jobs were supposed to lose almost two-thirds of their earnings in reduced grants, but the real tax rate was less than a third (Fraker, Moffitt, and Wolf 1985).

Welfare impacts are also understated because conventional evaluations capture mostly the "exit" effect of a work program—its ability to cause people already on the rolls to leave welfare faster. They miss much of the "entry" effects—the impact that a work program may have on whether people go on welfare in the first place. Entry effects may be positive if a work program attracts people onto welfare by removing the stigma of dependency or if eligibles think it will make them more employable. But on balance the effects are probably negative, because work requirements raise the "cost" of going on welfare in terms of time and trouble. One simulation found that full implementation of a demanding version of JOBS might depress the rolls by as much as 25 percent (Moffitt 1996).

It is difficult to study such effects experimentally. As mentioned, an evaluation where random assignment occurs at the time of registration for the work program misses diversion effects that occur beforehand. And even randomization at the time of application for welfare misses people who may be deterred even from approaching welfare. In the latter case, it is difficult even to define the population affected by the policies, let alone set up an experiment. A serious work or child support requirement might change the whole climate surrounding welfare, making dependency seem less acceptable and thus reducing the rolls (discussions of diversion and the research problems it poses are as yet rare; see Manski and Garfinkel 1992, chaps. 1, 6–7; Moffitt 1996). It has not appeared to MDRC that the institution of more serious work programs caused welfare applications to drop off, but these studies have produced no systematic information on the question (Gueron and Pauly 1991, 77, 183–84). Most of the projects occurred before work requirements were implemented sufficiently to affect the bulk of the caseload.

As it happens, JOBS was implemented in the midst of a substantial expansion of AFDC. Between 1989 and 1994, the rolls grew 30 percent nationally. This certainly implies that JOBS did not in any general sense restrain dependency. However, statistical analysis suggests that states that implemented JOBS forcefully suffered markedly less welfare growth than others, even controlling for differences among their caseloads, economics, and other factors (Mead 1995b).

These simulation and statistical results are not directly comparable to the impact findings from the MDRC evaluations. But they are in some rough sense stronger. They suggest that the evaluations do not capture all that welfare employment might do to drive caseloads down, especially if it is fully and forcefully implemented.

WELFARE DECLINE IN WISCONSIN

Wisconsin may well illustrate the capacity of work programs to reduce dependency in ways the public can see (the following discussion is based largely on Mead 1997a). During the 1989 to 1994 welfare boom, when the average state suffered a 34 percent increase in AFDC, Wisconsin was one of only four states to record a decline, of 8 percent. It achieved this despite paying among the highest benefits in the nation; the other three decliners—Arkansas, Louisiana, and Mississippi—were all southern states with low benefits. Over the longer period from 1987 to 1995, the caseload grew 29 percent in the average state but fell 27 percent in Wisconsin, or 9 points more than in the next-best state (Mississippi). According to more-recent state figures, from January 1987 to October 1996, Wisconsin cut its AFDC cases by 51 percent. Dependency fell 73 percent in the average county, more than 80 percent in some rural counties, and 25 percent even in Milwaukee, which has the state's largest and most nonwhite caseload.[24]

In the past few years, several states have outpaced Wisconsin in their rate of decline, but much of this is attributable to their late start as well as a favorable national economy. Wisconsin was the only northern, urban state to escape the recent boom and the only one that has reduced AFDC across an entire business cycle. Its record in reducing dependency is unparalleled.

THE REASONS FOR DECLINE

Most academic observers attribute this performance to the state's own favorable economy, which generates many jobs and low unemployment, and to a decline in its welfare benefits. Wisconsin suffered a much shallower recession in the early 1990s than much of the country, and Governor Tommy Thompson cut AFDC benefits 6 percent when he first took office in 1987. Nominal benefits have not been reduced since, but their real value has declined further with inflation, thus rendering fewer families eligible for aid (Wiseman 1996).

Observers within Wisconsin also mention the favorable economy, but seldom the decline in benefits. Instead, they mention the programs the state has undertaken to enforce work and otherwise promote self-reliance among welfare recipients. These include not only JOBS but also Learnfare, which requires welfare parents to keep their children in school, better enforcement of child support, and other initiatives. State officials credit these efforts with having "sent a message" to the dependent about the need for work. This, they say, caused many to leave welfare even when, as in the case of Learnfare, the immediate object was not necessarily to reduce the rolls.

These impressions are largely confirmed by statistical analysis. Time-series analysis does not show the caseload trend to be related clearly to unemployment rates or benefit levels.[25] However, a comparison of counties within Wisconsin shows the decline in caseloads to be greatest where the economy was most favorable and where the JOBS program was implemented most fully. The higher a county's level of participation in JOBS, the greater its decline in caseloads, even controlling for differences in the labor market and the demographics of the caseload. Effects probably varied over time; economic conditions apparently did most to depress the caseload in the late 1980s, JOBS in the early 1990s. The result is as valid for Milwaukee as elsewhere; the city has trailed the rest of the state in the fall in caseloads mainly because it did not enforce activity or work in welfare until recently, not because its caseload is unusually disadvantaged.

WORK PROGRAMS IN WISCONSIN

The Wisconsin experience confirms the arguments made earlier that the impact of work programs varies with their implementation and that much of the effect on dependency comes from diversion. The state obtained an early start on work enforcement by implementing improved welfare work programs with its own money in some localities in 1987 to 1989, prior to the Family Support Act. It then used JOBS money to expand programs further. Some officials in the state believe that this early buildup convinced recipients of the seriousness of work requirements and thus triggered the caseload fall. Counties that got this head start were better at reducing the caseload later.

Although work programs in Wisconsin have not been evaluated broadly, over time they have converged on the approach suggested by evaluations elsewhere, placing an emphasis on high participation and actual work. The counties typically enforce participation stringently. Many traditionally favored education and training as a service strategy. At first this probably retarded the fall in caseloads, but it gained the state a grip on its caseload that it later used to drive dependency down.[26]

The notable programs in the state emphasize both participation and work. The most exemplary is probably Kenosha, where most recipients have to work at least part-time before they qualify for training. In 1992 the National Alliance of Business chose Kenosha as the best JOBS program in the country. In 1993 Kenosha already had 40 percent of its clients working in private or government jobs, a level far above normal for JOBS (Mead 1995a, 21–22). In Kenosha and other leading counties, work program operations are highly paternalistic. Case managers follow up on clients closely to be sure they get the help they need to participate but also to verify that they fulfill their assignments and do not drop out.

In addition to implementing JOBS, the Thompson administration has launched experimental programs in some counties that are even tougher about demanding participation and work and that deliberately aim at diversion. These include Work First and Self-Sufficiency First, which demand that applicants for aid look for work before they get assistance, and Pay for Performance, which demands that recipients document hours of activity in job search or training in order to "earn" their benefits. Work First and Self-Sufficiency First station staff at welfare intake offices to try to persuade would-be applicants to get a job or help from their families rather than apply for aid. Work Not Welfare, operating in two counties, makes these demands and also limits aid to a total of twenty-four months; it is a pilot for Wisconsin Works, or W-2, the work-based aid system that was implemented statewide in September 1997. Because these projects were implemented mainly from 1994 on, they can explain little of the caseload fall since 1987 (Wiseman 1996). But their diversion effects appear to have accelerated the recent decline, especially in Milwaukee.

IS DIVERSION DENIAL?

Some might ask how diversion differs from simply denying people access to aid. Wisconsin might as well withdraw from TANF or reduce benefits to subsistence levels. Liberals have made this criticism ever since conservatives started building up fraud and abuse detection and work and child support requirements in welfare in the 1970s (Lipsky 1984; Brodkin 1986; Sosin 1986). But, at least in Wisconsin, diversion does not simply close the door to welfare. Applicants, if eligible, can still apply for aid and get it, and those who decide not to apply are not simply abandoned by government. Officials help them make arrangements alternative to welfare, including referring them to other programs, and government still accepts some responsibility for good outcomes. The new W-2 system offers novel health and child care subsidies to all working poor, on and off welfare. The new policies advise the needy about how to avoid dependency, and this is itself a service—one missing if welfare just goes out of business.

AN ECONOMIC RECKONING

Although the main issues in welfare are not economic, most work programs appear to save money for government and to be a rational investment for the community (the following discussion draws on Gueron and Pauly 1991; Riccio, Friedlander, and Freedman 1994; Kemple, Friedlander, and Fellerath 1995). Government must be willing to spend some money up-front in additional administration and support services such as child care to put welfare recipients to work.

But that investment is more than offset within three to five years. How much is saved and by whom, however, depends on the nature of the program.

In the nine programs studied by MDRC, government spent an additional $157 to $3,422 per experimental client, over and above what it was already spending.[27] In most cases, it recouped enough in reduced welfare and other economies to more than cover its costs. However, how much it saved depended on the nature of the program. Programs oriented to training or public employment, such as those in Baltimore, West Virginia, and some counties in California GAIN, lost money, while those oriented to job search and available employment, such as those in San Diego, saved two or three times what they cost. This was because the first group of programs spent heavily on education or government jobs, while the latter generated more gains in employment, earnings, and reduced welfare. Thus, the work-oriented model is generally preferable on grounds of both impact and cost.

From a broader, cost-benefit perspective, most of the programs again look successful, in that most produce more good for society than they cost. However, as with the budgetary reckoning, a positive result depends on generating enough gains in earnings and reduction in welfare to offset expenses. The few programs that did not net out positive were those where either the employment gains were too limited to do this (Florida) or unusually heavy costs were incurred for education and training without corresponding payoffs (Alameda and Los Angeles in California GAIN).

Gains and losses varied from different perspectives. Programs that generated large increases in earnings recorded gains for their clients, while those that produced large reductions in welfare sometimes yielded gains for the government budget or society while leaving the recipients worse off, because their earnings gains did not outweigh the loss of benefits. Parents from two-parent welfare cases, where they were served, often did worse than parents from the larger single-parent caseload. The former, often men, were often ushered off welfare, but they did not improve their earnings enough to recoup the loss. The latter, often single mothers, had more room to improve their working hours, so they often recorded large gains in earnings, more than enough to offset losses in benefits. In GAIN, for example, parents in two-parent cases lost $186, while single mothers gained $923 (Riccio, Friedlander, and Freedman 1994, 251–53, 264–66).

These results stem from conventional evaluations that calculate the effects on existing welfare recipients. The emergence of the diversion question alters the calculus. How are the economic gains and losses affected if we consider the propensity of tough programs to drive people off welfare or keep them from coming on it? One likely result is to increase budgetary savings, because reduced benefits for people who avoid welfare now are added to the benefits gained from putting existing recipients to work. Again, Wisconsin dramatizes the possibilities. The state has spent lavishly on administration and child care in order to move its welfare adults toward employment. Yet overall, welfare cost the state sixty-eight million dollars less in 1993/94 than it did in 1987/88. This was because the dramatic fall in caseloads over those years—driven, admittedly, by the economy as well as work policies—saved the state even more massive sums than it spent on reform (Mead 1997a, 25 n. 39).

It is less clear whether diversion benefits the recipients. The program evaluations suggest that, if the effect is to drive more of the dependents to go to work, they will emerge better off. But if it is merely to drive them off the rolls without going to work, they will emerge worse off, even if government and the overall society gain. As I note later in the chapter, limited evidence to date suggests that both things happen. The diversion question, thus, overhangs an economic assessment of welfare work programs, just as it does much else about them.

REFORM AS ADMINISTRATION

Experience to date suggests that the impacts of work requirements are limited, not so much by the nature of the programs as by the administrative capacities of government. In order to show sufficiency, work programs must reach the vast bulk of the adult recipients, and clients have to be supervised closely to be sure that they enroll and fulfill their assignments. This requires arranging support services such as child care. More critically, it requires hiring energetic case managers to track down people who drop out, and it requires establishing backup systems such as computer monitoring and adjudication. It requires creating financial incentives for staff and contractors to achieve results. It requires inspiring the whole organization with the work mission. All this takes leadership and money, although in the end the best programs save money (Bardach 1993; Mead 1997b).

The programs that garnered the highest impacts in the MDRC evaluations—San Diego's SWIM and Riverside GAIN—were well funded and conspicuously well organized and managed. San Diego drew on long experience with prior welfare employment programs (Hamilton 1988, 15–17). Equally, the programs that disappointed suffered from significant administrative problems. Cook County attempted to impose a work requirement on its entire caseload but lacked the resources to run job clubs (a successful work search strategy involving groups of clients) or to supervise individual job search closely (Quint and Guy 1986). Florida suffered a growing caseload and serious funding cuts in the middle of the program, leading to child-care shortages and an inability to monitor activities closely (Kemple, Friedlander, and Fellerath 1995, ES6–ES8; for details on the performance of these programs, see Table 11A.1).

One reason to think that Wisconsin's programs have impact is that they, like San Diego's SWIM and Riverside's GAIN, are unusually well run. In most if not all Wisconsin counties, JOBS staff are able and motivated, have adequate funding for child care and other support services, and enjoy effective reporting systems. The state has been running welfare work programs well for thirty years, and that prowess carries over to JOBS and the current Thompson experiments (the state was a model of the efficient WIN organization as set out in Mitchell, Chadwin, and Nightingale 1980, a pioneering study of the implementation of welfare employment). As a result, Wisconsin achieves among the highest participation rates of any state in JOBS. In 1994, 32 percent of its employable welfare adults met the JOBS participation standard, more than twice the rate required for that year and the tenth-highest figure in the country (U.S. Congress 1996, 425–27; other than Washington, all states that outperformed Wisconsin had smaller and less urban welfare caseloads). In 1990 Kenosha had already achieved participation rates by the JOBS measure of more than 50 percent, or more than twice the rate mandated for all states in 1995 (Wiseman 1991b).

The need for capable administration is an important constraint on work programs. Not all localities are able to implement them well enough to show impact, let alone sufficiency. But the same is true of most other social programs. Many compensatory programs judged successful by evaluators, including Perry Preschool, are hothouse plants—implemented only for small caseloads by unusually dedicated staff operating outside government. Among compensatory programs, welfare employment programs are unique in having shown impact on large populations even when run by regular government agencies. Even in instances, as in Kenosha, where much of service delivery is contracted out to private or nonprofit providers, the welfare department has ultimate responsibility for the program, and its capability is critical.

The Wisconsin experience suggests, if it does not prove, that work programs can achieve sufficiency. The Wisconsin programs not only have a real effect on welfare, they have enough effect so that the dependency problem is really changed. They reach the vast bulk of the caseload, and they have driven enough cases off the rolls so that dependency is fundamentally reduced, if not overcome. They have done this across the entire state, recently including even Milwaukee. It is likely that, forcefully implemented, work requirements have the power to change the expectations surrounding welfare and make it much more of a last resort for the needy than it is today. That is exactly what the public, in every state, wants welfare reform to achieve.

THE NEW WELFARE SYSTEM

Very likely, the use of work programs to deter entry to welfare will become even more important in future, under the welfare structure just enacted in Washington. PRWORA allows states to set the eligibility rules for federal assistance, not only the benefit level as they did under AFDC. JOBS was disestablished, and there is now no federally mandated welfare employment stricture. Yet Congress is still banking heavily on programs like JOBS to transform welfare. Under the TANF block grant, recipients must work within two years and cannot receive aid for more than five years, policies that presume states can move most current dependents toward employment (states are allowed to exempt up to a fifth of the caseload from the five-year limit).

THE NEW WORK REQUIREMENTS

To be sure they do this, 25 percent of adults receiving aid under TANF were supposed to be engaged in "work activities" by fiscal 1997, rising to 50 percent in 2002 and thereafter. That is more than four times the 20 percent standard that JOBS set for 1995, because the new rates apply to the entire caseload, not only the 44 percent of it judged employable in JOBS (U.S. Congress 1996, 425–27; JOBS normally exempted welfare mothers with a child less than three years old, while TANF allows states to exclude mothers with children less than one year old). The weekly hours of effort demanded to be a participant also rise, from the current twenty in 1997 to thirty in 2000 and thereafter. Even tougher standards are set for two-parent welfare cases. And "work activities" are defined to mean primarily actual work in private or subsidized jobs, disallowing the preference given to education and training in JOBS.

Such demands exceed the participation levels realized anywhere in the country. On their face, they look impossible—*assuming caseloads as they are now.* But Congress is assuming that caseloads will not remain as they are, that the enforcement of such demands will cause large diversion effects. This will deflate the caseload sharply, as is already happening in Wisconsin. Then states would have to realize the participation standards only for a much smaller caseload. As an incentive to do this, the participation rates that states have to meet each year are to be reduced by as many percentage points as they have cut their caseloads since 1995. Nationwide, the rolls have in fact declined by around a fifth since the end of the recent boom in 1994, easing the immediate pinch. That fall probably is driven by the same sort of political and administrative forces seen in Wisconsin, alongside a favorable economy, although the process is less advanced (Jason DeParle, "A Sharp Decrease in Welfare Cases Is Gathering Speed," *New York Times*, February 2, 1997, pp. 1, 18).

In later years, however, higher standards are bound to put severe pressure on states. The squeeze will tighten if the next recession slows or reverses the fall in caseloads. If states want federal funding, they face a Hobson's choice between enforcing work with unprecedented toughness or denying federal aid to much of the current caseload, which would then have to be supported on local funding or not at all. States cannot just ignore the standards, because failure to meet them triggers cuts in their federal grants of up to 21 percent. Distressed states might go to the courts or Congress and try to have the standards suspended or eased. But given the public will to change welfare, caseloads will probably be considerably reduced, even if the new standards are not fully met.

FROM IMPACT TO DIVERSION

The abrupt decline in the rolls in many states already makes impacts in the evaluator's sense seem less important than they once did. Today, the effects that work programs have on the caseload seem dwarfed by the effects they have off the caseload, in deterring applications for aid from the eligible population. Among experts, the big question is not the measured impact of programs, but what has happened to the people driven off the rolls by the new requirements, or who never came on them. Are they working or not, better off or not? What are the effects on children and families when parents are required to work?

To date, little is known. Preliminary indications from the few states that have terminated many clients are that outcomes are highly variable. When families lose TANF, some go to work, while others rely on other aid programs or on help from relatives and friends. Some end up worse off, some better off. So far, clear-cut hardship appears to be uncommon, primarily because people have other sources of support they can call on besides TANF, including other public benefits (U.S. General Accounting Office 1997; Fraker and others 1997).

To find out more will take methods less centered on programs than evaluators have usually used. Evaluations are accustomed to tracking clients using program sources or government wage reporting, but now researchers will have to search out the former recipients and survey them. Little research of this type exists, and it, too, suggests that the effects of cuts are various.[28] In a world of aggressive diversion, one cannot assume, as past evaluations often have, that the people receiving a program are representative of all eligibles. The nature of a program may effect who among the eligibles comes forward even to enter an evaluation (Wiseman 1997, 1–3). Indeed, one cannot assume that the effects of work policies are confined to present or even former recipients. To assess diversion fully, evaluators have to break free of program caseloads and survey the entire low-income population. Several such surveys are under way or planned to assess the effects of TANF, including a large effort by the Urban Institute with funding from the Annie E. Casey Foundation and others.

These shifts imply that the effectiveness of welfare work programs is less doubted today than it once was. The standard evaluation question, dating back to Rossi's Law and before, was whether an intervention had any effect at all. But if it did, that effect was presumed to be positive. Today, few seriously doubt that welfare work programs have effects, perhaps large ones. There is much more question about whether the effects are favorable. With diversion there is more concern about effects on families than when the spotlight was on economic impacts. In a few years, the effect of work policies will probably be sufficient for everyone to recognize. Dependency will be reduced visibly, and the debate will instead be over whether this is good.

APPENDIX 11A

Table 11A.1 Results of Main MDRC Welfare Employment Evaluations

Study Outcome in Final Year	Control Mean	Experimental-Control Difference	Percentage Change
Arkansas, 1983 to 1985			
Average earnings (dollars)	1,085	337	31
Percent employed at end of final year	18.3	6.2	34
Average AFDC payments (dollars)	910	−168	−18
Percent on welfare at end of final year	40.1	−7.3	−18
Baltimore, 1982 to 1985			
Average earnings (dollars)	2,989	511	17
Percent employed at end of final year	40.3	0.4	1
Average AFDC payments (dollars)	1,815	−31	−2
Percent on welfare at end of final year	48.4	−0.2	0
California GAIN, 1988 to 1993			
Average earnings (dollars)	2,523	636	25
Percent employed at end of final year	24.1	4.5	19
Average AFDC payments (dollars)	4,163	−331	−8
Percent on welfare at end of final year	55.5	−3.0	−5
Riverside GAIN, 1988 to 1993			
Average earnings (dollars)	2,552	1,010	40
Percent employed at end of final year	24.6	6.6	27
Average AFDC payments (dollars)	3,448	−584	−17
Percent on welfare at end of final year	45.8	−5.2	−11
Cook County (job search/work experience), 1985 to 1987			
Average earnings (dollars)	1,217	10	1
Percent employed at end of final year	21.4	1.3	6
Average AFDC payments (dollars)	3,146	−40	1
Percent on welfare at end of final year	80.8	−1.9	−2

(*Table continues on p. 306.*)

Table 11A.1 *Continued*

Study Outcome in Final Year	Control Mean	Experimental-Control Difference	Percentage Change
Florida, 1990 to 1993			
Average earnings (dollars)	3,138	80	3
Percent employed at end of final year	37.8	0.4	1
Average AFDC payments (dollars)	1,945	−113	−6
Percent on welfare at end of final year	53.6	−2.4	−4
San Diego (applicants in job search/ work experience), 1982 to 1985			
Average earnings (dollars)	1,937	443	23
Percent employed at end of final year	36.9	5.5	15
Average AFDC payments (dollars)	2,750	−226	−8
Percent on welfare at end of final year	47.9	−2.0	−4
San Diego, SWIM, 1985 to 1988			
Average earnings (dollars)	2,246	658	29
Percent employed at end of final year	29.3	5.4	18
Average AFDC payments (dollars)	3,961	−553	−14
Percent on welfare at end of final year	58.7	−7.4	−13
Virginia, 1983 to 1985			
Average earnings (dollars)	2,356	268	11
Percent employed at end of final year	34.1	4.6	13
Average AFDC payments (dollars)	1,295	−111	−9
Percent on welfare at end of final year	39.3	−2.6	−7
West Virginia, 1983 to 1986			
Average earnings (dollars)	435	16	4
Percent employed at end of final year	13.1	−1.0	−8
Average AFDC payments (dollars)	1,692	0.0	0
Percent on welfare at end of final year	72.5	−1.5	−2
Averages (excludes Riverside)			
Average earnings	1,992	329	16

Table 11A.1 Continued

Study Outcome in Final Year	Control Mean	Experimental-Control Difference	Percentage Change
Percent employed at end of final year	28.4	3.0	11
Average AFDC payments	2,409	−175	−7
Percent on welfare at end of final year	55.2	−3.1	−6

Sources: Gueron and Pauly (1991) 142–43; Kemple, Friedlander, and Fellerath (1995) E9–16; Riccio, Friedlander, and Freedman (1994) 120, 122.
Notes: Studies are weighted equally. Results are for AFDC, not AFDC-UP, and are for the last full year of the evaluations, which varied from one to three years in follow-up. Dates under the names of studies indicate the beginning of enrollment and the end of follow-up. "Percentage change" means the absolute impact as a percentage of the control-group mean. Averages for the percentage changes are means of the individual figures for percentage change, not calculated from the averages of the control means and experimental-control differences.

Table 11A.2 Experimental Versus Control Activity Levels in MDRC Evaluation Studies (Percent)

Activity	Experimentals	Controls
Studies using WIN data		
Baltimore (over twelve months)[a]		
Any employment and training activity	44.5	3.4
Job search or job club	25.0	2.0
Education and training	16.6	1.0
San Diego (over nine months)		
Any employment and training activity	46.4	6.1
Job search or job club	44.1	0.8
West Virginia (over nine months)		
Any employment and training activity[b]	30.2	6.9
Average		
Any employment and training activity	40.4	5.5
Job search or job club	34.6	1.4
Studies using other data		
Florida (over two years)		
Any employment and training activity	63.9	40.1

(*Table continues on p. 308*)

Table 11A.2 *Continued*

Activity	Experimentals	Controls
Job search or job club	42.7	18.7
Education and training	41.5	30.5
Cook County (over nine months)		
Any employment and training activity	47.2	16.9
Job search or job club	36.1	2.2
Education and training	16.9	15.9
California GAIN (over two to three years)		
Job search or job club	28.5	3.9
Education and training[c]	26.4	23.1
San Diego SWIM (over two to three years)		
Job search or job club	53.7	0.7
Education and training[d]	48.2	31.2
Virginia (over fifteen to twenty-eight months)[e]		
Education and training	15.8	12.7
Average		
Any employment and training activity	55.6	28.5
Job search or job club	40.3	6.4
Education and training	29.8	22.7

Sources: For Baltimore, Friedlander and others (1985) 62; for California GAIN, Riccio, Fried-lander, and Freedman (1994) 41; for Cook County, Friedlander and others (1987) 45; for Florida, Kemple, Friedlander, and Fellerath (1995) 51, 54; for San Diego, Goldman, Friedlander, and Long (1986) 194; for San Diego SWIM, Hamilton and Friedlander (1989) 38; for Virginia, Riccio and others (1986) 82; and for West Virginia, Friedlander and others (1986) 73.

[a] Figures cover AFDC and AFDC-U.

[b] Means Community Work Experience Program (CWEP) plus other activity.

[c] Means vocational plus postsecondary education.

[d] Means community college plus JTPA.

[e] Interval length is given in Hamilton and Friedlander (1989) 39.

The author gratefully acknowledges comments on the first draft of this paper from Jonathan Crane, Michael Wiseman, and an anonymous reviewer for Russell Sage.

NOTES

1. Adult recipients of Food Stamps are also subject to work requirements, and some pressures to enforce work have also appeared in Supplemen-

tal Security Income. But the TANF work programs are much the most well-developed, so only they are discussed here.

2. "Social program" here means a compensatory service program providing education or training that is supposed to enlarge the skills or earnings of clients. Transfer programs that distribute income, health care, or other direct benefits also have impacts, but these seem more apparent and have rarely been the subject of evaluation.

3. Experimental trials may be biased in other ways, for example because they fail to test the conditions that would exist if the experimental program were permanently and universally instituted.

4. Such claims were common at the conference on social programs that really work, where this chapter was first presented.

5. Some liberal analysts suggest that the goals are in conflict, because when recipients leave welfare they may lose more in income and other benefits, such as child and health care, than they gain. See Danziger, Sandefur, and Weinberg (1994), especially chapters 7 and 8. But research and experience show that the vast majority of welfare recipients who work are better off, at least in income terms, than they are without work, even if some remain poor. See Mead (1992, 71–72, 115–24).

6. Recipients may become mandatory for work, not only when they first enter welfare but also later. They have to recertify their eligibility every six months. At one of these reassessments, it may be discovered that they now meet the requirements for the work program, perhaps because their youngest child has passed some threshold age. They will then be referred to the program and could enter an evaluation, just like an initial applicant for aid.

7. Admittedly, the reported impacts of the four studies with early random assignment were not larger than those of the five studies with later randomization. Indeed, they were smaller. The late-randomizers included the formidable SWIM and GAIN studies. However, based on a t-test for difference of means, there is no statistically significant difference between the two groups.

8. The closer to program activities randomization is, the higher participation rates will be, because there are fewer stages at which clients may drop out before participating.

9. In practice, evaluators do not gauge impact by subtracting the raw mean of the control group from the mean for the experimentals; they estimate the difference using multivariate statistical models. With this method, impacts are more likely to be statistically significant, and they are adjusted for the slight demographic differences that may exist between the experimental and control groups. Due to random assignment, such models can be used without fear of selection bias.

10. The Family Support Act did not require that JOBS be mandatory. However, it gave states authority to compel recipients to participate, on pain of reducing their grants, and it levied participation standards on states that, in practice, forced most of them to use that authority.

11. In WIN in 1979, at the height of its implementation, 17 percent of clients were volunteers (Mead 1988, 274 n. 33). In JOBS, which lacks equivalent data, the proportion of volunteers might have been lower because required participation rates were higher. However, the proportion of volunteers might have been higher because the program had more education and training to offer, and this—rather than immediate work—is usually what volunteers seek.

12. There is some evidence that raising participation in welfare work programs may, in fact, depress the average quality of the jobs clients get. See Mead (1988, 272–73; 1997b, 120–21).

13. Such an effect, admittedly, would be limited if pressure to raise participation among experimentals in an evaluation tended to "spill over" to the controls. If the latter received a message that they ought to participate and work, they might seek out work or education or training more than otherwise. This would "raise the bar" for the experiment, making it less likely to show impact.

14. Some experts think that welfare employment programs should be voluntary, on the view that clients must be self-motivated to succeed. See Lynn (1989).

15. The third was served in the sense of participating in some way at some time in the course of a year. Analyses of participation in the MDRC studies usually use this standard. By it, the very tough SWIM program achieved participation rates of 52 percent (Hamilton 1988, xviii, 155–58, 162, 187). However, this criterion is more lenient than that in JOBS, which required that participants be scheduled for twenty hours a week and attend 75 percent of these hours, let alone in PRWORA, where the standard rises to thirty hours by 2000.

16. This is corroborated by one demonstration from 1979 to 1981. Five local WIN programs that raised their participation rates from 53 to 74 percent in these years also raised their job entries by 58 percent, in the face of a declining economy. See CSR, Inc., and Osora and Associates (1982). Such results tend to confirm the estimate that at least two-thirds of adults on the rolls are employable.

17. Statistical analyses also suggest that higher participation in WIN or JOBS is associated with stronger outcomes, particularly job entries and departures from welfare, even controlling for demographic features of the clients and the local labor market. See Mead (1988, 1997b).

18. The correlation between the year a study began and ended and its impacts is in fact slightly inverse, because of the strong results that Baltimore and San Diego recorded early in the sequence.

19. Freedman and Friedlander (1995, FS-5) say that Riverside did not dominate the national results.

20. An exception is Medicaid, the large and costly health program for the poor. However, most of its spending goes to the elderly and disabled, not the working-age poor and their children, who are the most affected by welfare work programs.

21. These measures were never drafted. Work was interrupted by the election of the Clinton Administration, which has postponed proposing measures until 1998 (Mead 1997b, 114).

22. Congress increased work incentives in 1962 and 1967 but cut them back sharply in 1981. The main criticism was that they did not raise work levels but did make it harder to close cases when recipients went to work.

23. I know of no research bearing on which effect dominates, but most welfare employment staff I have interviewed say that smoked-out recipients usually choose to leave welfare, implying that the jobs were worth more to them than aid.

24. The rates of decline in caseloads were calculated from state welfare caseload data in the *Green Book* (U.S. Congress, 1996) and data from the U.S. Administration for Children and Families. Wisconsin data are from the Wisconsin Department of Workforce Development.

25. A finding by Pawasarat and Quinn (1993) to the contrary is invalid because they did not adjust for the fact that the caseload trend is nonstationary. An analysis of the transformed series in Mead (1997a) did not show clear-cut unemployment or benefit effects.

26. An experimental test of a pre-JOBS work program in Rock County found that it increased dependency, probably by directing more clients into education and training and thus postponing their departure from the rolls (Pawasarat and Quinn 1993, chap. 11).

27. These figures refer to net cost of experimentals over controls, considering expenses to all government agencies serving the clients, including education and training agencies outside the work program proper. The wide range in costs partly reflects inflation—more recent programs cost more—and the varying length of the treatments.

28. One example is studies of families removed from AFDC by the 1981 Reagan eligibility cuts; the mothers generally worked more but still suffered net losses of income (Blank 1997, 137). Danziger and Kossoudji (1994/95) surveyed former general assistance recipients in Michigan who were cut from the program in 1991, finding limited employment and substantial hardship among them. The likeliest form of TANF reform, however, involves tougher work requirements rather than elimination of the program, and welfare mothers are on balance more employable than general assistance men, so these findings may not be applicable.

REFERENCES

Aaron, Henry J. 1978. *Politics and the Professors: The Great Society in Perspective*. Washington, D.C.: Brookings Institution.

Bane, Mary Jo, and David T. Ellwood. 1994. *Welfare Realities: From Rhetoric to Reform*. Cambridge, Mass.: Harvard University Press.

Bardach, Eugene. 1993. *Improving the Productivity of JOBS Programs*. New York: Manpower Demonstration Research Corporation.

Berrueta-Clement, John R., Lawrence J. Schweinhart, W. S. Barnett, A. S. Epstein, and David P. Weikart. 1984. *Changed Lives: The Effects of the Perry Preschool Program on Youths through Age Nineteen*. Monograph 8 of the High/Scope Educational Research Foundation. Ypsilanti, Mich.: High/Scope Press.

Blank, Rebecca M. 1997. *It Takes a Nation: A New Agenda for Fighting Poverty*. New York: Russell Sage; Princeton, N.J.: Princeton University Press.

Bloom, Howard S., Larry L. Orr, George Cave, Stephen H. Bell, and Fred Doolittle. 1992. *The National JTPA Study: Title II-A Impacts on Earnings and Employment at Eighteen Months*. Bethesda, Md.: Abt Associates.

Brodkin, Evelyn Z. 1986. *The False Promise of Administrative Reform: Implementing Quality Control in Welfare*. Philadelphia: Temple University Press.

CSR, Inc., and Osora and Associates. 1982. *Final Report: Evaluation of the WIN Total Registrant Involvement Project*. Washington, D.C.: CSR, Inc.

Danziger, Sandra K., and Sherrie A. Kossoudji. 1994/95. "What Happened to General Assistance Recipients in Michigan?" *Focus* 16(2, winter): 32–34.

Danziger, Sheldon H., Gary D. Sandefur, and Daniel H. Weinberg, eds. 1994. *Confronting Poverty: Prescriptions for Change*. New York: Russell Sage Foundation; Cambridge, Mass.: Harvard University Press.

Edin, Kathryn J. 1995. "The Myths of Dependence and Self-Sufficiency: Women, Welfare, and Low-Wage Work." *Focus* 17(2, fall/winter): 1–9.

Fraker, Thomas, Robert Moffitt, and Douglas Wolf. 1985. "Effective Tax Rates and Guarantees in the AFDC Program, 1967–1982." *Journal of Human Resources* 20(2, spring): 251–63.

Fraker, Thomas M., Lucia A. Nixon, Jan L. Losby, Carol S. Prindle, and John F. Else. 1997. *Iowa's Limited Benefit Plan: Summary Report*. Princeton, N.J.: Mathematica Policy Research.

Freedman, Stephen, and Daniel Friedlander. 1995. *The JOBS Evaluation: Early Findings on Program Impacts in Three Sites*. New York: Manpower Demonstration Research Corporation.

Friedlander, Daniel. 1988. *Subgroup Impacts and Performance Indicators for Selected Welfare Employment Programs*. New York: Manpower Demonstration Research Corporation.

Friedlander, Daniel, and Gary Burtless. 1995. *Five Years After: The Long-Term Effects of Welfare-to-Work Programs*. New York: Russell Sage Foundation.

Freidlander, Daniel, Marjorie Erickson, Gayle Hamilton, and Virginia Knox. 1986. *West Virginia: Final Report on the Community Work Experience Demonstration.* New York: Manpower Demonstration Research Corporation.

Friedlander, Daniel, Gergory Hoerz, David Long, and Janet Quint. 1985. *Maryland: Final Report on the Employment Initiatives Evaluation.* New York: Manpower Demonstration Research Corporation.

Friedlander, Daniel, Stephen Freedman, Gayle Hamilton, and Janet Quint. 1987. *Final Report on Job Search and Work Experience in Cook County.* New York: Manpower Demonstration Research Corporation.

Goldman, Barbara, Judith Gueron, Joseph Ball, and Marilyn Price. 1984. *Preliminary Findings from the San Diego Job Search and Work Experience Demonstration.* New York: Manpower Demonstration Research Corporation.

Goldman, Barbara, Daniel Friedlander, and David Long. 1986. *Final Report on the San Diego Job Search and Work Experience Demonstration.* New York: Manpower Demonstration Research Corporation.

Greenberg, David, and Michael Wiseman. 1992. "What Did the OBRA Demonstrations Do?" In *Evaluating Welfare and Training Programs*, edited by Charles F. Manski and Irwin Garfinkel. Cambridge, Mass.: Harvard University Press.

Gueron, Judith M. 1996. "A Research Context for Welfare Reform." *Journal of Policy Analysis and Management* 15(4, fall): 547–61.

Gueron, Judith M., and Edward Pauly with Cameran M. Lougy. 1991. *From Welfare to Work.* New York: Russell Sage Foundation.

Hamilton, Gayle. 1988. *Interim Report on the Saturation Work-Initiative Model in San Diego.* New York: Manpower Demonstration Research Corporation.

Hamilton, Gayle, and Daniel Friedlander. 1989. *Final Report on the Saturation Work Initiative Model in San Diego.* New York: Manpower Demonstration Research Corporation.

Harris, Kathleen Mullan. 1993. "Work and Welfare among Single Mothers in Poverty." *American Journal of Sociology* 99 (2, September): 317–52.

Herr, Toby, Robert Halpern, and Aimée Conrad. 1991. *Changing What Counts: Rethinking the Journey Out of Welfare.* Evanston, Ill.: Northwestern University, Center for Urban Affairs and Policy Research.

Kemple, James J., Daniel Friedlander, and Veronica Fellerath. 1995. *Florida's Project Independence: Benefits, Costs, and Two-Year Impacts of Florida's JOBS Program.* New York: Manpower Demonstration Research Corporation.

Lipsky, Michael. 1984. "Bureaucratic Disentitlement in Social Welfare Programs." *Social Service Review* 58(1, March): 3–27.

Lynn, Lawrence E., Jr., ed. 1989. "Symposium: The Craft of Public Management." *Journal of Policy Analysis and Management* 8(2, spring): 284–306.

Manski, Charles F., and Irwin Garfinkel, eds. 1992. *Evaluating Welfare and Training Programs.* Cambridge, Mass.: Harvard University Press.

Maynard, Rebecca A. 1995. "Subsidized Employment and Non-Labor Market Alternatives for Welfare Recipients." In *The Work Alternative: Welfare Reform and the Realities of the Job Market*, edited by Demetra Smith Nightingale and Robert H. Haveman. Washington, D.C.: Urban Institute Press.

Mead, Lawrence M. 1986. *Beyond Entitlement: The Social Obligations of Citizenship*. New York: Free Press.

———. 1988. "The Potential for Work Enforcement: A Study of WIN." *Journal of Policy Analysis and Management* 7(2, winter): 264–88.

———. 1992. *The New Politics of Poverty: The Nonworking Poor in America*. New York: Basic Books.

———. 1995a. *The New Paternalism in Action: Welfare Reform in Wisconsin*. Milwaukee: Wisconsin Policy Research Institute.

———. 1995b. "Taming Welfare Growth: The Role of the JOBS Program." Paper presented to the Association of Public Policy Analysis and Management, annual conference. Washington, D.C. (November 3, 1995).

———. 1997a. "The Decline of Welfare in Wisconsin." Paper presented to the Midwest Political Science Association, annual conference. Chicago, Ill. (April 11, 1997).

———. 1997b. "Optimizing JOBS: Evaluation versus Administration." *Public Administration Review* 57(2, March/April): 113–23.

Mitchell, John J., Mark L. Chadwin, and Demetra S. Nightingale. 1980. *Implementing Welfare-Employment Programs: An Institutional Analysis of the Work Incentive (WIN) Program*. U.S. Department of Labor R&D Monograph 78. Washington: U.S. Government Printing Office.

Moffitt, Robert. 1983. "An Economic Model of Welfare Stigma." *American Economic Review* 73(5, December): 1023–35.

———. 1996. "The Effect of Employment and Training Programs on Entry and Exit from the Welfare Caseload." *Journal of Policy Analysis and Management* 15(1, winter): 32–50.

Murray, Charles. 1984. *Losing Ground: American Social Policy, 1950–1980*. New York: Basic Books.

———. 1994. "What To Do about Welfare." *Commentary* (December): 26–34.

Pawasarat, John, and Lois M. Quinn. 1993. "Wisconsin Welfare Employment Experiments: An Evaluation of the WEJT and CWEP Programs." University of Wisconsin-Milwaukee, Employment and Training Institute, Milwaukee. September.

Piven, Frances Fox, and Richard A. Cloward. 1993. *Regulating the Poor: The Functions of Public Welfare*, updated ed. New York: Vintage.

Quint, Janet, and Cynthia Guy. 1986. *Interim Findings from the Illinois WIN Demonstration Program in Cook County*. New York: Manpower Demonstration Research Corporation.

Riccio, James, George Cave, Stephen Freedman, and Marilyn Price. 1986. *Final Report on the Virginia Employment Services Program.* New York: Manpower Demonstration Research Corporation.

Riccio, James, Daniel Friedlander, and Stephen Freedman. 1994. *GAIN: Benefits, Costs, and Three-Year Impacts of a Welfare-to-Work Program.* New York: Manpower Demonstration Research Corporation.

Rossi, Peter H. 1987. "The Iron Law of Evaluation and Other Metallic Rules." *Research in Social Problems and Public Policy,* vol. 4, edited by Joann H. Miller and Michael Lewis. Greenwich, Conn.: JAI Press.

Schorr, Lisbeth B., with Daniel Schorr. 1988. *Within Our Reach: Breaking the Cycle of Disadvantage.* New York: Anchor.

Sosin, Michael R. 1986. "Legal Rights and Welfare Change, 1960–1980." In *Fighting Poverty: What Works and What Doesn't,* edited by Sheldon H. Danziger and Daniel H. Weinberg. Cambridge, Mass.: Harvard University Press.

U.S. Congress. House Committee on Ways and Means. 1996. *1996 Green Book: Background Material on Programs within the Jurisdiction of the Committee on Ways and Means.* Washington: U.S. Government Printing Office.

U.S. General Accounting Office. 1997. *Welfare Reform: States' Early Experiences with Benefit Termination.* Washington: U.S. Government Printing Office.

Weissman, Evan. 1997. *Changing to a Work First Strategy: Lessons from Los Angeles County's GAIN Program for Welfare Recipients.* New York: Manpower Demonstration Research Corporation.

Wiseman, Michael, ed. 1991a. "Research and Policy: A Symposium on the Family Support Act of 1988." *Journal of Policy Analysis and Management* 10 (4, fall): 588–666.

———. 1991b. "Sample Family Support Act Job Opportunity and Basic Skills Training (JOBS) Participation Data (Revised)." Madison: University of Wisconsin, La Follette Institute of Public Affairs.

———. 1996. "State Strategies for Welfare Reform: The Wisconsin Story." *Journal of Policy Analysis and Management* 15 (4, fall): 515–46.

———. 1997. "Who Got New Hope?" Working Paper. New York: Russell Sage Foundation.

Index

Boldface numbers refer to tables and figures.

smoking. *See* cigarette smoking
social and environmental domain, 229, **231**, **232**
social competence: CPC program, 119, 124, **125**, 126, 127, **128**, **139**; and drug prevention programs, 25–27; LST program, 234, 235, 236; Perry Preschool results, 150–51, **152**, 154, 158; psychological factors as mediators for, 229, **230**, **232**, 233; TFC program, 269
social influence model, 201–2, 203–4, 233
social influences, and drug abuse prevention, 218–19, 220, 229, **231**, **232**. *See also* parental role; peer influences; teachers
social learning theory, 229
social programs for poor: definition, 309n2; erosion of public support for, 1; potential success of, 38–40. *See also* policy issues
sociocultural domain, 229, **231**, **232**
special education assignment: Abecedarian project, 172, **173**; CPC program, 124, **125**, 126, 130, **130**, **140**; Success for All, 52, 65–68; test scores as predictors of, 9–10, 21
Special Supplemental Nutrition Program for Women, Infants and Children (WIC), 23–24, **34–35**, 184–86. *See also* WIC (Women and Infants) Program
STaR (Story Telling and Retelling), 47
State funded welfare programs, 32, 303–4
statistically significant effects, and evaluation criteria, 2. *See also* size of effect
Story Telling and Retelling (STaR), 47
subjective interpretation, in social program evaluation, 2, 5
substance abuse. *See* drug use
Success for All: components, 46–53; costs, 68–69; effects, 57, **58**, 59, **60**, 61, **62–63**, 69; English language learners, 61, 64–65, **66**; evaluation design, 55–57; methodology, 54–55, 69–70; overview, 6–11, **34–35**, 37; program description, 45–46; special education, 52, 65–68
sufficiency criterion for welfare employment programs, 281, 302
supervision and discipline practices, in TFC program, 263–66, 268, 272
SWIM (Saturation Work Initiative Model), 30–31, 282, 289

teachers: costs of, 155; credentials of, 150; effectiveness in drug prevention, 243; empowerment of, 159; as mediating factors, 177–78; vs. peers as anti-drug coun-

selors, 206, 214, 216, 217; in Title I programs, 77; training of, 119, 240–41, 246. *See also* tutors, individual
teacher-student ratio, and CPC program, 119–20
Temple, J. A., 117, 127
Temporary Assistance for Needy Families (TANF), 277, 302–3
test scores and methodology, 8, 9–10, 11–12, 21–22. *See also* IQ (Intelligence Quotient); measurement methods
Texas Reading Initiative, 83
TFC (Treatment Foster Care) Program. *See* Treatment Foster Care (TFC) Program
timing of intervention: in drug abuse prevention, 227, 228, 235; vs. duration, 112–13, 131, 134. *See also* early intervention
Title I of Elementary and Secondary Education Act (ESEA) of 1965: allocation of funds from, 10, 14, 33, 81–82, 136–37; and CPC program, 113–14; failure of, 75–77
tobacco use. *See* cigarette smoking
training-oriented employment programs, 289–90, **290**, 293
Treatment Foster Care (TFC) Program: case study, 269–75; components of, 266–69; cost-benefit relationship, 260, 269; effects, 262–65, **263–64**, **266**; methodology, 259–62, 263–64; overview, 27–29, **34–35**; policy implications, 258, 265–66; potential of, 36–37
tutors, individual: as key to reading success, 7, 11–12, 78–79, 99–100, 101–2, 106; responsibilities of, 84–85; Success for All, 49–50, 67; training of, 51–52, 81, 91–92, 103–4

uniqueness of program, as criterion for evaluation, 5
unreported employment problem, 293–95
upscaling ability: CPC program, 16–17; as criterion for evaluation, 2, 6; LST program, 27; potential for, 36, 38–39; Reading One-to-One, 13–14; Success for All, 6; TFC program, 28–29; WIC program, 23–24

verbal ability. *See* reading skills
volunteer issue for welfare employment programs, 288–89, 310n11

War on Poverty, 279
Wasik, Barbara, 79, 80